W9-AJV-286

Civics

★ *Government and Economics in Action* ★

READING AND VOCABULARY STUDY GUIDE

PEARSON
Prentice
Hall

Needham, Massachusetts
Upper Saddle River, New Jersey

Pearson Prentice Hall™ is a trademark of Pearson Education, Inc.
Pearson® is a registered trademark of Pearson plc.
Prentice Hall® is a registered trademark of Pearson Education, Inc.

ISBN 0-13-181832-5

2 3 4 5 6 7 8 9 10   08 07 06 05 04

Contents

How to Use This Book

The Reading and Vocabulary Study Guide was designed to help you understand Civics content. It will also help you build your reading and vocabulary skills. Please take the time to look at the next few pages to see how it works!

The Reading Preview page gets you ready to read each section.

Objectives from your textbook help you focus your reading.

With each chapter, you will study a Target Reading Skill. This skill is introduced in your textbook, but explained more here. Later, questions or activities in the margin will help you practice the skill.

You are given a new Vocabulary Strategy with each chapter. Questions or activities in the margin later will help you practice the strategy.

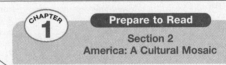

CHAPTER 1

Prepare to Read

Section 2
America: A Cultural Mosaic

Objectives

1. Explain what is meant by the American identity.
2. Discuss the contributions of European, Hispanic, African, Asian, and Native Americans to American society.
3. Describe the U. S. population today.

Target Reading Skill

Reread Rereading is another way to figure out the meaning of words and ideas that you do not understand. If what you read is not clear, try rereading it. As you read the text a second time, look for connections between words and sentences.

Read the following paragraph. Then reread it to find connections that help make the meaning of the word *immigrants* clear.

America is sometimes called a nation of <u>immigrants</u>. Immigrants not only brought their dreams for a better life to America, they also brought ways of life from their homelands.

Words and sentences in the paragraph help explain that immigrants are people who move from one country to make their homes in another.

Vocabulary Strategy

Using Word Parts Many words can be divided into parts. To find the meaning of a word with a prefix or suffix, put the meanings of the root and other word parts together. The suffix *-ness*, for example, means "quality or state." It can be added to many different roots.

Root	+	Suffix	=	Word
empty	+	-ness	=	emptiness "quality of being empty"
lonely	+	-ness	=	loneliness "state of being lonely"

Section Summary pages provide an easy-to-read summary of each section.

Provides a summary of the section's most important ideas.

Large blue headings correspond to large red headings in your textbook.

Reading Check questions mirror those in your textbook.

Key Terms, in blue within the summary, are defined at the bottom of the page.

✓ Reading Check

Underline the two sentences that explain why it is not correct to say that America is a melting pot.

Mark the Text

Vocabulary Strategy

Using Word Parts Use what you know about the meaning of the suffix -*ness* to explain the meaning of the underlined word.

_____

_____

_____

✓ Reading Check

Circle the sentence that tells whether European immigrants were more alike or more different.

Mark the Text

✓ Reading Check

List three areas in which Hispanic culture has affected culture in the United States.

1. _____

2. _____

3. _____

12 Reading and Vocabulary Study Guide

Section 2 Summary

People from many countries have made their homes in America. These different groups add to the <u>richness</u> of American society.

The American Identity

America has been called a nation of immigrants.
5 Immigrants have brought ways of life from their homelands. They also have brought dreams for a better life. Immigrants have helped make America diverse.

The United States is sometimes called a "melting pot." The idea is that immigrants melted into American
10 society. They gave up ways of life from the lands where they were born. But all Americans are not the same. Americans have kept parts of their different cultures. These differences add to what makes America great.

Americans are really part of a mosaic, not a melting
15 pot. A mosaic is made up of small tiles. The tiles are different sizes, shapes, and colors. Together the tiles make a whole picture. Together the groups in the United States form a whole nation.

European Americans

People from Europe were among the first immigrants
20 to come here. These people had different governments, languages, religions, and customs. The number of European immigrants is smaller today than in the 1800s and early 1900s. But European Americans are still the largest part of our population.

Hispanic Americans

25 Hispanic Americans, or Latinos, share a culture from Spanish-speaking countries. They can be of any race. After English, Spanish is the most common language in the United States. Latino foods, music, and architecture have added to United States culture.

Key Terms

immigrants (IM i gruhnts) *n.* people who move from one country to another

Questions and activities in the margin help you take notes on main ideas and practice the Target Reading Skill and Vocabulary Strategy.

was caused by **racism**. Since the 1960s, African Americans and others have worked for change. More choices in education, jobs, and housing are available to African Americans. But there is still work to be done.

Asian Americans and Native Americans

Some of the first Asians came here after the discovery of gold in 1849. Other groups said Asians were taking away jobs. In 1882 and 1907, **exclusion laws** were passed to keep immigrants from China and Japan from coming to America. These laws ended in 1952. Since then many Asian immigrants have come here.

Native Americans had been living here for thousands of years before Columbus. Then Europeans settled on land Native Americans used. Native Americans fought for their lands. But they were pushed west. By the late 1800s, thousands had died. Today, Native Americans are only a small part of the population.

Our Population Today

The 2000 **census** showed that about 25 percent of the United States population is not white, compared with 20 percent in 1990. Our ancestors come from all over the world. Each group adds to the richness of America.

Review Questions

1. Why is America like a mosaic? Explain.

2. What does the 2000 census show about the United States population today?

Key Terms

racism (RAY sih zum) *n.* the belief that your own race is better than others

exclusion laws (ek SKLOO shun LAWZ) *n.* laws that stopped people from China and Japan from moving to America

census (SEN sus) *n.* a count of people made every ten years

✓ **Reading Check**

Underline the sentences that give examples of discrimination against African Americans.

✓ **Reading Check**

Underline the sentence that explains what happened when the exclusion laws ended.

✓ **Reading Check**

Circle two words or phrases that tell how European settlers affected Native Americans in the 1800s.

✓ **Reading Check**

How did the United States population change between 1990 and 2000? List one possible social effect of this change.

Target Reading Skill

Reread Reread the paragraph under "Asian Americans" to understand why laws were passed to keep Asian immigrants from coming to America. Circle the sentence that explains the reason for the exclusion laws.

Chapter 1 Section 2 **13**

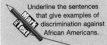

When you see this symbol, mark the text as indicated.

Use write-on lines to answer the questions. You can also use the lines to take notes.

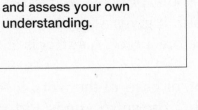

Questions at the end of each section and chapter help you review content and assess your own understanding.

Chapter 1 Assessment

e most Americans will work in
belt.
reas.
s.
jobs.

States is best described as a
pot.
e culture.
of different groups.
of immigrants.

following make up the largest ethnic group in the American population?
A. European Americans
B. Hispanic Americans
C. Native Americans
D. African Americans

4. Which of the following is *not* a basic American value?
A. equality
B. freedom
C. diversity
D. justice

5. We still need to work to make sure that all Americans enjoy equality, freedom, and justice because we
A. do not show equal respect to all.
B. have made a perfect nation.
C. have lived up to our values.
D. are different from each other.

Short Answer Question

In what ways are Americans alike and different from one another?

_____

_____

_____

_____

Chapter 1 Assessment **17**

Objectives

1. Discuss the variety of places where Americans live.
2. Find out how the American workforce is changing.
3. Learn why the average age of Americans is increasing.
4. Explore how our varied backgrounds contribute to what it means to be a United States citizen.

Target Reading Skill

Read Ahead As you read, you may come across words and ideas whose meanings are not clear to you. To understand the meaning of new words and ideas, it sometimes helps to read ahead in the text. As you continue to read, the meanings of new words and ideas often become clear. Read the following paragraph. Do not stop reading when you come to the under-lined words. Instead, read ahead to see if their meaning becomes clear.

Americans have always been on the move. At first most people lived on farms or in small towns. Later, people began to <u>concentrate</u> in <u>urban areas</u>. Why? They found jobs in factories and offices in cities and the large towns near them.

When you read ahead, it becomes clear that *concentrate* means "to gather together or come together in a place." You also find out that an urban area is a city and the towns around it.

Vocabulary Strategy

Using Word Parts You can use the meanings of word parts to help you figure out the meaning of words as you read. Roots, prefixes, and suf-fixes are word parts. A root is the base of a word. It gives a word its basic meaning. A **prefix** is a word part that comes before a root. A **suffix** is a word part that comes after a root.

Take the word *terrain*, for example. The root, or base, of the word ter-rain is *terr-*. The root *terr-* means "land or earth." The suffix *-ain* is added to *terr-* to make the word *terrain*. This added part means "having to do with." You might define *terrain* then simply as "land," "land feature," or "landform."

Section 1 Summary

¹ Not all Americans are alike. We can get information about who Americans are from the study of **demography**.

Where Americans Live

The United States is a huge country. Americans live in
⁵ all kinds of places, from high mountains to flat prairies. Americans also live in many different types of homes.

Americans have always been on the move. At first most people lived on farms or in small towns. Later, more people arrived. They and other settlers began to
¹⁰ move west, where there was more land. Little by little, people began to live and work in cities and the large towns near them. They found jobs in factories and offices. Today, four out of five Americans live in or near cities. Some Americans from the North and East
¹⁵ have moved to the South and West to live in the mild climate of the **Sunbelt**.

The Workforce

Americans have always worked hard. The first settlers from Europe cleared land to farm in the east. Since that time, Americans have farmed land on both coasts and
²⁰ in other places. Americans have built houses, stores, factories, and office buildings. We have made many kinds of products. These products are sold here and around the world.

About 60 million women and 70 million men make
²⁵ up the American workforce. They work at about 30,000 different jobs. Young people who work part-time or during the summer are also part of the workforce.

Key Terms

demography (dih MOG ruh fee) *n.* the study of the number of people in an area, the growth of that number, and the places where people live

Sunbelt (SUN belt) *n.* states where the weather is warm, such as Georgia, Florida, Texas, and Arizona

---

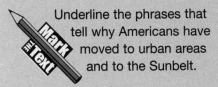

✓ **Reading Check**

Underline the phrases that tell why Americans have moved to urban areas and to the Sunbelt.

Target Reading Skill

Read Ahead The underlined sentence says that Americans have always worked hard, but it does not say how. Read ahead to get a clearer picture of the kinds of work Americans do. Circle ways that Americans worked in the past. Underline the kind of job most Americans will have in the future.

Describe how the American work force has changed over the last hundred years.

_____
_____
_____

✓ **Reading Check**

Circle the age group of the "baby boom generation." What effect has this group had on our society?

Mark the Text

_____
_____
_____

Vocabulary Strategy

Using Word Parts The root of the underlined word is *ethn-*. This root means "culture or nation." The suffix *-ic* means "having to do with." Use the root and suffix of the underlined word to explain what an ethnic group is.

_____
_____
_____

✓ **Reading Check**

Describe a challenge our diverse society may face in the future.

_____
_____

One hundred years ago, most Americans worked on farms and in factories. Modern machines have changed most jobs. By 2006, nearly 75 percent of American workers will have **service jobs**.

Ages of Americans

The number of Americans in different age groups has changed over time. In 1850, more than half of Americans were children. Today, there are more older Americans than ever before. There are different reasons for this. Better medical care helps people live longer. A large number of people were born during the **baby boom**. They are now between the ages of 40 and 60. People also have fewer children today. In the future, there may not be enough medical benefits and services for these aging Americans.

Americans' Varied Backgrounds

Americans are known for their **diversity**. Our jobs, hometowns, ages, and backgrounds show our differences. Our backgrounds differ because we are from different cultures. We also belong to different races and ethnic groups.

Review Questions

1. What kinds of jobs did most American workers have one hundred years ago?

_____
_____

2. Why are there more older Americans today than ever before?

_____
_____

Key Terms

service job (SER vis JAHB) *n.* a job in which a person does something for other people

baby boom (BAY bee BOOM) *n.* the rise in the number of babies born from 1946 to 1964

diversity (dih VER sih tee) n. differences

Prepare to Read

Section 2
America: A Cultural Mosaic

Objectives

1. Explain what is meant by the American identity.
2. Discuss the contributions of European, Hispanic, African, Asian, and Native Americans to American society.
3. Describe the U. S. population today.

Target Reading Skill

Reread Rereading is another way to figure out the meaning of words and ideas that you do not understand. If what you read is not clear, try rereading it. As you read the text a second time, look for connections between words and sentences.

Read the following paragraph. Then reread it to find connections that help make the meaning of the word *immigrants* clear.

> America is sometimes called a nation of <u>immigrants</u>. Immigrants not only brought their dreams for a better life to America, they also brought ways of life from their homelands.

Words and sentences in the paragraph help explain that immigrants are people who move from one country to make their homes in another.

Vocabulary Strategy

Using Word Parts Many words can be divided into parts. To find the meaning of a word with a prefix or suffix, put the meanings of the root and other word parts together. The suffix *-ness,* for example, means "quality or state." It can be added to many different roots.

Root	+	Suffix	=	Word
empty	+	-ness	=	emptiness "quality of being empty"
lonely	+	-ness	=	loneliness "state of being lonely"

✓ Reading Check

Underline the two sentences that explain why it is not correct to say that America is a melting pot.

Mark the Text

Vocabulary Strategy

Using Word Parts Use what you know about the meaning of the suffix *-ness* to explain the meaning of the underlined word.

_____

_____

_____

✓ Reading Check

Circle the sentence that tells whether European immigrants were more alike or more different.

Mark the Text

✓ Reading Check

List three areas in which Hispanic culture has affected culture in the United States.

1. _____

2. _____

3. _____

¹ People from many countries have made their homes in America. These different groups add to the <u>richness</u> of American society.

The American Identity

America has been called a nation of **immigrants**.
⁵ Immigrants have helped make America diverse.

The United States is sometimes called a "melting pot." The idea is that immigrants melted into American society. They gave up ways of life from the lands where they were born. But all Americans are not the same.
¹⁰ Americans have kept parts of their different cultures.

Americans are really part of a mosaic, not a melting pot. A mosaic is made up of small tiles. The tiles are different sizes, shapes, and colors. Together the tiles make a whole picture. Together the groups in the
¹⁵ United States form a whole nation.

European Americans

Europeans were among the first immigrants. These people had different governments, languages, religions, and customs. The number of European immigrants is smaller today than in the past. But European
²⁰ Americans are still the largest part of our population.

Hispanic Americans

Hispanic Americans, or Latinos, share a culture from Spanish-speaking countries. They can be of any race. Latino foods, music, and architecture have added to United States culture.

African Americans

²⁵ African Americans have suffered from **discrimination**. They could not attend schools with white people or live in neighborhoods with whites. Such unfair treatment

---

Key Terms

immigrants (IM i gruhnts) *n.* people who move from one country to another

discrimination (dih skrim i NAY shun) *n.* being unfair to one group

was caused by **racism.** Since the 1960s, African Americans and others have worked for change. More
30 choices in education, jobs, and housing are available to African Americans. But there is still work to be done.

Asian Americans and Native Americans

Some of the first Asians came here after the discovery of gold in 1849. Other groups said Asians were taking away jobs. In 1882 and 1907, **exclusion laws** were passed to
35 keep immigrants from China and Japan from coming to America. These laws ended in 1952. Since then many Asian immigrants have come here.

Native Americans had been living here for thousands of years before Columbus. Then Europeans set-
40 tled on land Native Americans used. Native Americans fought for their lands. But they were pushed west. By the late 1800s, thousands had died. Today, Native Americans are only a small part of the population.

Our Population Today

The 2000 **census** showed that about 25 percent of the
45 United States population is not white, compared with 20 percent in 1990. Our ancestors come from all over the world. Each group adds to the richness of America.

Review Questions

1. Why is America like a mosaic? Explain.

_____

_____

2. What does the 2000 census show about the United States population today?

_____

_____

Key Terms

racism (RAY sih zum) *n.* the belief that your own race is better than others

exclusion laws (ek SKLOO shun LAWZ) *n.* laws that stopped people from China and Japan from moving to America

census (SEN sus) *n.* a count of people made every ten years

✓ **Reading Check**

Underline the sentences that give examples of discrimination against African Americans.

✓ **Reading Check**

Underline the sentence that explains what happened when the exclusion laws ended.

✓ **Reading Check**

Circle two words or phrases that tell how European settlers affected Native Americans in the 1800s.

✓ **Reading Check**

How did the United States population change between 1990 and 2000? List one possible social effect of this change.

_____

_____

_____

Target Reading Skill

Reread Reread the paragraph under "Asian Americans" to understand why laws were passed to keep Asian immigrants from coming to America. Circle the sentence that explains the reason for the exclusion laws.

Prepare to Read

Section 3
The Values That Unite Us

Objectives

1. Learn why equal respect is part of the American Dream.
2. Describe the basic values that unite us as a nation.
3. Understand how Americans can help achieve our ideals.

Target Reading Skill

Paraphrasing Paraphrasing is another tool that can help you better understand what you read. Paraphrasing is putting what you have read in your own words. Read the sentence below out loud.

> Everyone, regardless of age, sex, race, wealth, opinions, or education, has worth and importance.

Now try paraphrasing what you have read by saying it again in your own words. One way to paraphrase the sentence is:

> Everyone is important. It does not matter what a person's age, sex, or race is. It does not matter what his or her views are. Worth is not measured by money or education.

Vocabulary Strategy

Using Word Parts Prefixes and suffixes can change the meaning of a word. Some prefixes, such as *un-*, *non-*, *dis-*, and *im-*, mean "not." When one of these prefixes is added to a root, it changes the root's meaning. Take the word *uncommon*, for example. When *un-* is added to the root *common* it changes the meaning to "not common."

Section 3 Summary

¹ America is a diverse nation. What brings us together as one people?

Equal Respect: The American Dream

Certain **beliefs** and **values** hold Americans together. Our nation was founded on these beliefs and values.
⁵ Many people from other countries have come here because of these beliefs. Immigrants to America often have dreams of a better life. They believe that people are important no matter what their age, sex, race, wealth, or education. This is a basic American belief.

Basic American Values

¹⁰ <u>Americans believe that everyone should have the same chance to become what he or she can be.</u> In other words, every person has the right to be treated with equal respect.

Three basic values stand behind the American belief
¹⁵ that all people deserve equal respect.

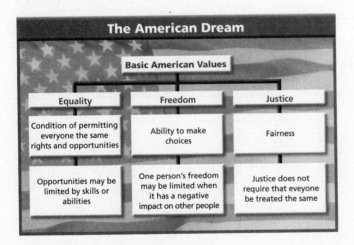

The American Dream

Basic American Values

Equality	Freedom	Justice
Condition of permitting everyone the same rights and opportunities	Ability to make choices	Fairness
Opportunities may be limited by skills or abilities	One person's freedom may be limited when it has a negative impact on other people	Justice does not require that eveyone be treated the same

In order for each person to become the best that he or she can be, there must be **equality**. Equality is one of our basic values. Part of equality is equal opportunity. This means that our race, gender, religion, back-
²⁰ ground, and opinions should not prevent us an equal

Key Terms

beliefs (bih LEEFS) *n.* things thought to be true

values (VAL yooz) *n.* things thought to be important

equality (ih KWAHL ih tee) *n.* having the same rights and chances

---

Underline the sentence that tells about the role, or part, that beliefs and values play in American society.

Target Reading Skill

Paraphrasing Paraphrase the underlined sentence.

_____

_____

_____

Give an example of each American value.

1. _____

2. _____

3. _____

Vocabulary Strategy

Using Word Parts Use what you know about the meaning of the prefixes *im-* and *dis-* to define the underlined words.

✓ Reading Check

Which of the following in Thomas's story shows that Americans need to work harder to give all equal respect? Circle the letter of the correct answer.

a. freedom

b. racism

c. equality

chance to succeed in life. **Freedom** is a second basic value. A third basic value is **justice**.

Citizens and the American Ideal

Our beliefs are an idea of how we want the United States to be. But our society is not perfect. It is <u>imper-</u>
25 <u>fect</u>. We try to live up to our beliefs and values. But we do not always reach these goals.

Thomas Pham came from Vietnam to live here. He heard that everyone in the United States has freedom and equality. He found out that this is not always true.
30 At school here, Thomas felt that people did not treat him the same as citizens who were born here. He was treated differently because of his race.

Not everyone in the United States shows equal respect for others. We sometimes <u>distrust</u> people who
35 are different. We still need to work to make sure that all Americans enjoy equality, freedom, and justice.

Review Questions

1. What beliefs and values bring Americans together as a nation?

_____

_____

2. How can Americans achieve our ideals?

_____

_____

Key Terms

freedom (FREE dum) *n.* being able to make choices

justice (JUS tis) *n.* fairness

1. In the future most Americans will work in
   A. the Sunbelt.
   B. urban areas.
   C. factories.
   D. service jobs.

2. The United States is best described as a
   A. melting pot.
   B. separate culture.
   C. mosaic of different groups.
   D. picture of immigrants.

3. Which of the following make up the largest ethnic group in the American population?
   A. European Americans
   B. Hispanic Americans
   C. Native Americans
   D. African Americans

4. Which of the following is *not* a basic American value?
   A. equality
   B. freedom
   C. diversity
   D. justice

5. We still need to work to make sure that all Americans enjoy equality, freedom, and justice because we
   A. do not show equal respect to all.
   B. have made a perfect nation.
   C. have lived up to our values.
   D. are different from each other.

Short Answer Question

In what ways are Americans alike and different from one another?

_____

_____

_____

_____

_____

Objectives

1. Learn why people form groups.
2. Describe the five major social institutions.

Target Reading Skill

Set a Purpose To better understand what you read, try setting a purpose for reading. Before starting, look at the headings and visuals in the text. Headings are short titles that tell about parts of the text. Visuals include all kinds of images such as photographs, tables, and maps. Headings and visuals give you information about the text. This information can give you a purpose, or focus, for reading what follows.

The title of this section is "Groups and Institutions." This title tells you the section is about groups and institutions. You know what a group is. One purpose for reading would be to find out what an institution is. You might also read to find out how groups and institutions affect you.

Vocabulary Strategy

Using Context Clues to Determine Meaning Sometimes you may read a word you recognize, but the word is used in a new way. To get a clearer idea of the meaning of the word, you can look at its context. The words, sentences, and paragraphs surrounding the word are its context. The context gives clues to the word's meaning.

For example, the word *dashes* commonly means "runs quickly." But it has a different meaning in this sentence: She *dashes* her new doll on the floor, breaking it into pieces." The clue is that the doll is broken into pieces. This clue tells you that here *dashes* means "throws down with force and anger."

Section 1 Summary

¹ Everyone has needs. People need food and shelter.
They need love and the company of others. They need
answers to questions about life and death.

People form groups to meet many of these needs.
⁵ We belong to some groups, such as family, just by
being born. Others we must join, such as school. We
choose to join some groups, such as clubs and <u>circles</u> of
friends. All these groups help us meet our needs.

Participating in a Group

People become members of a group through **socializa-**
¹⁰ **tion.** They learn to accept the values of the group. They
also learn the **rules** for how to behave in the group.
Rules are based on values.

Melissa became a member of a group at her school.
But she broke one of the rules by being late. The rule
¹⁵ was based on one of the group's values, which was to
be considerate of others. Melissa needed friendship,
and she wanted to accept the group's values. So she
changed how she behaved to stay in the group. The
group continued to meet her need for friendship.

Social Institutions

²⁰ Groups are important. But groups do not meet all our
needs. They do not give us food, clothing, or houses.
They do not make laws or govern our society. They
cannot do these things by themselves.

Social institutions take care of these needs. The
²⁵ values of social institutions shape our values. Their
rules tell us how to behave much of the time. Every
society has five main social institutions.

Vocabulary Strategy

Using Context Clues to Determine Meaning Use context to figure out the meaning of the word *circle* here. What clues do surrounding words, sentences, and paragraphs give about its meaning? What is its meaning?

_____

_____

_____

✓ Reading Check

Underline the needs that people meet by joining a group.

✓ Reading Check

Underline two sentences that tell how social institutions meet people's needs.

Key Terms

socialization (soh shuh luh ZAY shun) *n.* learning how to take part in a group

rules (ROOLZ) *n.* do's and don'ts

social institutions (SOH shul in stih TOO shuns) *n.* systems of values and rules that help to organize society

Set a Purpose Look at the heading and the visual on this page. What will you read about?

_____

_____

_____

_____

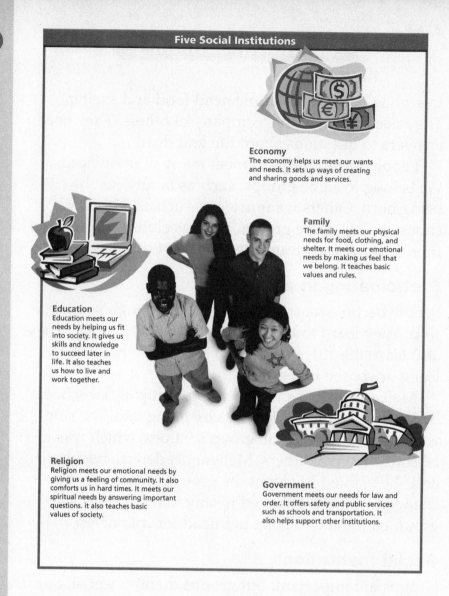

Five Social Institutions

Economy
The economy helps us meet our wants and needs. It sets up ways of creating and sharing goods and services.

Family
The family meets our physical needs for food, clothing, and shelter. It meets our emotional needs by making us feel that we belong. It teaches basic values and rules.

Education
Education meets our needs by helping us fit into society. It gives us skills and knowledge to succeed later in life. It also teaches us how to live and work together.

Religion
Religion meets our emotional needs by giving us a feeling of community. It also comforts us in hard times. It meets our spiritual needs by answering important questions. it also teaches basic values of society.

Government
Government meets our needs for law and order. It offers safety and public services such as schools and transportation. It also helps support other institutions.

Every society needs these five institutions. They provide a framework within which groups and organiza-
30 tions can exist.

Review Questions

1. Why do people form groups?

_____

_____

2. What are the five main social institutions?

_____

_____

CHAPTER 2

Prepare to Read

Section 2
Society's Training Grounds

Objectives

1. Identify the ways that families meet people's needs.
2. Explain the role of religion.
3. Describe the importance of education.

Target Reading Skill

Predict One way to set a purpose for reading is to predict what you will read. When you predict something, you tell what might happen before it happens. To make a prediction about what you will read, look at the headings, visuals, and anything else that stands out in the text. Use these parts of the text to make a prediction. Then read the text. Is it close to your prediction? If not, change your prediction to match what you learn.

Look at the title of this section, "Society's Training Grounds." Then look at the first heading in the section: "The Family." You might predict that families help train people to be part of society. You can test your prediction as you read the text.

Vocabulary Strategy

Using Context Clues to Determine Meaning Many English words have more than one meaning. You can use context clues to figure out which meaning of a word the author is using. In the sentences below, the word *back* has different meanings.

He wrote his answers on the back of the worksheet.
[*back* means "the other side"here]
She asked her friends to back her plan.
[*back* means "to support" here]

¹ The institutions of family, religion, and education help to shape our values.

The Family

The **family** is part of every society. You depend on your family for food, clothing, and shelter. Your family ⁵ makes you feel safe. It gives you a sense of belonging. It also teaches values you need to be part of society.

American families are smaller today than in the past. Some families include a father, mother, and children. Others have just one parent. Some families are ¹⁰ **blended families**.

Your family teaches you rules for daily life. These rules may include cleaning your room, doing homework, and not playing loud music. These rules are based on values such as being responsible, clean, and ¹⁵ respectful. There are punishments for breaking rules. And there are rewards for following them. Family rules often reflect a society's values. The family is a training ground for adults-to-be.

Religion

Religion is an important institution in our society. ²⁰ Religion is a comfort during hard times. It also answers questions about life and death. Religious groups create a feeling of community. Members of these groups are usually people who have similar goals and ways of looking at life. Religion also helps people decide how ²⁵ to live their lives.

<u>Every religion has a moral code, or a set of rules about how people should act.</u> These rules help people tell right from wrong. People who obey these rules feel confident that they are living good lives.

✓ Reading Check

Underline two sentences that tell how the family serves as a training ground for young people.

↻ Target Reading Skill

Predict Write a prediction about what you will learn under the heading "Religion." After you read, change your prediction if you need to.

_____

_____

_____

Vocabulary Strategy

Using Context Clues to Determine Meaning The word *act* has more than one meaning. It can mean "do something." It also means "play a part" and "behave." Look at the underlined sentence. Which meaning is correct in this sentence?

_____

_____

Key Terms

family (FAM uh lee) *n.* a group of related people, such as parents and children

blended families (BLEN did FAM uh leez) *n.* families that include adults and their children from different marriages

30 Religion teaches values. These include charity, sympa-
thy, and loyalty to friends and family. These values
cannot be written into laws. But when people follow
these values, life is better for everyone.

Americans belong to many religious groups. There
35 are more than 1,200 religious groups in the United
States today. All groups do not share the same rules.
Some people belong to no religious group at all. Your
own beliefs sometimes make it difficult to let others
believe as they wish. These conflicts can test our ideal
40 of equal respect.

Education

Education teaches skills and other rules. Like most
people, you probably hope to have a career. A career is
work that uses your skills and talents. It allows you to
earn money. It also gives you a feeling of importance.
45 To have a career, you need an education. Education
prepares you for your life as a working adult. School is
also a place where you meet people. They may have
different backgrounds and values. In school you learn
it is important to respect others.

50 The institution of education serves our society.
Society needs to train people to run all kinds of services. Society also needs to prepare people to live
together. Schools teach us about our history, culture,
and government. In school we learn about the ideal of
55 equal respect. We also learn the values of freedom,
equality, and justice. Through education, American
society makes sure that our country continues to be
free and democratic.

Review Questions

1. How does religion help guide, or direct, people's
lives?

_____

_____

2. Why is education important?

_____

_____

✓ Reading Check

Circle the paragraph that describes the contribution that religion makes to American society.

✓ Reading Check

Underline the sentence that tells why meeting people from different backgrounds is an important part of education.

Vocabulary Strategy

Using Context Clues to Determine Meaning The under-lined word means "land outside cities and towns." It also means "nation." What meaning does the word have here?

_____

_____

_____

Objectives

1. Explain the characteristics of the American economy.

2. Identify American economic freedoms.

3. Describe your role in the American economy.

Target Reading Skill

Preview and Ask Questions Asking questions before reading will help you better understand what you read. First get an idea of what the section is about. You can do this by previewing, or looking at, the headings and visuals in the section before you read. Also pay attention to anything else that stands out in the text. Ask some questions based on what you see. Then look for the answers to your questions as you read.

Look at the vocabulary terms that stand out under the heading "The American Economy." You might ask the following questions before reading: What is an economy? What do goods and services have to do with an economy? What is a consumer? What is a market? How do prices work in an economy?

Vocabulary Strategy

Using Context Clues to Determine Meaning How can you figure out the meaning of a word you do not recognize as you read? As you have learned, words, phrases, and sentences around the word sometimes give clues to its meaning. The information in the second sentence below helps you understand what the word *consume* means.

As consumers, we consume goods and services to satisfy our wants. We use gasoline when we want to run our cars; we use the barber when we want a haircut.

The second sentence tells us that consume means "to use."

Section 3 Summary

¹ Suppose one day you make brownie bars. Then you get an idea. You could make a lot of brownie bars. You could call them BarWonders. You could trade them for goods and services that you need or want.

The American Economy

⁵ Every society has an **economy** to make and provide goods and services. In our economy, each person is a **consumer**. In other words, we consume, or use, goods and services to satisfy our wants. Most people are also workers who make goods or provide services.

¹⁰ People trade goods or services in a **market**. Stores are one kind of market. In a store, people meet face-to-face to <u>exchange</u> what they have for what they want. Usually, they trade money for some item such as a slice of pizza or a t-shirt. In other kinds of markets, such as ¹⁵ a stock exchange, buyers and sellers never meet.

In a market, you a pay a **price** for a good or service. When you trade your BarWonders for goods and services, you are bartering. Bartering is one way to pay for what you want. Usually people use **money** to pay for ²⁰ goods and services. Money can be anything, from beads to coins to checks.

The American economy is based on the basic value of freedom. Like all institutions, our economy has rules that people must follow. Some rules of the economy ²⁵ protect important freedoms.

✓ Reading Check

Underline the sentence that explains what an economy does.

Target Reading Skill

Preview and Ask Questions
Preview the underlined heading. Then write two questions based on the heading. Look for answers to your questions as you read.

_____

_____

_____

Vocabulary Strategy

Using Context Clues to Determine Meaning Circle one word in the text that helps you figure out the meaning of the underlined word.

Key Terms

economy (ih KAHN ih mee) *n.* a system for making things and offering services to meet people's wants

consumer (kun SOO mer) *n.* a person who uses goods and services to meet his or her wants

market (MAR kit) *n.* a place where people trade goods or services

price (PRĪS) *n.* what you pay for goods or services in a market

money (MUN ee) *n.* anything taken as payment for goods or services

Using Context Clues to Determine Meaning
Underline the phrase in the chart that helps define the word *profit*.

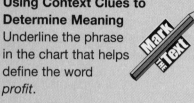

Target Reading Skill

Preview and Ask Questions
Write a question you might ask after previewing the underlined heading.

_____

_____

_____

✓ Reading Check

Underline the sentences that tell how people benefit from the American economy.

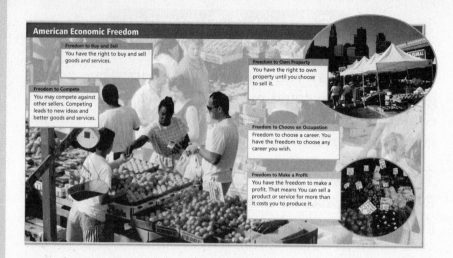

American Economic Freedom

Freedom to Buy and Sell
You have the right to buy and sell goods and services.

Freedom to Compete
You may compete against other sellers. Competing leads to new ideas and better goods and services.

Freedom to Own Property
You have the right to own property until you choose to sell it.

Freedom to Choose an Occupation
Freedom to choose a career. You have the freedom to choose any career you wish.

Freedom to Make a Profit
You have the freedom to make a profit. That means You can sell a product or service for more than it costs you to produce it.

The rules of our economy are based on the idea of fairness. If you make an agreement to do a job, sell a product, or pay a worker, you may not break it. You also may not make something that does not work the way
30 that you say it does.

America's Economy and You

Our economy works well for the most part. It supplies the goods and services we want. We also are free to try to reach our dreams—to have careers and ways of life that we choose. We benefit from the United States
35 economy in these ways.

Review Questions

1. What freedoms are protected in the American economy?

_____

_____

2. What part do you play in the American economy?

_____

_____

CHAPTER 2

Prepare to Read

Section 4 Government: Meeting Society's Needs

Objectives

1. Learn why government is needed.
2. Explain how three different forms of government work.
3. Describe the roles of law in government.

Target Reading Skill

Use Prior Knowledge To understand new information better, use what you already know. Take a look at the headings and images in the text before you start to read. Then ask yourself: What do I already know about what I see?

Take the heading "Political Socialization," for example. What does *political* mean to you? What have you learned about socialization?

Heading or Image	What I Already Know
Political Socialization	Socialization is learning how to be part of a group.

Vocabulary Strategy

Using Context Clues to Determine Meaning Always look at words, phrases, and sentences around a word for clues to its meaning. The underlined words in the paragraph below offer clues to the meaning of the word *chaos*.

Without government, daily life would be filled with chaos. There would be no order to the way roads were built or towns and cities planned. People would disagree about ways to settle arguments and deal with crime.

Unfamiliar Word	Clues	Meaning
chaos	no order, disagree	no order, confusion

✓ **Reading Check**

Underline the information in the chart that tells about the part courts play in our government.

Target Reading Skill

Using Prior Knowledge Name a form of government and write something you know about it.

_____

_____

_____

Vocabulary Strategy

Using Context Clues to Determine Meaning In the paragraph that begins "In a dictatorship," circle the details that offer clues about the meaning of *military*.

✓ **Reading Check**

Underline one sentence about monarchy and one sentence about dictatorship that tells the main difference between the two.

¹ Our government was formed to protect our rights. In some countries, people's rights are not protected and they live in fear.

The Role of Government

Government helps brings order to people's lives.

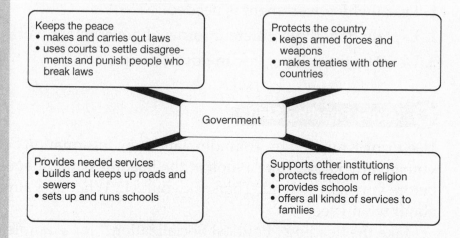

Keeps the peace
- makes and carries out laws
- uses courts to settle disagreements and punish people who break laws

Protects the country
- keeps armed forces and weapons
- makes treaties with other countries

Government

Provides needed services
- builds and keeps up roads and sewers
- sets up and runs schools

Supports other institutions
- protects freedom of religion
- provides schools
- offers all kinds of services to families

Forms of Government

⁵ There are many forms of government. Three common forms today are monarchy, dictatorship, and democracy.

In a **monarchy,** one person has all or most of the power. That person is the monarch. The monarch's power is hereditary. That means it is passed down in a ¹⁰ family. Monarchies in which one person holds all the power are not common today. The kingdom of Saudi Arabia is one example.

In a **dictatorship,** one person, called a dictator, controls the government. A dictator usually takes power ¹⁵ by force. Often dictators are <u>military</u> leaders. They use the armed forces and police to keep power. They do not pay attention to laws. Saddam Hussein of Iraq was a modern example of a dictator.

Key Terms

monarchy (MAH nar kee) *n.* a government in which one person, called a monarch, holds all or most of the power

dictatorship (dik TAY ter ship) *n.* a government controlled by one person called a dictator

In a **democracy,** power is shared by all the people.
20 Democracy means "government by the people." The people decide how the government will meet their needs and protect their rights and freedoms. They do this by voting and choosing leaders. The United States was the first modern democracy.

Laws: The Rules of Government

25 Laws are government rules for how to behave. A document called the Constitution contains our most basic and important laws. Town, county, state, and national governments also can make laws. These laws cannot go against the Constitution.

Laws affect almost everything we do. When we fol-
30 low laws, we help protect the rights of others. We also help to keep order. Breaking the law leads to different kinds of punishment.

People in a democracy can share their opinions. They can work with others to make new laws. They
35 also can try to change laws they think are unfair.

Political Socialization

Terrorists attacked the United States on September 11, 2001. After that, people across the country showed their **patriotism** in many ways. We learn how to behave politically and patriotically from our parents,
40 teachers, church, the media, and others. This process is called **political socialization**.

Review Questions

1. How does government bring order to people's lives?

_____

_____

2. Name three common forms of government.

_____

_____

Key Terms

democracy (dih MAHK ruh see) *n.* government by the people

patriotism (PAY tree uh tiz um) *n.* the show of love for one's country

political socialization (puh LIT ih kul soh shuh luh ZAY shun) *n.* the process of learning how to behave politically

Use Prior Knowledge What do you already know about laws that matches their definition as rules of government?

_____

_____

_____

✓ **Reading Check**

Describe how people in a democracy help to make the laws.

_____

_____

_____

_____

✓ **Reading Check**

Circle four groups that help teach people about patriotism.

1. People form groups to
   A. start clubs.
   B. meet needs.
   C. have work.
   D. all of the above

2. Which of the following is *not* a social institution?
   A. government
   B. family
   C. religion
   D. transportation

3. School is where we learn American values and
   A. get a comfortable life.
   B. meet different kinds of people.
   C. experience equal respect.
   D. serve our society.

4. The American economy includes consumers, workers, and
   A. markets.
   B. prices.
   C. money.
   D. all of the above

5. In a democracy,
   A. one person controls the government by force.
   B. all or most of the power is in the hands of one person.
   C. power is shared by all the people.
   D. power is passed down in a family.

Short Answer Question

Identify the five institutions that help to shape our values. In your own words, describe each of the institutions.

_____

_____

_____

_____

Prepare to Read

Section 1
What It Means To Be a Citizen

Objectives

1. Discuss who a citizen is and how a person becomes an American citizen.

2. Discuss what the office of citizen is and what important powers citizens possess.

Target Reading Skill

Identify Main Ideas The main idea is the most important point the writer makes in a paragraph or section. Sometimes the writer states the main idea in a sentence. This sentence may appear at the beginning, end, or middle of a paragraph or section. Read the paragraph below out loud.

> <u>People from other countries can become citizens of the United States by going through a process called naturalization.</u> They learn English and study American history. They also learn the values, laws, rights, and duties of American citizens.

The underlined sentence tells the main idea of the paragraph. You can tell that it is the main idea because the other sentences in the paragraph give details that support it.

Vocabulary Strategy

Using Roots and Suffixes As you already know, a **root** is the word part that gives a word its basic meaning. A **suffix** is a word part that is added after the root. When you know the meanings of a word's root and suffix, you can often figure out the meaning of the word as you read.

Take the word *government*, for example. It can be divided into two parts: *govern + ment*. The root is *govern-*. The suffix *-ment* means "result or action." When you add the suffix to the root, you know the meaning of *government* is "the result or action of governing."

Section 1 Summary

Target Reading Skill

Identify Main Ideas
Underline the sentence that states the main idea of the last paragraph under "Who Is a Citizen?"

Vocabulary Strategy

Using Roots and Suffixes The suffix *-ship* means "state or condition." Now use what you know about this suffix to explain the meaning of the underlined word.

_____

_____

✓ Reading Check

Underline the sentences that tell how the rights and duties of naturalized citizens differ from the rights and duties of citizens by birth.

¹ A United States **citizen** is an official member of his or her town, state, and nation.

Who Is a Citizen?

The Constitution says that a person can be a citizen of the United States by birth or by choice.

You are an American citizen if
You were born in the United States or its territories.
or
At least one of your parents was a United States citizen when you were born.
or
You have been naturalized.
or
You were under age eighteen when your parents were naturalized.

₅   **Aliens** can become United States citizens by going through the naturalization process. They study American history and English. They also learn the values, laws, rights, and duties of citizens. **Naturalized** citizens have all the rights and duties of citizens by ₁₀ birth with one exception: They do not have the right to be President or Vice President.

   Once a person is a citizen, he or she will always be a citizen except in a few special cases. A person can decide to give up his or her <u>citizenship</u>. Or a person ₁₅ can become a citizen of another country. Citizenship may be taken away from a person who tries to overthrow the U.S. government by force.

Key Terms

citizen (SIT uh zun) *n.* a person with certain rights and duties under a government

alien (AY lee un) *n.* a citizen of one country who lives in another country

naturalized (NA chuh ruh līzd) *v.* having taken the steps to become a citizen

The Office of Citizen

Citizens hold the power in our country. Abraham Lincoln said that we have a government "of the peo-
20 ple, by the people, [and] for the people." He meant that our government does what its citizens want it to do. That includes making laws, building roads, collecting taxes, and making <u>agreements</u> with other countries. Citizens have the power to decide what our govern-
25 ment will and will not do.

As citizens, we elect **representatives**. We choose members of Congress. We elect the President. We also elect office holders such as city council members, mayors, governors, and many judges. We give these people
30 power to make decisions and to pass laws.

Our leaders stay in office only as long as we want them to. We give our power to them only for that time. The real power belongs to us. In this way, each of us holds an office. Our office is the "office of citizen."
35 Being a citizen is the most important office in our society. Citizens hold this office for as long as they live.

Review Questions

1. How does a naturalized citizen of the United States differ from a citizen by birth?

_____

_____

_____

2. What is the most important office in the United States? Why?

_____

_____

_____

Target Reading Skill

Identify Main Ideas Underline the sentence that tells the main idea of the first paragraph under the heading "The Office of Citizen."

Vocabulary Strategy

Using Roots and Suffixes Use what you know about the root and suffix of the underlined word to explain its meaning.

_____

_____

_____

✓ Reading Check

How do American citizens give their representatives power in government? Circle the best answer.

(a) They elect representatives to office.

(b) They make representatives citizens.

(c) They choose representatives they like.

Key Terms

representatives (rep rih ZEN tuh tivz) *n.* people chosen by citizens to speak and act for them in government

Prepare to Read

Section 2
Rights, Duties, and Responsibilities

Objectives

1. Explore some of the many rights guaranteed to American citizens.
2. Learn about the many duties and obligations citizens share.
3. Find out about some of the responsibilities citizens honor to keep our country strong and united.

Target Reading Skill

Identify Supporting Details A detail is a point related to the main idea. It gives information to fill in a picture more completely. Writers use details to support main ideas. Identifying supporting details can help you figure out what the main idea of a paragraph or section is. In the paragraph below, the main idea is in dark type. The supporting details are underlined once.

> **Having a driver's license gives you certain rights and duties.** You have <u>the right to drive on public roads and highways</u>. It is also your <u>right to park where the law allows</u>. Your <u>duties include obeying traffic signals and signs</u>. You also must make sure that you <u>do not drive over the speed limit</u>.

Vocabulary Strategy

Using Roots and Suffixes Knowing the meanings of different roots and suffixes can help you understand words you have never seen before. To figure out what a word means, try dividing it into root and suffix. Then combine the meanings of the root and suffix. Look at these words with the suffix -*ity*, which means "state or condition."

Word	=	Root	+	Suffix,	Meaning
ability	=	able	+	ity,	state of being able
possibility	=	possible	+	ity,	state of being possible

Section 2 Summary

¹ Citizens have rights, duties, and responsibilities.

Rights of Citizens

American citizens have many rights.

Some Rights of American Citizens

- the right to vote and hold elected office
- the right to say what you think in speech or writing
- the right to follow your own religion
- the right to have a fair trial
- the right to be protected by the government when you work or travel in other countries

---

Our rights are based on the beliefs and values of equal respect, freedom, equality, and justice. The ⁵ Constitution stands behind these rights, and laws and courts protect them.

Duties of Citizens

Citizens also have duties. Duties go along with our rights as citizens. When we carry out our duties, we help our government to meet our needs.

¹⁰ Obeying the law is one of our duties. Laws help to keep order. Everyone in a democracy, including government officials, must obey the law. This idea is called the **rule of law**. The rule of law makes sure that the government does not take power away from the people.

¹⁵ Helping to protect our country is another duty. When you are eighteen or older, you may volunteer to serve in the military. Young men must register for military service when they are eighteen.

Target Reading Skill

Identify Supporting Details
Where would you look for supporting details for the main idea of this section?

_____

_____

_____

✓ Reading Check

How do the rights held by American citizens suggest the importance of "equal rights for all"?

_____

_____

_____

_____

✓ Reading Check

Circle the sentence that explains why it is important for government officials to obey laws like other citizens.

Key Terms

rule of law (ROOL UV LO) *n.* a government in which the law rules, rather than men or women

Vocabulary Strategy

Using Roots and Suffixes The suffix -*dom* means "state or condition." Underline the word with this suffix. Then divide the word into its root and suffix and explain its meaning.

_____

_____

Target Reading Skill

Identify Supporting Details List details that support the underlined main idea.

1. _____

2. _____

3. _____

✓ Reading Check

Circle the words that tell why it is important to get information on issues that are decided in elections.

Serving on a jury at a trial is another duty. The
20 Constitution says that anyone accused of a crime may have the case decided by a **jury of peers**. During the trial, lawyers may call **witnesses** to prove their case. Paying taxes and attending school are other duties.

Responsibilities of Citizens

Citizens also have responsibilities. Responsibilities are
25 different from duties. We are not required by law to carry them out. Instead, we choose to do them.

One responsibility is working toward the **common good.** We do this by acting to protect others' rights and freedoms. We also work to make our communities,
30 states, and nation good places to live.

Voting is another responsibility. To vote wisely, citizens need to learn about issues. Holding government office or helping a **candidate** run for office are other ways to be a responsible citizen.
35 Citizens also show responsibility by trying to convince government to act in a cause they believe in. Citizens do this by sharing their opinions. They write letters to representatives. They write letters to newspapers. They speak at government meetings. They join or
40 form groups that influence government.

Review Questions

1. What are some rights American citizens have?

_____

_____

2. What is a basic responsibility of every citizen?

_____

_____

Key Terms

jury of peers (JER ee UV PEERZ) *n.* ordinary people who hear a court case and decide whether a person is innocent or guilty

witnesses (WIT nis iz) *n.* people who have seen events connected to a crime or who have special information that may tell whether a person is guilty or innocent

common good (KAHM un GUD) *n.* the well being of all members of society

candidate (KAN dih dayt) *n.* a person running for office

Prepare to Read

Section 3
Citizenship and Our Other Roles in Society

Objectives

1. Learn about playing social roles.
2. Discuss how social roles involve expected behaviors.
3. Consider the different levels of participation involved in social roles.
4. Explore how to play the role of citizen.

 Target Reading Skill

Identify Implied Main Ideas Sometimes the main idea of a paragraph is not stated directly. It is implied, or suggested, instead. When the main idea is implied, you have to figure out what it is. To do this, look at the details in the paragraph and decide what idea they support. Read the paragraph below and pay close attention to the underlined details. What main idea do they suggest?

> You play a part in society as a citizen, student, family member, and friend. You may also act as a worker. You may be a member of a club or team. You also act as your own person by making many choices during the course of a day.

The implied main idea is the following: You have many roles in society.

Vocabulary Strategy

Using Roots and Suffixes Remember, knowing the meaning of roots and suffixes can help you figure out the meaning of words you do not understand. Many words are formed by adding the suffix *-ion* after a root. The suffix *-ion* means "act of, state of, or result of."

Word	Root	Suffix	Meaning
completion	complet-	-ion	act of completing, state of being complete
selection	select-	-ion	act of selecting, state of being selected
creation	creat-	-ion	act of creating, result of creating

Section 3 Summary

¹ People have many roles in society. They play different parts within a family. They also play parts with friends, people they work with, neighbors, and other citizens.

Playing Social Roles

⁵ Jean Reardon, for example, plays <u>many social roles every day</u>. She plays <u>the role of family member</u>. She helps her daughter with homework and spends time with her husband. She plays <u>social group roles</u> as a carpool member and student. When she reads the news-¹⁰paper to learn about issues, Jean plays <u>the citizen role</u>. Jean also plays <u>worker and friend roles</u>. When she goes shopping, Jean plays the <u>consumer role</u>. <u>All day</u> she plays <u>the self role</u>.

We choose some social roles, such as being a friend, ¹⁵club member, or consumer. We are born into family roles. We have to play other roles at different times in our lives, such as student.

Roles as Expected Behaviors

People behave, or act, differently in different roles. Other people's <u>expectations</u> about how you should act ²⁰in a certain role help you know how to act. The way you act also depends on what you want. It depends on the kind of person you are, too.

Roles and how people play them change over time. Sometimes, you may play the same role in different ²⁵ways. For instance, you may play the role of friend differently with different friends. As time passes, you also may stop playing a role.

Key Terms

social roles (SOH shul RŌLZ) *n.* parts that people play in real life

Social roles sometimes overlap. They do this when you play more than one role at the same time.
30 Sometimes roles conflict with each other. When that happens, you may have to decide which role to play.

Level of <u>Participation</u>

You have to choose how active you want to be in each social role. You make choices based on what is important to you. Then you must accept the consequences, or
35 results, of taking part or not taking part. When people participate fully in a role, most feel satisfaction and get a better sense of who they are.

The Citizen Role

The citizen role is important. Some citizens play a very active part. They may run for government office. Or
40 they may work for political campaigns. Some people spend less time in the citizen role. They stay informed, vote, or give money to support candidates and issues.

The citizen role is not limited to government activities. Many people play the role by adding to the com-
45 mon good. They do this by serving their communities in various ways.

How much time and energy will you give to being a responsible citizen? To decide, look at other roles you play. How important are they to you? Your decision
50 will also be based on your stage of life, values, talents, and interests. Playing an active role can give you a sense of satisfaction and fulfillment. Taking a less active role can mean you are dissatisfied or unfulfilled.

Review Questions

1. What determines the social roles we play?

_____

_____

2. How do people play the citizen role?

_____

_____

✓ **Reading Check**

Describe changing or conflicting social roles you have played.

_____

_____

_____

Vocabulary Strategy

Using Roots and Suffixes What is the root and suffix of the underlined word? What does the word mean?

_____

_____

Target Reading Skill

Identify Implied Main Ideas Use the details under the heading "Levels of Participation" to figure out the main idea of the section. Write a sentence that states the main idea.

_____

_____

_____

✓ **Reading Check**

Bracket the sentences that explain the consequences of participating passively rather than actively in a social role.

1. If you are not an American citizen by birth, you can become a citizen by
   A. being under age eighteen when your parents were naturalized.
   B. working in the United States or going to school here.
   C. serving in the armed forces.
   D. being elected to Congress or running for President.

2. Which of the following is a duty of every American citizen?
   A. voting in elections
   B. having a fair trial
   C. obeying the law
   D. following your religion

3. Citizens of the United States show responsibility by
   A. voting for representatives and on issues.
   B. speaking at government meetings.
   C. making their communities good places to live.
   D. all of the above

4. How you play a social role depends on
   A. how you want to play it.
   B. the kind of person you are.
   C. what people expect.
   D. all of the above

5. People choose how actively they want to take part in social roles based on
   A. what roles are available.
   B. what is most important to them.
   C. how many people are taking part.
   D. how large their community is.

Short Answer Question

Explain the difference between a citizen's duties and a citizen's responsibilities.

_____

_____

_____

_____

_____

Prepare to Read

Section 1
The Colonial Experience

Objectives

1. Learn how the colonists acquired a voice in their government.
2. Understand the meaning of citizenship in the colonies.
3. Explore some roots of individual freedom in America.
4. Describe the colonists' signs of discontent with English rule.

Target Reading Skill

Recognize Multiple Causes A cause is an event that makes another event happen. It can also be a situation that leads to a new situation. Sometimes there is more than one cause for an event or new situation. In the 1700s, the American colonies became unhappy with the English government. There were many reasons for this. As you read about the colonies, look for the causes of their anger toward England.

Vocabulary Strategy

Using Word Parts Many words can be divided into parts. Understanding the meanings of a word's parts can help you figure out the meaning of the whole word. Roots, prefixes, and suffixes are all word parts.

Take the word *unknown,* for example. It can be divided into two parts: *un + known.* The prefix *un-* means "not." Knowing the meaning of that word part helps you define *unknown* as "not known."

[1] Many American traditions began in the colonies. What happened to the colonists is important. It is part of our nation's **heritage**.

A Voice in Government

The colonists were used to having a say in the govern-[5]ment. This was one of their rights as citizens of England. In each colony citizens elected leaders to a **legislature**. This kind of self-government was unusual at that time.

England was busy fighting wars in the 1600s and [10] early 1700s. The colonists mainly governed themselves. But they did not completely control their government. The English king set up each colony through a **charter**. If the people of a colony questioned England's power, the colony could lose its charter.

[15] <u>The citizens in the colonies sometimes had to stand up against the colonial governors.</u> The governors did not have to pay attention to the colonists' rights. They were not elected. That means the colonists did not choose them.

Citizenship in the Colonies

[20] Being an English citizen in the colonies was different from being an American citizen today. Only white men who owned land could vote or hold office. Colonists were like citizens today in that they worked for the common good. They served on juries. They served in [25] the local volunteer army. They supported education.

✓ Reading Check

Underline the sentences that explain why the American colonists were able to govern themselves.

⊙ Target Reading Skill

Recognizing Multiple Causes Identify two causes that led to the underlined situation. Number the causes where you find them in the text.

Vocabulary Strategy

Using Word Parts Circle the word under "A Voice in Government" that begins with the prefix un-. Write a definition of the word below.

_____

_____

_____

✓ Reading Check

Explain what it meant to be a citizen in the American colonies.

_____

_____

_____

Key Terms

heritage (HAYR ih tij) *n.* ways and beliefs passed down from parents to their children

legislature (LEJ is lay cher) *n.* a group of people chosen to make the laws

charter (CHAR ter) *n.* a document giving permission to create a government

Some Roots of Freedom

For most of history, people did not have freedom of religion. They did not have freedom of speech. The colonists worked to win these freedoms.

30 The colonists lived at a time when religion was often closely tied to government. For example, all English citizens had to support the Church of England. Many colonists left England because they did not agree with that church. Most colonies allowed religious freedom. "Religious freedom" in colonial times differed from reli-
35 gious freedom today. It usually meant that people could belong to any Christian church. Still, the colonists took a step that led to freedom of religion for all Americans.

An early fight for freedom of the press took place in 1735. Under English law, newspapers could not com-
40 plain about the government. John Peter Zenger printed articles that complained about the government. So he was sent to jail. Zenger's lawyer was Andrew Hamilton. Hamilton argued that Zenger was innocent if what he wrote was true. Hamilton said that freedom of the press
45 was a basic right. The jury found Zenger not guilty. This case made colonists fight for freedom of the press.

Signs of Discontent

In the 1770s, England tightened control of its colonies. Many colonists were angry with their governors. The governors used too much power. The colonists often
50 used the word tyranny when talking about the governors. Many colonists began to wonder whether England might try to take away their rights and their voice in government.

Review Questions

1. How did the colonists get a voice in government?

_____

_____

2. What was one sign that the colonists were not happy about the government?

_____

_____

Key Terms

tyranny (TEER uh nee) *n.* bad use of power

✓ Reading Check

Underline two sentences that help explain how important freedom of religion was to the colonists. Underline two sentences that explain how important freedom of the press was.

Vocabulary Strategy

Using Word Parts Explain the meaning of the underlined word.

_____

_____

Target Reading Skill

Recognizing Multiple Causes List two causes of the underlined situation.

1. _____

_____

2. _____

_____

✓ Reading Check

Why do you think England tightened its control over the colonies?

_____

_____

_____

Prepare to Read

Section 2
Roots of American Government

Objectives

1. Discuss how the colonists looked to ancient Greece and Rome for models of government.

2. Examine how the English tradition influenced American government.

3. Understand how relying on reason helped shape the American government.

Target Reading Skill

Identify Causes and Effects As you have read, a cause makes something happen. An effect is what happens. Identifying causes and effects helps you understand the connections between events. Look at the cause-and-effect chart.

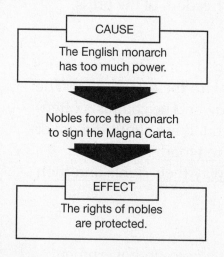

Vocabulary Strategy

Using Word Parts The root of a word is the part that gives the word its basic meaning. Prefixes and suffixes added to the root add to the meaning of the root. Look at the word *democracy,* for instance:

Root	+	Suffix
dem-	+	*-cracy*
"people"	+	"rule by"

Democracy means "rule or government by the people."

Section 2 Summary

¹ American colonists based their new government on the experiences of others.

Looking to Ancient Greece and Rome

The ancient Greek city of Athens was an example for American government. Powerful kings ruled Athens
⁵ for hundred of years. Then the people set up the world's first **direct democracy**. They had meetings. They discussed how to improve life for their community. Later, American colonists set up their own form of direct democracy. They held town meetings to vote on
¹⁰ issues.

The English Tradition

The colonists believed that Athens and the **republic** of Rome were examples of good government. Both were supposed to stop tyranny.

A struggle in England led to the government we
¹⁵ have today. For hundreds of years, kings had complete power over the English people. The people were not citizens. They were subjects. That means they were under the king's command. Some kings were fair. Others were not. In 1215, English nobles limited the
²⁰ power of their <u>monarch</u>, or king. They forced the king to sign the Magna Carta. This document gave rights to the people that the king could not take away. It was an important step in helping to give basic rights to many English people, including the colonists.

✓ Reading Check

Circle the term that tells what colonial governments had in common with the government of ancient Athens.

Vocabulary Strategy

Using Word Parts The root *mon-* means "one." The suffix *-arch* means "ruler." Use this information to explain the meaning of the underlined word.

_____

_____

Key Terms

direct democracy (dih REKT dih MAHK ruh see) *n.* a form of government in which the people make the laws

republic (rih PUB lik) *n.* a government in which leaders are elected by the people to make laws

Identifying Causes and Effects
Underline a sentence that describes an effect of the English Bill of Rights.

✓ **Reading Check**

What does history suggest about how the English people felt about government?

_____

_____

_____

✓ **Reading Check**

Explain how Locke and Montesquieu might have felt about each other's ideas and why.

_____

_____

_____

25　　In the 1200s, England set up a legislature to make laws. It was called Parliament. Parliament became more powerful than the king. In 1689, it passed the English Bill of Rights. It listed the rights of all English citizens, not just the rich. It also protected against

30 unfair rulers. English citizens, including the colonists, were glad to have their rights protected.

Relying on Reason

The colonists also learned new ideas from European writers. Many writers wrote about reason. Reason means being able to think clearly. The writers also

35 believed that people had **natural rights**.

　　One important writer was John Locke. He argued that government should serve the people, not the other way around. He said government should protect people's natural rights—the rights to life, liberty, and

40 property. Any government that abuses its power should not be obeyed.

　　Another important writer was the French writer Montesquieu. He wrote about the **separation of powers**. Under this system, the legislature makes the laws.

45 An executive, such as a governor, carries out the laws. And judges explain the laws. This system guards against tyranny. It does not give one person or part of government too much power.

Review Questions

1. What idea for government did Rome give the colonists?

_____

_____

2. What two English documents helped shaped American government?

_____

_____

Key Terms

natural rights (NACH er ul RĪTS) _n._ rights people are born with that government cannot take away

separation of powers (sep uh RAY shun UV POW erz) _n._ dividing government power among legislative, executive, and judicial branches

Prepare to Read

Section 3
Moving Toward Nationhood

Objectives

1. Explain the clash of views that brought the colonists into open conflict with England.
2. Summarize the Declaration of Independence.
3. Describe how Americans organized a new government.
4. Understand the challenges that a struggling American government would have to face.

 Target Reading Skill

Understand Effects An effect is what happens as a result of an event or action. To identify effects of an event or action, ask: What happened as a result of this event? In this section, for instance, ask: What happened when England tightened its control over the colonies? As you read, look for the effects of this action.

Vocabulary Strategy

Using Word Parts You know that a prefix comes before the root of a word and a suffix comes after the root. To understand the meaning of a word with a prefix or a suffix, combine, or bring together, the meanings of this part and the word's root. Look at these examples.

Word	Prefix	Root	Suffix	Meaning
pianist		pian- "having to do with the piano"	-ist "someone involved in"	"someone who plays the piano"
inactive	in- "not"	-act- "do"	-ive "inclined to"	"not inclined to do," "not active"

Vocabulary Strategy

Using Word Parts Tell what you think the root of the underlined word means. Then add the meaning of the suffix to explain the meaning of the word.

_____

_____

_____

Target Reading Skill

Understanding Effects What was the effect, or result, of Thomas Paine's writings?

_____

_____

✓ Reading Check

Why do you think Thomas Paine called some of his writings about independence *Common Sense?*

_____

_____

_____

✓ Reading Check

Underline sentences that help explain the purpose of the Declaration of Independence.

---

¹ The colonies and England did not agree. These disagreements led to war. And war led to independence.

A Clash of Views

The American colonies and the English government disagreed on important issues. For example, Parliament
⁵ let the colonists trade only with England. The <u>colonists</u> wanted to sell their products to any country.

Parliament taxed the colonies. It needed money to pay for the French and Indian War. But the colonists did not want to pay taxes unless their leaders
¹⁰ approved them. To get people to pay, Parliament gave colonial governors more power.

The colonists took steps to become independent. In 1774 they sent leaders to the First Continental Congress. A year later they held the Second
¹⁵ Continental Congress. Some colonists began fighting English soldiers. Others were not ready to fight. Thomas Paine's writings changed their minds. His pamphlet about independence was called *Common Sense.* He argued that England was too far away to
²⁰ govern American properly.

The Declaration of Independence

The Second Continental Congress voted for independence. A group wrote a document. It announced the colonies' independence. This Declaration of Independence called attention to natural rights. It described
²⁵ the purpose of government. It said that people give power to the government only if that government protects their rights. If the government misuses power, people can change the government.

The document was approved in Philadelphia. The
³⁰ date was July 4, 1776. It made the colonies "free and independent states."

Organizing a New Government

Each state had to create its own government. People remembered that some of the first settlers had made a

compact. Each state created its own constitution, or
35 plan of government.

The states were 13 separate governments. Conflicts with the king and Parliament had made the colonists afraid. They did not want to give power to a central government.

40 The Continental Congress planned for a loose confederation. A *confederation* is an alliance of <u>independent</u> states. This plan was called the Articles of Confederation. There would be no executive or judicial branches. The legislature, known as Congress, was not given the power
45 to tax or enforce laws. Most power stayed with the states. The Articles needed the **ratification** of all 13 states. The articles were approved in 1781.

A Limping Government

The new government faced problems after the war. Congress and the states did not have enough money to
50 pay their debts. Congress did not have the power to control trade with England.

Farmers faced problems, too. They had debt and taxes on their land. In 1786, angry Massachusetts farmers started a rebellion. Their leader was Daniel Shays.
55 Congress did not have the power to stop the rebellion. Many Americans called for a stronger national government that could keep law and order. They also wanted to solve the problems that had led to Shays' Rebellion.

Review Questions

1. On what two issues did the American colonies and the English government have different views?

_____

2. How were the states organized at first? What was this plan for government called?

_____

_____

Key Terms

compact (KAHM pakt) *n.* a written agreement to make and obey laws for the good of the group

ratification (ra tuh fuh KAY shun) *n.* approval

Vocabulary Strategy

Using Word Parts Use what you know about the meaning of the prefix *in-* to explain the meaning of the underlined word.

_____

_____

✓ Reading Check

Underline the sentence that explains why the states did not want to give power to a central government.

⟳ Target Reading Skill

Understanding Effects Circle the name of the event that was an effect, or result, of the problems farmers faced.

✓ Reading Check

Underline the phrase in the text that completes this sentence.

Shays' Rebellion led to calls for _____.

1. To be a citizen in the colonies, you had to be a white man and
   A. work for the common good.
   B. own land.
   C. serve in the army.
   D. represent England's interests.

2. Which freedom did the colonists help make part of our heritage?
   A. freedom of religion
   B. freedom of the press
   C. both of the above
   D. none of the above

3. The American colonists found ancient examples of good government in the democracy of Athens and
   A. Parliament of England.
   B. the legislature of each colony.
   C. the republic of Rome.
   D. their own town meetings.

4. American government used Locke and Montesquieu's ideas of
   A. natural rights and separation of powers.
   B. responsible government and citizens' rights.
   C. the rights to life, liberty, and property.
   D. representative government and the power of reason.

5. The Declaration of Independence called attention to natural rights and
   A. set up a separation of powers.
   B. described the purpose of government.
   C. organized the government of the United States.
   D. changed the colonists' minds about independence.

Short Answer Question

Why did the colonists take steps to gain independence from England?

_____

_____

_____

_____

_____

CHAPTER 5

Prepare to Read

Section 1
The Constitutional Convention

Objectives

1. Discuss the debate among delegates over the kind of national government that was needed.
2. Understand the compromises made as the national government was created.
3. Describe the powers granted to the executive and judicial branches.

Target Reading Skill

Use Context Clues What can you do when you come to a word you do not know while reading? Look for clues to its meaning in the context, or the surrounding words and sentences. Read the paragraph below. What clues do you find to the meaning of *revise*?

> Under the Articles of Confederation, Congress did not have the power to deal with all the country's problems. In 1787, a convention was called to revise the Articles of Confederation.

The first sentence says that the Articles of Confederation did not give Congress enough power. It suggests that *revise* means "change."

Vocabulary Strategy

Recognizing Signal Words Signal words can help you figure out the order in which events happened. Signal words include *before, after, first, then,* and *next.* Read the following sentence and think about what it tells you about the order of events.

> After Shays' Rebellion, people called for a stronger national government.

The signal word *after* tells you that the call for stronger government followed Shays' Rebellion.

[1] The Articles of Confederation did not give Congress enough power. In 1787, a convention was called. Its job was to revise the Articles of Confederation.

Agreement and Disagreement

Delegates both agreed and disagreed about issues. Most [5] agreed that a national government was needed. They also wanted to guard against abuse of power. They did not agree about how many representatives each state should have. They also did not agree about how much power the national government should have.

Getting Organized *and* Madison's Plan

[10] The Constitutional Convention took place in Pennsylvania. The delegates set rules for the debates. They decided to keep the discussions secret. This way, the delegates would be free to change their minds. They also could think about the good of all states, not [15] just the people they represented.

Delegates wanted a new plan for government. James Madison suggested a strong national government. It would have legislative, executive, and judicial branches. The legislative branch would have two parts: [20] a House of Representatives and a Senate. The number of members would be based on a state's population.

Sharing Power

Delegates argued about how the national government and the states would share power. They decided that the national government would have some powers. [25] The states would have others. Both would share some powers.

One issue was whether a state could protect or end the slave trade. Northern and southern states did not agree about this. They finally said that the national [30] government could control trade in general. It was not allowed to control the slave trade until 1808.

Reaching Compromise

At first there were two plans for representation in Congress. One was the Virginia Plan. This plan based the number of representatives on state population. The

---

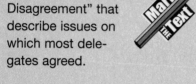

✓ Reading Check

Underline the sentences under "Agreement and Disagreement" that describe issues on which most delegates agreed.

Target Reading Skill

Use Context Clues
Circle the word or sentence that is a clue to the meaning of the underlined word.

✓ Reading Check

What did the delegates decide about keeping the convention secret?

_____

_____

_____

✓ Reading Check

Circle the information that tells how Madison wanted the legislative branch to be organized.

✓ Reading Check

In the text, number the two parts of the compromise the delegates reached about slavery.

35 other was the New Jersey Plan. It called for each state to have the same number of representatives.

Then, Roger Sherman of Connecticut suggested a new plan. He wanted a **bicameral** legislature. The number of members of the House of Representatives
40 would be based on state population. Each state also would have two senators, no matter what its population. This plan is known as the **Great Compromise.** The **Three-Fifths Compromise** solved the problem of whether to count slaves as part of a state's population.

Executive and Judicial Branches

45 Executive and judicial branches were added to the government. This allowed a separation of powers. The President would hold executive power. A Supreme Court would interpret the laws.

The delegates did not agree about who should elect
50 the President and Congress. Some wanted direct election by the people. Others said the people were not informed enough to choose. The delegates decided that all citizens would elect members of the House. State legislatures would select senators. The Electoral
55 College would select the President.

The Signing

On September 17, 1787, 39 delegates signed the Constitution. Over the years changes have been made to the Constitution but the basic plan of government is the same.

Review Questions

1. On what issues did delegates agree? Disagree?

_____

_____

2. What was Madison's plan for the government?

_____

_____

Key Terms

bicameral (bī KAM er uhl) *adj.* with two houses, or parts

Great Compromise (GRAYT KAHM pruh mīz) *n.* the plan for representation in Congress that gave each side something it wanted

Three-Fifths Compromise (three FIFTHS KAHM pruh mīz) *n.* an agreement to count each slave as three fifths of a person

Recognizing Signal Words Which came first, the New Jersey Plan or the Great Compromise? Circle the word or words that tell you the order of these plans.

_____

_____

✓ Reading Check

Underline the sentence that explains the purpose of the Three-Fifths Compromise.

✓ Reading Check

Why did some delegates not want direct election of the President?

_____

_____

✓ Reading Check

Explain how our government today is similar to the one outlined by the Framers.

_____

_____

_____

_____

Prepare to Read

Section 2
The Struggle for Ratification

Objectives

1. Identify the views of the Federalists.
2. Discuss the views of the Anti-Federalists.
3. Explore the role of *The Federalist* in the debate over the Constitution.
4. Learn the outcome of the struggle over ratification.

 Target Reading Skill

Interpret Nonliteral Meanings Writers sometimes use nonliteral language, such as images or comparisons, to get ideas across to readers. Images and comparisons can help to make ideas clearer. In doing so, they can help to make a point in the text. Read the following sentence.

> The debate over the Constitution dragged on.

The phrase *dragged on* creates an image in the reader's mind of a very slow, long process.

Vocabulary Strategy

Recognizing Signal Words The words *first, then, next,* and *finally* can signal steps in a process or event. Read these sentences that describe the process of the Constitution becoming the law of the land.

> The Constitution did not go into effect right away. First it was debated. Then it was ratified, or approved, by the states.

The signal word *First* tells the first step in making the Constitution the law of the land. *Then* points to the second step.

Section 2 Summary

¹ The Constitution had to be **ratified** by at least nine states. The states that approved it would become part of the new nation. The Constitution created <u>a storm of debate</u>. Some people liked the new plan. Others were ⁵ firmly against it.

The Federalists

The **Federalists** supported the Constitution. They said a strong national government could protect the nation against other countries better than the states could alone. It would also keep order, control trade, and pro-¹⁰ tect the rights of citizens. It would pay the nation's debts. It would make sure American money had value at home and around the world.

The Anti-Federalists

The **Anti-Federalists** were against the Constitution. They said that a national government would be too far ¹⁵ away from local communities. Anti-Federalists did not want to give Congress the power to make laws "neces-sary and proper." They said this could lead to trouble for the states. They also feared that a strong national government would take away liberty. They were trou-²⁰ bled that there was no bill of rights.

Target Reading Skill

Interpret Nonliteral Meanings
What does the underlined phrase tell you about people's reactions to the Constitution?

_____

_____

✓ **Reading Check**

Underline the sentence that tells the Federalist position on the Constitution.

✓ **Reading Check**

Bracket the sentence that explains why the Anti-Federalists wanted a bill of rights.

Key Terms

ratified (RAT uh fīd) *v.* approved

Federalists (FE druh lists) *n.* people who liked the new Constitution and supported a strong national government

Anti-Federalists (AN tī FE druh lists) *n.* people who did not like the new Constitution and who were against a strong federal government

Target Reading Skill

Interpret Nonliteral Meanings
Reread the sentence in brackets. What do you think the meaning of *born* is?

_____

_____

_____

Vocabulary Strategy

Recognizing Signal Words What does the underlined word tell you about this step in creating a new government?

_____

_____

✓ **Reading Check**

Circle the word in the last sentence that explains why it was important for all 13 states to ratify the Constitution.

The *Federalist* Papers

James Madison, Alexander Hamilton, and John Jay were Federalists. They wrote news articles. These articles explained why the Constitution was a good idea. They were gathered in a work called *The Federalist.* In
25 one, James Madison said that the Constitution would protect liberty. *The Federalist* also pointed out the problems that America faced. It was a weak, young nation on a large continent. Other countries might overpower them if they did not unite.

Ratification

30 Many Americans decided to support the Constitution. The arguments of the Federalists' helped to convince them. The support of George Washington and Benjamin Franklin also helped. Many more were convinced after the Federalists agreed to add a bill of
35 rights.

In 1788, New Hampshire ratified the Constitution. It was the ninth state to do so. But the Constitution still needed the support of the four other states. These states were home to more then 40 percent of the
40 nation's people. By 1790, all 13 states had ratified the Constitution. [The new government was born.] <u>Finally,</u> the loose union of states had become the United States of America.

Review Questions

1. Why were the Anti-Federalists against the Constitution?

_____

_____

2. How many states finally ratified the Constitution?

_____

_____

Prepare to Read

Section 3
The Supreme Law of the Land

Objectives

1. Learn the goals of our government stated in the Preamble to the Constitution.
2. Explore the Articles of the Constitution.
3. Analyze the principles of limited government.

Target Reading Skill

Use Context Clues Remember, surrounding words, sentences, and even paragraphs may give clues to the meaning of words you do not recognize. Read these sentences and look for a clue to the meaning of the word *amendments*.

> Amendments can be made to the Constitution. Each <u>change</u> must be the will of the people.

The underlined word helps explain the meaning of amendments.

Vocabulary Strategy

Recognizing Signal Words Some words signal that an example is going to be given. Read this paragraph.

> The powers delegated, or assigned, to Congress are known as delegated powers. Most of these powers—<u>such as</u> the power to coin money, to declare war, and to regulate trade—are listed in Article 1 of the Constitution.

The words *such as* signal that examples of the delegated powers of Congress are going to be given. Other words signaling examples are listed below.

Words That Signal Examples				
for example	for instance	such as	like	specifically

Target Reading Skill

Use Context Clues
Circle the context clue that tells you what the Preamble to the Constitution is.

✓ Reading Check

Circle the goal of government that promises to protect our freedoms.

✓ Reading Check

List the main duties of the legislative, executive, and judicial branches.

Legislative _____

Executive _____

Judicial _____

[1] The Constitution sets up our form of government. Our government is a republic. In a republic, the citizens elect their representatives. The Constitution is the land's highest law. It guards citizen's rights. It also [5] gives rules for both national and state governments.

The Goals of Our Government

The Constitution begins with an introduction. This Preamble lists six goals of our government.

Goals of Our Government					
Unite the 13 separate states under a strong national government.	Use fair ways to settle disagreements between individuals, states, and governments.	Set up a peaceful society in which people are protected from unlawful acts.	Protect citizens from attacks by other countries.	Create conditions that will help all Americans.	Make sure that our freedoms and those of future Americans are protected.

The Articles

The plan for our government is organized in seven parts called articles.

[10] **Article 1: The Legislative Branch.** Congress makes the laws for our nation. It is divided into two houses: the House of Representatives and the Senate.

Article 2: The Executive Branch. The President heads the executive branch. The President's job is to carry out [15] the laws.

Article 3: The Judicial Branch. A national court system settles arguments between states. Important cases on which lower courts do not agree can be sent to the Supreme Court. The Supreme Court makes the final [20] decision.

Article 4: The States. Each state must honor the laws of other states.

Article 5: Amending the Constitution. Amendments can be made to the Constitution. Three fourths of the [25] states must approve a change.

Key Terms
amendments (uh MEND munts) *n.* changes

Article 6: The Supremacy of the Constitution. No state law may go against the Constitution.

Article 7: Ratification. This article explains the process of ratification, or approval, of the Constitution.

30   The first ten amendments are the Bill of Rights. They were approved in 1791. Since then, seventeen other amendments have been added.

Limited Government

The Constitution creates a government with <u>limited</u> powers. Federalism, separation of powers, and checks 35 and balances restrict the government's power.

    Under **federalism,** some powers belong to the national government. Some belong to the states. And some are shared by both. They include delegated powers, **concurrent powers**, and **reserved powers**.

40   The Constitution divides power among the executive, legislative, and judicial branches. This separation of powers helps to keep the branches from abusing power.

    The Constitution also protects against abuse of power by **checks and balances.** For instance, the 45 President can stop the actions of Congress by vetoing a bill. The courts decide whether a law is constitutional. The House can **impeach** the President. Checks and balances help the branches work together.

Review Questions

1. Where in the Constitution are the three branches of government and their powers described?

_____

2. What three principles limit the power of government?

_____

Key Terms

federalism (FE druh li zum) *n.* type of government in which powers are divided between the national government and the states

concurrent powers (kun KER unt POU erz) *n.* powers shared by the federal and state governments

reserved powers (ri ZERVD POU erz) *n.* powers that the Constitution neither gives to Congress nor denies to the states

checks and balances (CHEKS AND BAL un sus) *n.* gives each branch of government ways to limit the powers of the others

impeach (im PEECH) *v.* accuse

Target Reading Skill

Use Context Clues Circle the word that gives a clue to the meaning of *limited*.

Vocabulary Strategy

Recognizing Signal Words
Underline one word or group of words in the last paragraph that signals an example. Tell what the example explains.

_____

_____

_____

✓ **Reading Check**

In the text, number two reasons why checks and balances are important to our system of government.

1. The delegates to the Constitutional Convention kept their discussions secret so that they could
   A. organize the national government.
   B. disagree on important issues.
   C. consider the good of all the states.
   D. all of the above

2. The Great Compromise was a plan for government that
   A. set up a Senate with two senators for each state.
   B. was dependent entirely on a state's population.
   C. did not take into account a states population.
   D. counted slaves in the states population.

3. The Federalists believed that a strong national government
   A. was not government by consent of the people.
   B. put people's liberties in danger.
   C. would protect the nation against other nations.
   D. should be limited by a bill of rights.

4. In which part of the Constitution are the goals of our government described?
   A. Preamble
   B. Bill of Rights
   C. Article 4
   D. amendments

5. Federalism limits government by giving
   A. all power to the national government.
   B. certain powers to both the national government and the states.
   C. no powers to the states.
   D. all of the above

Short Answer Question

How does the separation of powers protect against abuse of power?

_____

_____

_____

_____

Prepare to Read

Section 1
Adding the Bill of Rights

Objectives

1. Understand the amendment process.
2. Learn about the debate in Congress over the Bill of Rights and its ratification.

Target Reading Skill

Understand Sequence Looking at the sequence of events will help you understand and remember the events. **Sequence** is the order in which events happen. This diagram shows the sequence of events leading up to the adoption of the Bill of Rights.

The Creation of the Bill of Rights

Madison says that a bill of rights is needed.

⬇

Congress begins working on the idea.

⬇

A group writes 12 amendments.

⬇

Congress approves the list.

⬇

The states approve ten of the amendments.

⬇

These ten become our Bill of Rights.

Vocabulary Strategy

Using Roots and Prefixes You know that a prefix is a word part that is added before a root. A root is the word part that gives a word its basic meaning. A word with both a root and a prefix brings together the meanings of both.

For example, the prefix *pro-* means "forward, in front of, or for." The root "duc" means to lead. "Produce" means to lead forward or bring forth.

Target Reading Skill

Understand Sequence Reread the bracketed paragraph. Which happens first: Do the states ratify an amendment or is an amendment proposed to the states?

_____

_____

Vocabulary Strategy

Using Roots and Prefixes Use the prefix and root of the underlined word to explain its meaning. The root means "put."

_____

_____

✓ Reading Check

Why is having a formal amendment process important?

_____

_____

_____

[1] The **Bill of Rights** became part of the Constitution after the states approved it. The Federalists had promised that a bill of rights would be added to the Constitution. This change in the Constitution was the [5] first test of the **amendment process.**

The Amendment Process

Amendments to the Constitution must be approved at both the national and state levels. First an amendment is approved at the national level. Next, it is proposed to the states. Then, the states either ratify or reject it.
[10] An amendment can be <u>proposed</u> to the states in two ways. Congress may propose an amendment, but only if it has been approved by a vote in the Senate and the House of Representatives. Congress has proposed 27 amendments that are now part of our Constitution. A [15] national **convention** may also propose an amendment. The convention must be called for by two thirds of state legislatures. A national convention has not yet been used to propose an amendment.
There are two ways for the states to ratify an [20] amendment. Usually an amendment is approved by three fourths of the state legislatures. It can also be approved by special conventions in three fourths of the states. Congress chooses which way an amendment will be approved.

Key Terms

Bill of Rights (BIL UV RĪTS) *n.* a list of the people's rights that was added to the Constitution after it was ratified

amendment process (uh MEND munt PRAH ses) *n.* the way in which changes are made to the Constitution

convention (kun VEN shun) *n.* a gathering of people

The Debate in Congress

25 The amendment <u>process</u> for the Bill of Rights began in Congress. In 1789, James Madison told members of the House that a bill of rights was needed. Many Americans believed that the Constitution did not protect their rights. Madison argued that a bill of rights

30 would "make the Constitution better" for those people.

After some debate, Congress began to work on a bill of rights. It made a list of rights. The list drew from the English Bill of Rights, state constitutions, and other documents. Members of Congress also discussed where to

35 place the Bill of Rights. Madison wanted it within the articles of the Constitution. That would show its connection to limits already placed on the government. Most members of Congress voted to put the Bill of Rights at the end. They did not want the list to have the

40 same importance as the original Constitution.

A committee in Congress wrote 12 amendments. Ten of these protected the people's rights. Congress approved the amendments. It then proposed them to the states. People who did not trust the new govern-

45 ment before welcomed the amendments. Two amendments did not get enough support. By 1791, the states had ratified the ten amendments that protected citizens' rights. The Bill of Rights had become part of the Constitution.

Review Questions

1. Describe the two ways that an amendment can be proposed to the states.

_____

_____

_____

2. Explain where different groups wanted the Bill of Rights to be placed in the Constitution and why.

_____

_____

_____

✓ Reading Check

Bracket the sentence(s) that explain the debate over where to place the Bill of Rights in the Constitution.

Vocabulary Strategy

Using Roots and Prefixes Look at the word *process*. Its root, *cess*, means "go." Use the word's parts to help explain its meaning.

_____

_____

CHAPTER 6

Prepare to Read

Section 2
Protections in the Bill of Rights

Objectives

1. Understand how the First Amendment protects individual freedoms.
2. Find out how the Bill of Rights protects people against abuse of power by the government.
3. Learn how the Bill of Rights protects people accused of crimes.
4. Discuss the protections of other rights outlined in the Ninth and Tenth Amendments.

Target Reading Skill

Understand Sequence You have learned that sequence is the order in which events happen. But sequence is not just time order. It can also be order of importance. Or it can be some other order that organizes ideas or other items. As you read, consider the order of and the information in the first ten amendments. The First Amendment, for example, deals with different freedoms.

Vocabulary Strategy

Using Roots and Prefixes Remember, a prefix is added before the root of a word. As you read, pay attention to prefixes and roots of words you do not recognize. These word parts can often help you figure out the meaning of a word. If you do not know the meaning of a prefix or root, look it up in a dictionary. Then see if you can combine the meaning of the prefix with the meaning of the root to unlock the word's meaning.

Word	Prefix	Root	Meaning
protect	pro- "in front"	tect "cover"	"guard, defend"

Section 2 Summary

The first ten amendments are known as the Bill of Rights. They were added to the Constitution to protect citizens' rights. The Bill of Rights did not change any basic ideas of the Constitution. It describes basic rights that are protected under our form of government.

Protections of Individual Freedoms

The First Amendment protects a number of freedoms for every American.

First Amendment

Freedom of Religion
• the right to follow the religion of your choice, or not to practice any religion
• separation of church and state

Freedom of Speech
• the right to speak and write freely
• people are not free to slander, or tell lies about, a person

Freedom of the Press
• the right to print or publish information and opinions
• people are not free to libel, or print lies about, a person

Freedom of Assembly
• the right to assemble, or meet together
• gatherings must be peaceful and not go against others' rights

Freedom of Petition
• the right to ask a government representative to change a law, make a new law, or solve problems in other ways
• ways to petition, or make a request, include letters, e-mail, telephoning, and petitions

✓ **Reading Check**

List ways you use the basic freedoms of the First Amendment every day.

_____

_____

_____

_____

Target Reading Skill

Understand Sequence
Circle the sentence that describes the First Amendment. Why do you think such rights were described in the first amendment in the Bill of Rights?

_____

_____

_____

Key Terms

separation of church and state (sep uh RAY shun UV CHERCH AND STAYT) n. the idea that the government may not be involved in anything related to religion

Vocabulary Strategy

Using Roots and Prefixes Use a dictionary to find the meaning of the prefix in the underlined word. Then circle the letter of the correct meaning of the word.

a. good use

b. bad use

c. no use

d. none of the above

✓ Reading Check

Explain how the amendments that protect against abuse of power also protect Americans' right to privacy.

_____

_____

_____

✓ Reading Check

Why is it important for all people to have due process of law?

_____

_____

_____

✓ Reading Check

How might the Ninth and Tenth amendments have helped form a lasting Constitution?

_____

_____

_____

Protections Against Abuse of Power

The Second Amendment deals with people's right to own guns. The Third says the government must get permission to let soldiers use citizens' homes. The Fourth says the police cannot search people (or their homes) without good reason. The Fifth protects citizens from abuse of the power of **eminent domain.**

Protections of an Accused Person's Rights

The Fifth, Sixth, Seventh, and Eighth Amendments describe the rights of an accused person. The Constitution says that citizens are allowed **due process of law.**

The Fifth Amendment says that an accused person cannot be forced to confess. It also protects citizens from **double jeopardy.** The Sixth protects a citizen's right to a speedy, public, and fair trial. The Seventh permits jury trials. The Eighth protects accused persons from "cruel and unusual punishments."

Protections of Other Rights

The Ninth Amendment says that citizens' rights are not limited to the rights listed in the Constitution. The Tenth says that the powers not mentioned in Article 1 belong to state governments or to the people.

Review Questions

1. Which amendments describe the rights of an accused person?

_____

2. What does the Ninth Amendment say?

_____

_____

Key Terms

eminent domain (EM uh nent do MAYN) *n.* the power to take private property for public use

due process of law (DOO PRAH ses UV LAH) *n.* the system in which government must treat accused persons fairly

double jeopardy (DUB ul JEP er dee) *n.* being placed on trial twice for the same crime

---

CHAPTER 6

Prepare to Read

Section 3
Interpreting the Bill of Rights

Objectives

1. Determine the role of the courts in interpreting citizens' rights.
2. Examine the definition of freedom of speech and students' rights in the *Tinker* case.
3. Describe how the courts protected freedom of expression for extreme groups in the *Skokie* case.
4. Understand that protecting the rights of citizens is a continuing challenge for all.

Target Reading Skill

Recognize Words That Signal Sequence Signal words can help you understand how ideas or events are related, or connected. The words in the chart signal the sequence, or order, of events. The word *in* followed by a date also points out the order of events.

Sequence Signal Words						
first	next	last	then	before	during
after	finally	second	third	later	when

Vocabulary Strategy

Using Roots and Prefixes Several prefixes mean "not."

Prefixes with the Meaning "Not"			
dis-	in-	non-	un-

As you read, use what you know about the meaning of these prefixes to figure out the meaning of words you do not recognize. Read this sentence:

What happens when people <u>disagree</u> about the meaning of our rights under the Constitution?

When you know that *dis-* means "not," you know that *disagree* means "do not agree."

Chapter 6 Section 3 **67**

Section 3 Summary

Mark the Text

_____

_____

_____

_____

_____

Target Reading Skill

Recognize Words That Signal Sequence What does the under-lined phrase tell you about the _Tinker_ case?

_____

_____

✓ **Reading Check**

List some other symbols that are protected by the First Amendment.

_____

_____

_____

¹ The rights of citizens are often hard to interpret, or explain. The first ten amendments to the Constitution do not say how rights apply in every case. Sometimes certain rights have to be weighed against others. The
⁵ meaning of **freedom of the press** and **freedom of speech,** for example, may be different in different cases.

The Role of the Courts

Judges must decide whether laws go against people's rights. The two cases below are **case studies.** They show how ideas in the Constitution apply to real events.

Students and Free Speech

¹⁰ The _Tinker_ case involved two questions. What is meant by "speech" in freedom of speech? What rights do stu-dents have under the Constitution?

In 1965, Mary Beth Tinker, her brother, and another student wore black armbands to school. They were
¹⁵ protesting the Vietnam War. School officials said the students could not wear armbands and suspended the students. The Tinkers' parents argued that the school was not allowing the students freedom of speech. School officials said the armband rule helped to keep
²⁰ order. They also argued that schools were not places for political protests.

The case went before a local court first. It decided that the rule against armbands was needed. A higher court agreed. Then the Supreme Court heard the case.
²⁵ It decided the students were right. It said that symbols such as armbands are forms of speech. It also said that the protest did not interfere with other students' right to an education. Most importantly, the Court ruled that students have a basic right to free speech.

Key Terms

freedom of the press (FREE dum UV THUH PRES) _n._ the right to print newspapers, magazines, and other materials without gov-ernment control

freedom of speech (FREE dum UV SPEECH) _n._ the right to say what you think

case studies (KAYS STUD eez) _n._ descriptions of events and issues and how they were handled

The *Skokie* Case: Freedom for Nazis?

30 In 1977, members of the American Nazi Party applied for a permit to march in Skokie, Illinois. Forty thousand Jews lived in the town. Many had survived the death camps of World War II. These camps had been set up between 1938 and 1945 by the German dictator
35 and Nazi party leader Adolf Hitler. The city of Skokie tried to stop the march. It made the marchers buy insurance that would help the city pay if the march caused any damage or injuries. The marchers planned a rally to protest the insurance. A county court ruled
40 that they could not hold a protest.

A long court battle began. The question was difficult. Does the First Amendment protect groups that spread a message of hate? There were strong arguments on both sides. The marchers took the case to the
45 Supreme Court. The Supreme Court said the Illinois Supreme Court and the U.S. District courts had to hold a hearing on their ruling against the Nazis. [These courts finally decided that the Skokie law requiring insurance went against the First Amendment.] It also
50 decided that the Nazis had a right to hand out material expressing their message. The Skokie case showed that the First Amendment protects even <u>unpopular</u> beliefs.

The Continuing Challenge

Protecting the rights of citizens is a challenge that we all share. Our rights are not protected just because they
55 are in the Constitution. Citizens play a key role in protecting people's rights through their actions and respect for each other.

Review Questions

1. How do courts interpret the meaning of citizens' rights?

_____

_____

2. How did the Supreme Court define "speech" in the *Tinker* case?

_____

_____

✓ Reading Check

Underline a sentence that helps explain how the *Skokie* case showed that courts are needed to interpret our rights.

↻ Target Reading Skill

Recognize Words That Signal Sequence Circle the sequence signal word in the bracketed sentence. What does it tell you about the order of events?

_____

_____

_____

Vocabulary Strategy

Circle the prefix in the underlined word. Then use the prefix to explain the word's meaning.

_____

_____

_____

✓ Reading Check

List some ways you can help protect the rights of others.

_____

_____

Chapter 6 Assessment

1. An amendment to the Constitution can be proposed by Congress or by
   A. the Senate.
   B. the President.
   C. a national convention.
   D. a special election.

2. The Bill of Rights drew ideas from
   A. the Magna Carta.
   B. the English Bill of Rights.
   C. colonial charters.
   D. all of the above

3. The idea of due process of law comes from
   A. state constitutions.
   B. English legal tradition.
   C. the House and Senate.
   D. all of the above

4. The Ninth Amendment says citizens' rights are
   A. limited to what the Constitution lists.
   B. not limited to what is in the Constitution.
   C. decided by state governments.
   D. described in state constitutions.

5. In the *Tinker* case, the Supreme Court ruled that
   A. students have a right to free speech.
   B. schools have a right to suspend students.
   C. students have a right to an education.
   D. schools have a right to control behavior.

Short Answer Question

What five kinds of rights does the First Amendment to the Bill of Rights protect?

_____

_____

_____

_____

_____

CHAPTER 7

Prepare to Read

Section 1
Changing the Law of the Land

Objectives

1. Learn how slavery was abolished.
2. Find out more about how African Americans gained the right to vote.
3. Explore how women gained the right to vote.
4. Discuss how young adults gained the right to vote.
5. Learn how the Constitution adapts to the needs of society.

Target Reading Skill

Analyze Word Parts Breaking a word you do not know into parts may help you figure out the word's meaning and pronunciation. Prefixes, roots, and suffixes are word parts that contribute to a word's meaning. Pronunciation is how you say a word out loud.

Take the word *convention*, for example. It can be broken into three parts:

Prefix	Root	Suffix
con- "together"	ven "come"	-tion "act of"

When you put the meanings of the parts together, you understand that *convention* means "the act of coming together."

Vocabulary Strategy

Using Context Clues You know that the words, sentences, and paragraphs around a word make up its context. Context often gives clues to a word's meaning. Read this paragraph.

> Originally, the Constitution let the states decide who was **qualified** to be a citizen. Most states gave citizenship only to white men who owned property. Today, however, anyone born or naturalized in the United States is a citizen.

The underlined sentences offer clues to the meaning of the word *qualified.* The information in these sentences tells you that *qualified* means "able."

Section 1 Summary

Vocabulary Strategy

Using Context Clues
Circle the word that gives a clue to the meaning of *abolish*.

✓ Reading Check

Underline the sentence that tells why the Supreme Court's decision in the *Dred Scott* case was a victory for supporters of slavery.

Target Reading Skill

Analyze Word Parts The word *illegal* can be divided into these parts:

Prefix	Root	Suffix
il-	leg	-al

The root *leg* means "law." What do you think the prefix *il-* means? (Hint: *Il-* is related to the prefixes *in-* and *un-*.)

_____

_____

✓ Reading Check

Why is the Fourteenth Amendment sometimes called the "second Bill of Rights"?

_____

_____

_____

---

¹Since the Bill of Rights was written, 17 other amendments have been added. Most of them helped the Constitution adjust to changing times. Some made changes in citizenship and voting rights.

Abolishing Slavery

⁵The issue of slavery divided our nation for a long time. Enslaved African Americans worked on farms in the South. In many northern states, slavery was not allowed. Both northern and southern states had to ratify the Constitution. So a compromise was made on ¹⁰slavery. The Constitution did not abolish, or end, slavery. It did not even mention slavery.

Then, in 1857, the Dred Scott case came to the Supreme Court. The Court ruled that slaves were property. The Court said the Constitution allowed slavery. ¹⁵Change finally came after the Civil War. In 1865, the Thirteenth Amendment was added to the Constitution. It ended slavery in the United States.

African Americans and the Right to Vote

In 1868, the Fourteenth Amendment was added to the Constitution. It said that African Americans were citi-²⁰zens. It said the states—not just Congress—must respect citizens' rights. The Fourteenth Amendment is sometimes called the "second Bill of Rights."

In 1870, the Fifteenth Amendment was added. It promised **suffrage** for African Americans. Even so, ²⁵some states still kept African Americans from voting. They did this by making some people pay a **poll tax.** Those who could not pay the tax could not vote. In 1964, the Twenty-fourth Amendment made poll taxes against the law. This was a big step in protecting the ³⁰rights of African Americans. It also helped to undo past unfairness to African Americans.

Key Terms

suffrage (SUF rij) *n.* the right to vote

poll tax (POHL TAKS) *n.* money that must be paid in order to vote

Women and the Right to Vote

From the founding of our country, most people believed that a woman's place was in the home. Because of such traditional ideas, women were not allowed to vote. They also could not run for political office.

In the late 1800s, more women took jobs outside their homes. More women became active in social and political issues. Women asked for the right to vote. Supporters known as suffragists joined them. For 40 years, Congress refused to pass an amendment to allow women to vote. Finally, the House and Senate approved it. It became the Nineteenth Amendment. The states approved the amendment in 1920.

Youth and the Right to Vote

Until the middle of the 1900s, the voting age was 21. But many Americans believed that citizens old enough to fight in a war should have the right to vote. In 1970, Congress passed a new law. It allowed 18-year-olds to vote in national, state, and local elections. The Supreme Court ruled that Congress could only set the voting age for national elections. To let 18-year-olds vote in all elections, the Constitution had to change. In 1971, Congress approved the Twenty-sixth Amendment. This lowered the voting age to 18.

The Voice of the People

The voting rights amendments show that the Constitution can be changed as views and needs change. The Thirteenth, Fourteenth, and Fifteenth Amendments were the result of the Civil War. All the other changes were made through the peaceful work of citizens. The United States is truly a government by the people. The citizens decide what will be the law of the land.

Review Questions

1. Why didn't the Constitution abolish slavery?

_____

_____

2. How did women gain the right to vote?

_____

_____

Vocabulary Strategy

Using Context Clues Explain a traditional idea about women. Circle a context clue that would help you figure out the meaning of *traditional*.

_____

_____

✓ Reading Check

List two ways women showed they deserved the right to vote.

1. _____

_____

2. _____

_____

✓ Reading Check

Underline the sentence that explains why many Americans supported lowering the voting age to 18.

✓ Reading Check

Circle the words that tell who can propose changes to the Constitution.

Objectives

1. Discuss the role of the Supreme Court.

2. Explore how equality and segregation were at odds in our nation's history.

3. Consider equality and affirmative action in our nation's history.

4. Take a look at women and equality.

5. Understand how the Constitution provides a framework for the future.

Target Reading Skill

Recognize Word Origins A word's origin is where the word comes from. Many English words come from Latin or Greek. The word *segregation*, for example, comes from Latin. Its prefix *se-*, its root *greg*, and its suffix *-ation*, are all from Latin. When you know their meanings, you can figure out the meaning of *segregation*.

Prefix	Root	Suffix
se-	greg	-ation
"apart"	"herd"	"act of"

The Latin word parts tell you that *segregation* means "being apart from the herd or crowd." Knowing about word origins can help you figure out the meanings of words.

Vocabulary Strategy

Using Context Clues Remember, when you come across a word you do not recognize while reading, you can look for clues to its meaning in its context. Surrounding words, sentences, and paragraphs often make the meaning of unknown words clear. Read this paragraph.

> **The Framers** of the Constitution understood that specific instructions for running a government **in 1787** might not work years **later**. The Framers gave general ideas and let **later** generations fill in the details.

Clues to the meaning of the word *generations* appear in dark type. They tell you that *generations* means "people who lived after the Framers

Section 2 Summary

¹ The Constitution is a <u>flexible</u> document. It gives us general ideas for running the government. It does not have to change to meet every new issue our nation faces.

The Role of the Supreme Court

The Supreme Court decides if a law or action follows
⁵ the Constitution. Its decisions must be obeyed. Even the President and Congress must obey them. But decisions may be changed. There may be an amendment to the Constitution. A later court decision also may change them.

Equality and Segregation

¹⁰ How the Supreme Court interprets the Constitution can change, too. The right to **equal protection** set out in the Fourteenth Amendment is an example. In the 1896 case of *Plessy* v. *Ferguson*, the Court ruled that **segregation** of African Americans was allowed. They also
¹⁵ said the separate places for blacks and whites had to be of equal quality. This "separate but equal" idea was used to support segregation for more than 50 years.

In the 1950s, some new cases came to the Supreme Court. These cases forced the Court to decide if "separate but equal" places really gave "equal protection."
²⁰ One major case was *Brown* v. *Board of Education*. The Supreme Court changed its mind about segregation. It ruled that segregation went against the Constitution. This decision <u>overturned</u> *Plessy* v. *Ferguson*. It said that
²⁵ all segregation laws are unconstitutional.

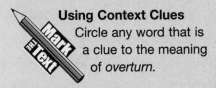

Target Reading Skill

Recognizing Word Origins The root of the underlined word is Latin and means "bend." What do you think the meaning of the word is?

_____

_____

Vocabulary Strategy

Using Context Clues Circle any word that is a clue to the meaning of *overturn*.

✓ Reading Check

Underline the sentences that explain how Supreme Court decisions can be overturned.

✓ Reading Check

How did the result of *Brown* v. *Board of Education* affect segregation?

_____

_____

_____

Key Terms

equal protection (EE kwul pruh TEK shun) *n.* the idea in the Constitution that says that people must be treated fairly, though not in exactly the same way

segregation (seg rih GAY shun) *n.* the separation of one group or race from another, especially in public places such as hotels, schools, and trains

© Pearson Education, Inc., Publishing as Pearson Prentice Hall. All rights reserved.

Recognizing Word Origins The word *affirmative* includes the Latin root *firm*, which has the same meaning as the word in English. What do you think the Latin root means? What might *affirmative* mean?

_____

_____

✓ Reading Check

Underline the phrase that tells what affirmative action was originally designed to counteract.

✓ Reading Check

How was the equal protection clause applied by the Supreme Court in the *Phillips* case?

_____

_____

_____

✓ Reading Check

Circle the words that tell to whom the principle of equal protection applies.

Equality and Affirmative Action

After the *Brown* case, Congress passed laws against discrimination. But these laws could not undo past discrimination. In the 1960s, the government said companies and schools had to take **affirmative action.** This
30 was meant to give equal chances to various groups.

Some people said that affirmative action did not give equal treatment. They said it was reverse discrimination. One case was *Regents of the University of California* v. *Bakke.* In this case, the Supreme Court was
35 to decide if affirmative action was fair. The Court said a college could not discriminate against whites because of race. Equal protection applies to all people. It also said schools could consider race when trying to create diversity among students.

Women and Equality

40 The Supreme Court has also looked at equal protection for women in the workplace. One case was *Phillips* v. *Martin Marietta.* The Court said that companies could not have one set of rules for hiring men and another for women. Women had to be treated equally.

A Framework for the Future

45 The Supreme Court applies the general ideas of the Constitution to new issues. Amendments may be needed from time to time. Still, the sturdy framework of the Constitution is not likely to change.

Review Questions

1. What part does the Supreme Court play in interpreting the Constitution?

_____

_____

2. Explain how the Supreme Court allowed segregation in *Plessy* v. *Ferguson.*

_____

_____

> **Key Terms**
>
> **affirmative action** (uh FER muh tiv AK shun) *n.* a plan of steps to work against the effects of past discrimination

1. Slavery was abolished by
   A. the Constitution.
   B. the Supreme Court.
   C. the Thirteenth Amendment.
   D. the Bill of Rights.

2. Even after the Fifteenth Amendment, African Americans
   A. were not counted as American citizens.
   B. did not have the right to vote.
   C. were enslaved in southern states.
   D. were kept from voting by poll taxes.

3. The Nineteenth Amendment gave women
   A. the right to vote.
   B. equal pay.
   C. political office.
   D. more jobs.

4. Supreme Court decisions must be obeyed by
   A. Congress.
   B. the President.
   C. citizens.
   D. all of the above

5. Segregation laws were made unconstitutional by
   A. *Regents of the University of California* v. *Bakke.*
   B. *Plessy* v. *Ferguson.*
   C. *Brown* v. *Board of Education of Topeka.*
   D. *Phillips* v. *Martin Marietta Corporation.*

Short Answer Question

How does the Constitution provide a framework for the future?

_____

_____

_____

_____

_____

Prepare to Read

Section 1
The Members of Congress

Objectives

1. List the responsibilities of lawmaking.
2. Describe the day of a member of Congress at work.
3. Explore the jobs of representatives and senators.
4. Identify the requirements, salaries, and benefits of being a representative or senator.

Target Reading Skill

Identify Signal Words Certain words signal, or point out, relationships between ideas, people, places, and things. Writers can use signal words to compare or contrast. Read this sentence.

Like senators, members of the House of Representatives are elected to office.

The word *like* compares senators to members of the House. Other words signaling comparison or contrast are *alike, unlike, similar, similarly, different, same, opposite.*

Vocabulary Strategy

Using Roots and Prefixes A prefix is a word part added before the root. The root carries the basic meaning of the word. A prefix adds to or changes the meaning of the root. Study these prefixes and their meanings.

Prefix	Meaning
re-	again, back
un	not
over	above, past, beyond

Now think about the meaning of *overlap* in this sentence:

The terms of senators overlap the terms of other senators.

Overlap means "run past or go beyond."

Section 1 Summary

1 Congress is the legislative branch of the government. It is made up of the Senate and the House of Representatives. The job of Congress is to make laws.

The Responsibilities of Lawmaking

Members of Congress have responsibilities to different
5 groups. Each member is responsible to the group of citizens he or she represents. These **constituents** expect senators and representatives to be their voice in Congress.

Members of Congress are also responsible to their political party. Each party works to elect members.
10 Members are expected to support the issues that are important to that party. One way members do this is to bring a **bill** before Congress.

Members of Congress who want to run for reelection need support and money. They often get help from
15 **interest groups.** Interest groups work to get members of Congress to support bills that help their group. Interest groups use **lobbyists** to do this. A member of Congress must also be a servant of the people. This means they give information and help to those who
20 need it. This is an important role because it helps constituents and wins votes in the next election.

Members of Congress at Work

Members of Congress spend a lot of time learning about issues. They listen to and give speeches. They also vote on bills. Every day, they go to meetings with each other
25 and with lobbyists and constituents. Members of Congress prepare bills. They study reports. They read letters, too. Staff members help them.

Key Terms

constituents (kun STICH oo ents) *n.* the people a member of Congress represents

bill (BIL) *n.* a proposed law

interest groups (IN trist GROOPS) *n.* people who work together to accomplish a goal on which they all agree.

lobbyists (LAHB ee ists) *n.* people who work for interest groups

---

✓ **Reading Check**

Underline the sentence that explains the phrase *servant of the people.*

Vocabulary Strategy

Using Roots and Prefixes Circle the word in the third paragraph under "The Responsibilities of Lawmaking" that includes the prefix *re-.* Explain its meaning.

_____

_____

✓ **Reading Check**

Bracket the text that explains what a senator or representative does on a typical day in Washington.

Representatives and Senators

There are 435 representatives in the House. Each serves for two years. Representatives may run for reelection.
30 The number of representatives for each state depends on the state's population.

The Constitution calls for a census. The census counts the number of people in each state. It is used to decide how many representatives each state has. Each state is
35 divided into **congressional districts**. All congressional districts must have about the same number of people.

Senators

There are 100 members in the Senate. Each state has two. A senator focuses on the interests of the whole state, not just one district. Senators are elected for six-
40 year terms. One third of the senators are elected every two years. The terms of senators overlap, unlike the terms of representatives. That means there are always some experienced members in the Senate.

Requirements, Salary, and Benefits

Senators and representatives must live in the states in
45 which they are elected. Representatives must be at least 25 years old. Senators must be at least 30 years old. A representative must have been a citizen for at least seven years. A senator must have been a citizen for at least nine years.
50 Benefits include offices in Washington and in each district or state. Members receive money for their offices, staff, and travel. They also have free use of the mail to write to constituents.

Review Questions

1. To whom are members of Congress are responsible?

_____

_____

2. List some duties of a member of Congress.

_____

_____

> **Key Term**
>
> **congressional district** (kun GRE shuh nul DIS trikt) *n.* the part of a state that a member of the House represents

Objectives

1. List and describe the powers given to Congress.

2. Identify limits on the powers of Congress.

Target Reading Skill

Make Comparisons When you compare two or more things, you see how they are alike. The following words and phrases are often used to make comparisons.

similar to   the same as   alike

Read this sentence:

Senators and representatives have the same job in Congress—to make laws.

Note that the word *same* is used to compare the jobs of senators and representatives.

Vocabulary Strategy

Using Roots and Prefixes Many prefixes in English words come from the Greek and Latin languages. Here are some examples of Greek and Latin prefixes with the same meaning.

	Meaning
Greek Prefixes syn-, sym-, syl-, sys-	together, with
Latin Prefixes co-, col-, com-, con-, cor-	

Knowing the meaning of these prefixes will help you understand the meaning of many words. Take the word *synagogue,* for example. It refers to a place where people of the Jewish faith worship. *Congress* refers to the group that comes together to make laws for our nation.

Target Reading Skill

Making Comparisons
The underlined signal word compares the powers of Congress. Bracket the sentence that explains how these powers are the same.

Vocabulary Strategy

Using Roots and Prefixes Circle a word with the prefix *col-* or *com-*. Use the prefix to explain the word's meaning.

_____

_____

¹ Local and state governments have the power to solve some problems. The Constitution gives Congress the power to solve other problems, such as national issues. But there are limits to these powers.

Powers Given to Congress

⁵ The powers given to Congress are the <u>same</u> in one way. They all reflect one or more of the goals in the Preamble to the Constitution. Some of these goals are "to form a more perfect union, establish justice, and insure domestic tranquility." Other goals are to "pro-
¹⁰ vide for the common defense, promote the general welfare, and secure the blessings of liberty."

Congress helps the general welfare, or well-being of the people. It does this by making laws that help people live better. Congress has the power to collect taxes
¹⁵ and borrow money. It has the power to decide how the money it collects will be spent. It has final approval of the government's **budget.**

Congress provides for the defense of the nation. It has the power to set up an army and a navy. Only
²⁰ Congress has the power to declare war.

Congress also helps establish justice. It has the power to create federal courts below the Supreme Court. Congress also has the power to impeach an official such as the President or a federal judge. Only the
²⁵ House can impeach. The Senate has the power to put the impeached person on trial. The person is removed from office if he or she is found guilty.

The Constitution does not list all the powers of Congress. The elastic clause gives Congress unnamed
³⁰ powers. It allows Congress to make all laws that are "necessary and proper" for carrying out the listed powers. The elastic clause makes the government flexible. That helps it to change with the times.

Key Terms
budget (BUJ it) *n.* a plan for raising and spending money

The Constitution gives Congress important powers
35 that do not have to do with making laws. Congress also has the power to investigate matters related to the government. It can gather information to make laws. It can also find out how the executive branch is enforcing laws.

Limits on the Powers of Congress

Limits on the powers of Congress are both general and
40 specific. The system of checks and balances sets general limits. Article 1, Section 9 of the Constitution lists specific limits.

The most important of these specific limits protects the rights of citizens. If you are in jail without a charge,
45 a lawyer or friend can get a writ of habeas corpus. This paper orders the police to bring you into court. The court decides if the police have enough evidence to keep you in jail. If not, you must be let go. The Constitution says that Congress cannot take away this
50 right except during invasion or civil war.

The Constitution also does not allow Congress to pass a **bill of attainder.** This convicts a person of a crime without a trial. In addition, Congress cannot pass an ex post facto law. Such a law makes a particu-
55 lar act a crime. Then it punishes people who did the act before the law was passed.

Review Questions

1. What do the powers given to Congress have in common?

_____

_____

2. What places general limits on the powers of Congress?

_____

_____

Key Terms

bill of attainder (BIL UV uh TAYN der) *n.* a law that finds a person guilty of a crime without a trial

---

✓ Reading Check

Underline the major powers the Constitution grants the Congress.

Vocabulary Strategy

Using Roots and Prefixes
Use what you know about prefixes to find the word in the first paragraph under "Limits on the Powers of Congress" that means "a group of things that together form a whole." Underline the word and circle the part that means "together."

✓ Reading Check

Underline the sentence that explains why the Constitution places specific limits on the powers of Congress.

Prepare to Read

Section 3
How Congress Is Organized

Objectives

1. Identify the leaders of both houses of Congress.
2. Describe the work of congressional committees.
3. Describe the President's role in legislation.

Target Reading Skill

Identify Contrasts When you contrast two or more things, you see how they are different. The following words and phrases are often used to point out differences.

unlike   in contrast to   than

Consider the contrast made in this sentence:

The House of Representatives has more members than the Senate.

The word *than* is used to contrast the two houses of Congress.

Vocabulary Strategy

Using Roots and Prefixes The roots of many English words come from the Latin language. The chart below shows some common Latin roots and their meanings.

Root	Meaning
-duc-	lead
-fer-	bring, bear
-ject-	throw

Remember, a prefix added to a root adds to or changes the root's meaning. The word *introduce,* for example, combines the prefix *intro-* with the root *duc-.* The prefix can mean "in" or "into." You could understand the meaning of *introduce* as "lead into."

Section 3 Summary

¹ The meeting periods of Congress are called terms. Each two-year term is divided into two sessions. There is one session for each year.

Members of Congress often work in committees to
⁵ make laws. A committee is a small working group.

Leadership in Congress

The Constitution says that the House of Representatives must choose the **Speaker of the House.** It says that the Vice President serves as the president of the Senate. It also directs the Senate to choose a **president pro tem-**
¹⁰ **pore.** This officer is called president pro tem, for short.

The Democratic and Republican parties decide who the leaders will be. The party with more members is called the majority party. The one with fewer members is the minority party.

¹⁵ The majority party in the House chooses the Speaker of the House. The Speaker is the most powerful member. The Speaker chooses committee members and sends bills to committees. The Speaker also leads sessions.

²⁰ The Vice President is in charge of sessions of the Senate. Unlike the Speaker, the Vice President cannot take part in debates. The Vice President votes only to break a tie. The majority party in the Senate chooses the president pro tem. This officer usually leads the
²⁵ Senate sessions. That is because the Vice President is busy with executive duties.

Floor leaders must guide bills through Congress. They work closely with committee leaders and party members. Assistant floor leaders are called whips.
³⁰ They help the floor leaders.

Key Terms

Speaker of the House (SPEE ker UV THUH HOWS) *n.* the officer who
³⁵ leads the House of Representatives

president pro tempore (PREZ i dent PRO TEM puh ree) *n.* the officer who leads the Senate when the Vice President is not there

floor leaders (FLOR LEE derz) *n.* main officers of the majority and minority parties in Congress

---

Target Reading Skill

Identify Contrasts Underline a word in the fourth paragraph under "Leadership in the House" that signals contrast. Then circle the two things that are being contrasted.

✓ Reading Check

Circle the names of the leaders of the Senate.

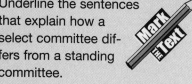
Working in Committees

Committees do much of the work of making laws. A bill introduced in the House or Senate is sent to a standing committee. These are permanent committees. Each deals with one area, such as banking. Each has
35 Democratic and Republican members. The chairperson of each committee belongs to the majority party.

Committees control what happens to a bill. First, a standing committee studies it. Next, it holds hearings about the bill. The committee may suggest changes.
40 Finally, the committee decides whether to send the bill to the entire House or Senate. If the committee does not send the bill, the bill expires or dies.

The House or Senate sometimes forms a select committee. This committee deals with a problem not covered
45 by a standing committee. Members of both the House and the Senate make up a joint committee.

A bill must pass in both houses. Then it can go to the President to be signed. Sometimes the houses cannot agree. Then a conference committee is formed. <u>It is dif-</u>
50 <u>ferent from a standing committee because it is tempo-</u>
<u>rary.</u> It tries to settle the differences between the houses.

The President's Role

A bill is sent to the President after it has been passed by both houses. The President can sign the bill into law. He also may veto, or reject, a bill. The President may send
55 the bill back to Congress unsigned. Congress can still pass the bill by a two-thirds vote of both houses.

A bill can also become law if the President holds it for ten days without signing or vetoing it. This is another way the President can veto a bill. It is called a
60 pocket veto.

Review Questions

1. What is the name of the person who leads the House?

_____

65 **2.** What does a standing committee do with a bill?

_____

> **Key Terms**
>
> **pocket veto** (POK it VEE tō) *n.* when the President rejects a bill by keeping it for 10 days, during which Congress ends its session

Prepare to Read

Section 4
Following a Bill in Congress

Objectives

1. Describe the process of stopping a bill from being passed.
2. Discuss how compromise bills are accepted and become law.
3. Explain how a bill dies in committee.

Target Reading Skill

Compare and Contrast Comparing and contrasting help you sort out and understand information. When you compare two things, you look at similarities. When you contrast them, you look at differences.

As you read this section, compare and contrast the paths that different minimum-wage bills took toward becoming a law. Use a diagram like this to note similarities and differences between bills.

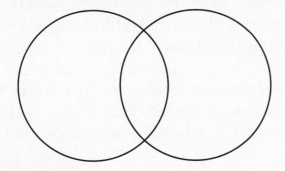

Vocabulary Strategy

Using Roots and Prefixes The Latin roots *minor-* and *major-* have opposite meanings.

Root	Meaning	Root	Meaning
minor-	smaller	major-	greater

Use this information to understand the meaning of the underlined term in this sentence:

The Republicans stopped the bill although they were the <u>minority</u> party in the Senate.

Now you know that the minority party is the smaller political party.

Using Roots and Prefixes The underlined word is related to the Latin root *minor-*. It means "smallest, least, or lowest." What do you think a minimum wage is?

_____

_____

_____

✓ Reading Check

Underline the sentence that explains how the Republicans kept the minimum-wage bill from coming to a vote.

Mark the Text

¹ The process a bill goes through in becoming a law takes time. Every bill is studied and debated carefully. Bills face many problems. If members of Congress disagree on the issue, a bill can be stopped. Later, they ⁵ may agree on a compromise bill. A bill can also die in committee.

Stopping a Bill

Senator Edward Kennedy introduced S.837, a <u>minimum-wage</u> bill, in 1987. It was given to the Labor and Human Resources Committee. Senator Kennedy led the commit- ¹⁰ tee. The committee held hearings on the bill. Then it sent the bill to the full Senate to be approved. This step is called reporting the bill.

The Senate began its debate on the bill. Senator Orrin Hatch opposed the bill. He thought it would ¹⁵ hurt the economy. He and other Republicans started a **filibuster** to block passage of the bill. Filibusters do not happen in the House. The House has time limits for debates. The Democrats tried to stop the filibuster by calling for **cloture.** A three-fifths vote is needed for clo- ²⁰ ture. The Democrats tried twice to get the number of votes needed for cloture. They failed. The Senate could not vote on the bill. That is because the filibuster did not end. The Republicans stopped the bill this way.

Key Terms

filibuster (FI luh bus ter) *n.* when senators give long speeches to try to stop the Senate from voting on a bill

cloture (KLO chur) *n.* when senators vote to stop a filibuster by ending the debate on a bill

Compromise Bills

Senator Kennedy introduced a new minimum-wage
25 bill, in the next Congress. This bill had several changes
in it. Some Republicans liked it better. The Senate
passed it.

The House also passed a minimum-wage bill. The
Senate and House bills were not exactly alike. A confer-
30 ence committee formed to work on a compromise bill.
Both houses passed this bill. It was sent to the
President. President George H. W. Bush thought an
increase in the minimum wage would hurt the economy. He vetoed the bill.

35 Congress could not override the veto. It worked on
another compromise bill. The President liked the new
bill. He signed it into law.

Another minimum-wage bill was introduced in the
House in 1996. It was sent to the Committee on Ways
40 and Means. The committee approved it and sent it to
the full House. The Senate passed a similar bill several
weeks later. A conference committee worked out a
compromise bill. Both houses of Congress passed it.
President Clinton signed the bill.

A Bill Dies in Committee

45 Senator Kennedy introduced another minimum-wage
bill in 1998. The bill was sent to the Labor and Human
Resources Committee. The committee now had a
Republican senator as its leader. It did not get the support of the majority of committee members. The bill
50 "died" when the 105th session of Congress ended.

Review Questions

1. How can members of the Senate stop a bill?

_____

_____

2. How do compromise bills become law?

_____

_____

Target Reading Skill

Compare and Contrast
Underline the sentence that contrasts the Senate and House minimum-wage bills.

✓ **Reading Check**

Circle the sentence that explains why a confer-ence committee was formed.

Target Reading Skill

Compare and Contrast
Underline the sentence that tells what hap-pened to Senator Kennedy's 1998 minimum wage bill.

✓ **Reading Check**

Why do you think Senator Kennedy wanted to raise the minimum wage?

_____

_____

_____

1. The number of representatives each state has in Congress is decided by
   A. the state.
   B. a census.
   C. the President.
   D. the people.

2. Why is the elastic clause important?
   A. It gives Congress unlisted powers.
   B. It is both general and specific.
   C. It is studied and debated carefully.
   D. all of the above

3. Who serves as president of the Senate when the Vice President cannot?
   A. Speaker of the House
   B. president pro tempore
   C. majority whip
   D. floor leader

4. Who can introduce a bill in Congress?
   A. a member of Congress
   B. an interest group
   C. a citizen
   D. the executive branch

5. Cloture is a way to
   A. report a bill.
   B. override a veto.
   C. stop a filibuster.
   D. make a law.

Short Answer Question

Identify five powers of Congress.

_____

_____

_____

_____

_____

Prepare to Read

Section 1
The Roles of the President

Objectives

1. Learn why the Framers of the Constitution created the office of President with limits.

2. Describe the various roles of the President.

3. Identify which of the President's roles have been created by tradition.

Target Reading Skill

Read Ahead Reading ahead helps you understand words and ideas in the text. Try reading ahead if a word or idea is not clear. Information in the next paragraph or two may help explain the meaning of the word or idea. Read this paragraph.

> The President is chief executive. That means the President is head of the executive branch of our nation's government. The President's main job is to execute, or carry out, the laws.

The meaning of the first sentence may not be clear to you right away. If you read ahead, you get more information. This information explains what it means to be chief executive.

Vocabulary Strategy

Using Word Parts Breaking a word into parts can help you understand its meaning. Word parts include prefixes, roots, and suffixes.

- A root is the base of the word. It has meaning by itself.
- A prefix is added before the root. It changes the meaning of the word.
- A suffix is added after the root. It changes the word's meaning and its part of speech. Also note that there may be a change in the spelling of the root when a suffix is added.

> Take the word *execute*, for example. *Execute* is a verb that means "carry out." When you add the suffix *-ive* to the root *execute*, you get the word *executive*. This new word is an adjective. Its meaning is "having to do with carrying out."

✓ Reading Check

Bracket the sentence that tells for how many years a President's term lasts.

Target Reading Skill

Read Ahead Keep reading to find out the meaning of *commander in chief*. Underline the sentence that explains this role of the President.

¹ The President is the head of the **executive branch.** Carrying out laws is only part of the job. The President's most important duty is to set goals for the nation and develop policies. Policies are ways of reach-
⁵ ing goals. The President must make final decisions on many important issues.

Creating the Office of President

The Constitution sets limits on the office of President. One limit on the President's power is the term of office. The President is elected for a term of four years. No
¹⁰ President may hold office for more than two terms.

The separation of powers also limits the President's power. The President only carries out laws. Congress makes laws. The Supreme Court decides if a law agrees with the Constitution.
¹⁵ Another limit is the system of checks and balances. Congress must approve many of the President's deci- sions. It can remove the President from office in cases of serious wrongdoing. The Supreme Court can decide if actions taken by the President agree with the
²⁰ Constitution.

A Leader with Many Roles

The President serves as chief executive. This means he or she is head of the executive branch. The President executes the laws, or makes sure they are carried out.

The President is commander in chief. That means
²⁵ the President leads the armed forces. The President makes the most important decisions when the nation is at war. The President may send troops to another country—even if Congress has not declared war. The War Powers Resolution says that the troops cannot
³⁰ stay more than 60 days. Congress must approve longer stays.

Key Terms

executive branch (eg ZEK yuh tiv BRANCH) *n.* the part of govern- ment that must carry out the law

The President is our chief diplomat. The President takes the lead in making **foreign policy.** But the Senate must approve treaties the President makes with other
35 countries. It also must approve **ambassadors** the President chooses. The President is free to make **executive agreements**.

Each year, the President gives the State of the Union speech to Congress. This speech includes ideas about
40 foreign policy and **domestic policy.** The President gets Congress to turn policy into laws in various ways. For example, the President calls and meets with members of Congress to <u>convince</u> them to support programs.

<u>The President has some judicial powers.</u> The
45 President chooses justices for the Supreme Court and judges for other federal courts. The President can also reduce the punishment of someone convicted of a federal crime. The President can even give pardons. A pardon is a release from punishment.

Roles Created by Tradition

50 The Constitution does not mention two other roles. They are party leader and chief of state. As party leader, the President supports party goals and candidates. As chief of state, the President speaks for the whole nation.

Review Questions

1. How are the President's powers limited?

_____

_____

2. Give an example of a judicial power of the President.

_____

Key Terms

foreign policy (FOR un POL uh see) *n.* a set of plans for helping our nation get along with other nations

ambassadors (am BAS uh derz) *n.* people who act for our nation in a foreign country

executive agreements (eg ZEK yuh tiv uh GREE muntz) *n.* agreements with other countries that do not need Senate approval

domestic policy (duh MES tik POL uh see) *n.* a set of plans for helping our nation deal with events and issues at home

Circle the text that tells how the President influences the making of laws.

Target Reading Skill

Read Ahead Read the underlined sentence. Then read ahead to find how many judicial powers the President has.

_____

_____

_____

Vocabulary Strategy

Using Word Parts The root of *convince* comes from the Latin word *vincere,* meaning "to overpower or conquer." The prefix *con-* or *com-* means "together or with." Use these word parts to write a definition of *convince.*

_____

_____

_____

✓ **Reading Check**

In the text, number the description of the two roles the President has taken on over time that are not in the Constitution.

Objectives

1. Learn about the Executive Office of the President.
2. Identify the executive departments.
3. Identify the independent agencies.
4. Understand the civil service system.

Target Reading Skill

Paraphrase Try paraphrasing to make sure that you understand what you have just read. Paraphrasing is putting something you have read into your own words. Read this paragraph.

> The duty of the Department of Homeland Security is to safeguard our country from terrorism. In this role, the department coordinates the antiterrorist activities of many federal agencies.

You might paraphrase the paragraph like this:

> What does the Department of Homeland Security do? Its job is to keep our country safe from terrorism. It does this by directing other government groups to work against terrorists.

Vocabulary Strategy

Using Word Parts When you come across a word you do not know while reading, break it into parts. The meaning of parts of the word can help you understand the meaning of the word as a whole.

Some words that relate to government contain the suffix *-cracy*, for example. This word part means "rule or government by." The word *democracy* contains this suffix. *Demo-* means "people." The meanings of the root and suffix tell you that *democracy* means "government by the people."

Section 2 Summary

¹ Today the executive branch is the government's largest branch. It has become a **bureaucracy.** The President has an **administration** to help direct the bureaucracy. Members of the administration lead the three main
⁵ parts of the executive branch. These are the Executive Office of the President, the executive departments, and the independent agencies.

The Executive Office of the President

The President chooses most of the people in the Executive Office of the President (EOP). Their main job
¹⁰ is to advise the President.

<u>The EOP includes the White House staff. It also includes the Vice President. It also includes special groups that help the President to make decisions about issues at home and abroad. The President's most trust-</u>
¹⁵ <u>ed advisers and assistants make up the White House staff.</u> The President chooses these people. They do not need Senate approval. The President decides what the Vice President does. The Vice President may play an active role. He or she may become President if the
²⁰ President dies. The Vice President may also serve as "acting President." That happens if the President becomes seriously ill.

The Executive Departments

The executive departments form the largest part of the executive branch. They help to carry out laws and to
²⁵ run government programs. Each department helps do one or more of the President's jobs. The Department of Defense helps the President as commander in chief. The Department of Homeland Security helps keep us safe from terrorism.

Key Terms

bureaucracy (byoo RAH kruh see) *n.* a large group of departments and offices that are part of a government

administration (ad min uh STRAY shun) *n.* the group of people chosen to work with the President

---

Vocabulary Strategy

Using Word Parts If *bureau* means "department or office," what does *bureaucracy* mean?

_____

_____

Target Reading Skill

Paraphrase How would you paraphrase the underlined text?

_____

_____

_____

✓ Reading Check

Circle the two groups and one person who make up the Executive Office of the President.

✓ Reading Check

Underline the sentence that explains the role of the executive departments in the President's Cabinet.

✓ Reading Check

In the text, number the three types of independent agencies.

✓ Reading Check

Bracket the sentence that explains how civil servants get their jobs today.

30 Each executive department has a leader, or head. The President chooses these heads. The Senate must approve each choice. Most department heads are called secretaries. The department heads are the main members of the **Cabinet.**

The Independent Agencies

35 Independent agencies do other jobs in the executive branch. There are three types.

- Executive Agencies. The President controls these. The National Aeronautics and Space Administration (NASA) is one example. The Environmental
40 Protection Agency (EPA) is another.

- Regulatory Commissions. Congress has formed 12 of these. The Consumer Product Safety Commission (CPSC) is an example. It sets safety rules for household products.

45 • Government Corporations. These agencies are like private businesses. They try to make a profit. Our postal service is an example. Most provide public services. The services may be too risky or costly for a private business to take on.

The Civil Service System

50 The civil service system helps to create trained government workers. These workers are called civil servants. They must pass tests to get their jobs.

Review Questions

1. What is the main job of people in the Executive Office of the President?

_____

_____

2. Give an example of each type of independent agency.

_____

_____

_____

Key Terms

Cabinet (KAB uh nit) *n.* the leaders of the executive departments who give the President advice

Prepare to Read

Section 3 Presidents and Power

Objectives

1. Understand the limits of the President's freedom to take action.
2. Discuss how government leaders seek a balance between strong Presidential leadership and the needs of democracy.
3. Learn how past Presidents have used the power of the office.

Target Reading Skill

Reread Rereading can help you understand words and ideas in a passage. If a passage was not clear the first time you read it, try rereading it. When you reread, look for connections between words, sentences, and ideas. Read this paragraph.

> Suppose, however, that a President often made important decisions without asking Congress or thinking about whether the actions were constitutional. Clearly, the need for strong presidential leadership must be balanced against the need to protect ourselves against abuse of power.

Now reread it. Do you see the connection between the first sentence and the second sentence? The first sentence explains why there is a need for the balance described in the second sentence. Rereading slowly and carefully also can help you to make sense of a long, complex sentence—like the first sentence in the paragraph above.

Vocabulary Strategy

Using Word Parts Remember, breaking a word you do not know into parts can help you understand its meaning. You may find roots, prefixes, or suffixes when you break a word into parts. A root is the base of the word. It has meaning by itself. A suffix comes after the root. It changes the word's part of speech and meaning.

You will read the word *opportunity* in this section. The suffix *-ity* shows that the word is a noun. If you know the meaning of *opportune*, you can figure out what *opportunity* means.

opportune   +   ity   =   opportunity

✓ Reading Check

Circle two examples of a President's freedom to take action.

Mark the Text

Vocabulary Strategy

Using Word Parts If *opportune* means "favorable," what is an opportunity?

_____

_____

✓ Reading Check

In the text, check the reason that the President should be able to act without seeking the approval of Congress.

Mark the Text

1 The President's actions affect our nation. They also affect nations all over the world.

Freedom to Take Action

The President has a lot of freedom. The President can hold talks with officials from other nations, for exam-
5 ple. Some talks lead to executive agreements. The Senate does not have to approve these. Other talks lead to **treaties**. The Senate can reject any treaty. But it is hard for the Senate to say no after the President agrees to a treaty. **Executive privilege** protects the President's
10 freedom to act.

Seeking a Balance

Why should the President be free to act without the other branches of government? The President must be able to act quickly in a crisis. The President also may need to take an opportunity that might be lost while
15 waiting for approval. The need for strong leadership must be balanced against the need for protection against abuse of power.

Presidential Power

The actions of three Presidents show how leaders have used their power.

20 • President Jefferson had a chance in 1803 to buy land from France. This Louisiana Territory would double the size of the United States. But the Constitution did not say the President could buy land. Jefferson knew he had to act quickly. Secretary of State
25 Madison believed that the President's power to make treaties gave Jefferson the right to buy the land. Jefferson decided to buy it. The Senate approved the treaty with France. Congress then paid France for the land.

Key Terms

treaties (TREE teez) *n.* formal agreements between nations

executive privilege (eg ZEK-yuh tiv PRIV uh lij) *n.* the President's right to keep some information secret from Congress and the courts

30 • President Truman faced a problem in 1952. Steel was
needed to make weapons for the Korean War.
Steelworkers would not work unless their demands
were met. The companies would not meet the
demands. The President gave an executive order. It
35 gave control of the mills to the government for a
time. The companies said the President could not
take control of private property. Truman said he was
acting as commander in chief to protect our troops.
The Supreme Court ruled the President could not
40 use executive orders to make his own laws.

• President Nixon left office in 1974. He left because
of the Watergate <u>scandal</u>. He and his staff were
accused of covering up a break-in. Burglars were
caught in the Democratic National Committee head-
45 quarters. They had broken in to get information
about the Democrats' campaign plans. The information would help to re-elect Nixon. A special committee investigated. They asked for tapes the President
had made of his conversations. Nixon refused. He
50 claimed executive privilege. The Supreme Court
ruled that he must turn over the tapes. It said that
executive privilege is not unlimited. It cannot be
used to hide criminal acts.

These three examples show that the President does not
55 govern alone. The three branches of government share
power. The system of checks and balances helps to
make sure the government acts in the best interests of
the people.

Review Questions

1. What limits a President's freedom to make treaties?

_____

_____

2. What powers did Presidents Truman and Nixon use?

_____

_____

Reread What do you think that
the underlined word means?
Reread to find out.

_____

_____

Vocabulary Strategy

Using Word Parts Like -*ity*, the
suffix -*ion* makes a word a noun. If
investigate means "look into carefully to get information," what is an
investigation?

_____

_____

✓ Reading Check

Look at the three examples of how
Presidents have used
power. Write O next to
an example if it is an
opportunity. Write C if
it is a crisis.

Chapter 9 Assessment

1. As commander in chief, the President
   - A. makes treaties with other countries.
   - B. carries out the laws of our country.
   - C. leads the U.S. armed forces.
   - D. gives the State of the Union speech.

2. The President is party leader and chief of state as a result of
   - A. tradition.
   - B. election.
   - C. duty.
   - D. action.

3. Which of the following is chosen by the President?
   - A. administration
   - B. Cabinet
   - C. justices of the Supreme Court
   - D. all of the above

4. The Vice President is part of the
   - A. Executive Office of the President.
   - B. Department of State.
   - C. government corporation.
   - D. civil service system.

5. Which protects the President's freedom to act?
   - A. executive department
   - B. executive privilege
   - C. executive branch
   - D. executive agreement

Short Answer Question

Briefly explain why the executive branch is an important part of our government.

_____

_____

_____

_____

_____

Prepare to Read

Section 1
The Role of the Federal Courts

Objectives

1. Understand the need for laws and courts in our society.
2. Learn what courts do.
3. Discuss and compare the roles of state courts and federal courts.

Target Reading Skill

Use Context Clues Context clues can help you understand words you do not recognize while reading. Look at words and sentences around the unfamiliar word. They often give clues to the word's meaning. Read this sentence. Pay attention to the underlined words.

A legislative body <u>makes a law</u> against one person damaging another's property.

The underlined words give clues to the meaning of *legislative body*. They tell you that a legislative body is a group that makes laws.

Vocabulary Strategy

Recognizing Word Origins A word's origin is where the word comes from. Words in this section contain the Latin roots *-put-*, *-jur-*, and *-dic-*. The chart shows what these roots mean.

Latin Root	Meaning
-put-	think
-jur-	law
-dic-	say

Knowing these roots can help you figure out the meanings of words in which they appear. As you read, use the context and what you know about these Latin roots to figure out what *dispute* and *jurisdiction* mean.

Target Reading Skill

Use Context Clues Circle two context clues that hint at the meaning of the underlined word. Then explain its meaning.

_____

_____

✓ **Reading Check**

Bracket the text that describes the purpose of a legal system.

✓ **Reading Check**

Write *CIV* next to the names of the two parties in civil trials. Write *CRIM* next to the names of the parties in criminal trials.

¹ The Supreme Court and other federal courts make up the <u>judicial</u> branch of the federal government. Judges are the most important members of this branch.

Laws and Courts

⁵ The legal system in our society helps to solve disagreements that involve laws. A legal system is needed to answer questions in serious conflicts.

What Courts Do

Courts of law solve legal conflicts. The two kinds of legal conflicts are criminal cases and civil cases. In a ¹⁰ criminal case, a court decides if a person is innocent or guilty of breaking the law. The court also decides what the punishment will be if the person is guilty. In a civil case, a court settles a disagreement.

In a civil case, one side, the **plaintiff**, usually brings ¹⁵ the case to court. The other party is called the **defendant**. In a criminal case, the **prosecution** brings the case to court. The prosecution is called "The People." The other side in a criminal case is called the defendant.

The judge decides which side's argument is most in ²⁰ keeping with the law. The judge does not take a side. A jury also takes part in many cases. The jury decides the facts of a case. The Constitution says that a person accused of a crime has the right to a trial by jury.

Courts have the important job of deciding what the ²⁵ law means. Courts also may have to decide if the Constitution allows a law. A court's decision can set a **precedent**. A precedent makes the meaning of a law or the Constitution clearer. It also tells how the law should be applied.

Key Terms

plaintiff (PLAYN tuf) *n.* a person or group who complains against someone in a law case

defendant (dih FEN dunt) *n.* a person or group against whom a complaint is made in a law case

prosecution (prah si KYOO shun) *n.* a government body that makes a criminal charge against a person or group accused of breaking the law

precedent (PREH suh dunt) *n.* a court decision that may be used to help decide a future case

State Courts and Federal Courts

30 Our legal system has both state courts and federal courts. Most cases begin in a lower court, often at the state level. State courts decide most legal arguments and <u>violations</u> of the law.

Most state court systems have three levels. These
35 are trial courts, appeals courts, and a court of final appeals. The court to which a legal case goes first has **original jurisdiction.** This court determines the facts in a case. This often happens during a trial with a jury.

The plaintiff or defendant may believe that the deci-
40 sion made by a trial court is unfair. Then he or she has the right to **appeal.** Each state has appeals courts to hear cases from lower state courts. These courts have **appellate jurisdiction.** An appeals court reviews the legal issues in a case.

45 An appeals court may agree with the lower court's decision. Or it may decide that the trial was unfair. It also may overturn the lower court's decision. Then the appeals court may order another trial. The Constitution does not allow double jeopardy. This means that you
50 cannot be tried for the same crime after being found innocent.

The Supreme Court hears cases appealed from the state courts. It makes sure that all 50 state court systems interpret the Constitution in the same way. It also makes
55 sure that the rights of all Americans are protected.

Review Questions

1. What do courts do?

_____

_____

2. Compare the roles of state courts and federal courts.

_____

_____

Key Terms

original jurisdiction (uh RIJ uh nul jer us DIK shun) *n.* the right to hear a case first

appeal (uh PEEL) *v.* to ask a higher court to review the decision made in a case

appellate jurisdiction (uh PEH lut jer us DIK shun) *n.* the right to hear an appeal

---

Target Reading Skill

Use Context Clues What do you think *violations* means? Circle any clues to its meaning.

_____

_____

Vocabulary Strategy

Recognizing Word Origins
Review the meanings of *-jur-* and *-dic-*. What does *jurisdiction* mean?

_____

_____

✓ Reading Check

How does a case go from a trial court to the Supreme Court?

_____

_____

_____

Prepare to Read

Section 2 The Organization of the Federal Courts

Objectives

1. Learn what district courts do.
2. Discuss the role of the courts of appeals.
3. Consider the purpose of the Supreme Court.
4. Examine what federal court judges do.

 **Target Reading Skill**

Interpret Nonliteral Meanings Literal language means exactly what it says. Nonliteral language uses images or comparisons to express an idea or make a point. Read this sentence.

The district courts are the workhorses of the federal court system.

This sentence describes the district courts as workhorses. What idea does this image express? It suggests that the district courts do most of the work in the federal court system.

Vocabulary Strategy

Recognizing Word Origins Suffixes from the Latin language appear on many English words. As you know, a suffix is a word part that is added after the root of a word. It changes the word's part of speech. The chart shows two Latin suffixes and their meanings.

Latin Suffix	Meaning
-ate-	having, being
-or-	someone who does

Knowing these Latin suffixes and their meanings will help you understand the meanings of words in this section.

Section 2 Summary

¹ Article III of the Constitution contains the framework for the federal court system. It does not set up lower courts. Congress created district courts and courts of appeals in 1789 through the Judiciary Act.

The District Courts

⁵ The district courts do most of the work in the federal court system. There are 94 district courts. Each state has at least one. Some larger states have four. District courts are courts of original jurisdiction. That makes them the first to hear cases involving federal issues. A ¹⁰ judge directs what goes on in a district court. The court may call witnesses. A jury usually decides the facts in a case.

The Courts of Appeals

The **courts of appeals** are the next highest level of the federal court system. There are 12 <u>appellate</u> courts. ¹⁵ Each takes cases from a group of district courts within an area. This area is called a circuit. The courts of appeals often are called **circuit courts**.

A court of appeals has no jury. It calls no witnesses. It does not look at any evidence. Lawyers make argu-²⁰ments in front of a panel of three judges. The judges can agree with the lower court's decision. Or they may disagree and reverse it. The courts of appeals decide whether the original trial was fair.

> ✓ **Reading Check**
>
> Circle the name of the courts that do most of the work in the federal court system.

> **Vocabulary Strategy**
>
> **Using Word Origins** Recall the meaning of the suffix *-ate*. Also look at the context, or words and sentences around *appellate*. What do you think *appellate* means?
>
> _____
>
> _____

> ✓ **Reading Check**
>
> Underline three sentences that explain how a court of appeals works.

Key Terms

courts of appeals (KORTZ UV uh PEELZ) *n.* federal courts that review the decisions of lower district courts

circuit courts (SER ket KORTZ) *n.* federal courts of appeals

Target Reading Skill

Interpret Nonliteral Meanings
Restate the underlined sentence in your own words.

_____

_____

Vocabulary Strategy

Using Word Origins If *legislate* means "to make law," what is a legislator? (Hint: remember what the suffix *-or* means.)

_____

_____

The Supreme Court

The Supreme Court is the highest court in the federal
25 court system. Its main job is to be the final court of
appeals for both the state and federal court systems. It
has original jurisdiction over a few special kinds of
cases. These include cases involving foreign governments and arguments between state governments.
30   There are many other federal courts. These include
the Court of Claims, the Court of Customs and Patent
Appeals, and the Tax Court. Congress set up these special courts. Appeals from some of these courts are sent
directly to the Supreme Court. Others must first pass
35 through a court of appeals or a higher special court.

Federal Court Judges

Federal judges do the work of the judicial branch. A
judge settles individual cases. He or she must not favor
one party. Judges help define and clarify the work of
lawmakers by applying the law to specific cases. The
40 President chooses all federal judges for the district
courts, courts of appeals, and Supreme Court. The
Senate must approve the choices. The judges serve life
terms. They can be removed only by being impeached.
   <u>Federal judges shoulder great responsibility</u>. They
45 must balance the rights of individuals with the interests of the whole nation. Often they have to make decisions that seem unfair to one side.
   The nine Supreme Court justices have the most
responsibility. They decide specific cases, often involv-
50 ing just one or two people. Their decisions may have
important consequences for the nation.

Review Questions

1. What is the job of the courts of appeals?

_____

_____

2. What do federal court judges do?

_____

_____

Objectives

1. Analyze the importance of judicial review.
2. Learn about the Supreme Court justices and the work they do.
3. Explore some of the influences on judicial decision making.
4. Describe how the Supreme Court is a changing court.
5. Understand the relationship between the Supreme Court and the other branches of government.

Target Reading Skill

Use Context Clues You can use context while reading to understand words you do not know. Context is the words, phrases, and sentences around a word. Look to see if the context restates the word. Context may also give an example or make a comparison that helps you understand an unfamiliar word. Look at the context of the word *constitutional* in this sentence, for example.

> The Supreme Court has the final say about what laws are constitutional, or <u>allowed by the Constitution</u>.

The underlined words explain the meaning of *constitutional*.

Vocabulary Strategy

Recognizing Word Origins Some English words contain word parts from ancient Greek. The suffix *-ism*, for example, comes from Greek. It has various meanings, including "act or practice." Use what you know about this suffix to understand unfamiliar words as you read. Remember, a suffix is added after the root of the word. It changes the part of speech of the word. The suffix *-ism* makes a word a noun.

✓ Reading Check

Underline the sentence that explains why judicial review is an important power of the Supreme Court.

⊙ Target Reading Skill

Use Context Clues
What is the meaning of the underlined word? Circle words or phrases that helped you figure out its meaning.

_____

_____

✓ Reading Check

Bracket the sentences that tell how Supreme Court justices are chosen.

✓ Reading Check

Circle the text that explains what decides the outcome of a case heard by the Supreme Court.

---

¹ The Supreme Court has the final say about what the Constitution means and what laws are allowed. A Supreme Court decision sets the broadest and longest-lasting precedent in our legal system.

Judicial Review

⁵ **Judicial review** is one of the most important powers of the Supreme Court. It gives the judicial branch the final say over whether a law is allowed by the Constitution. The Court took the power during the case of *Marbury* v. *Madison*. Marbury sued Secretary of
¹⁰ State Madison because he did not get a government job. Marbury took his case directly to the Supreme Court.

The Court looked at the law that allowed Marbury to bring his case before the Court. This law was the
¹⁵ Judiciary Act of 1789. Part of the Judiciary Act gave the Court original jurisdiction. The Court decided that this was unconstitutional. This decision gave the Supreme Court the power of judicial review.

The Justices

The President chooses Supreme Court <u>justices</u> from
²⁰ among the most respected judges, lawyers, and legal scholars in the country. The Senate must then approve the President's choices. The Supreme Court is made up of a Chief Justice and eight associate justices.

The Work of the Supreme Court

The Court chooses which cases to hear. It usually
²⁵ chooses cases about important constitutional issues.

Each side gives briefs, or written arguments. Lawyers present oral arguments before the Court. Then the justices meet to discuss the case. The Chief Justice summarizes the case and offers an opinion. Each jus-
³⁰ tice has a chance to comment. Finally, the Chief Justice calls for a vote. A majority decides the case.

> **Key Term**
> **judicial review** (joo DISH ul rih VYOO) *n.* the power of the Supreme Court to overturn any law that goes against the Constitution

Most Supreme Court decisions come with an **opinion**. The opinion shows how the law must be applied or how the Constitution must be interpreted.

Influences on Judicial Decisions

35 Various factors affect how the justices vote in a court case. The justices consider <u>precedent</u>, or past court decisions. They try to understand what lawmakers were thinking when they made laws.

A Changing Court

The Supreme Court has had three "personalities" since 40 the 1950s. The "Warren Court" was known for defending the rights of people accused of crimes. Its decisions are examples of **judicial activism.** Many "Burger Court" decisions are examples of **judicial restraint**. The Court today is the "Rehnquist Court." It has made 45 decisions that limit the government's authority.

The Court and Other Branches of Government

Judicial review gives the Supreme Court an important check on the power of the legislative and executive branches. The President's power to choose justices is one check on the Supreme Court. The Senate can check 50 the power of the President and the Supreme Court. It can refuse to approve justices chosen for the Court.

Review Questions

1. Explain why judicial review is important.

_____

_____

2. List three factors that affect how Supreme Court justices vote on a case.

_____

_____

Key Terms

opinion (uh PIN yun) *n.* a written statement that explains the reasons for a Supreme Court decision

judicial activism (joo DISH ul AK tih vih zum) *n.* an effort by judges to take an active role in making policy by overturning laws

judicial restraint (joo DISH ul rih STRAYNT) *n.* an effort by judges to avoid overturning laws

Target Reading Skill

Use Context Clues Circle the words that help you understand the meaning of *precedent* in context.

Vocabulary Strategy

Recognizing Word Origins What does activism mean if *-ism* means "act or practice"?

_____

_____

✓ Reading Check

Why do justices try to determine the intentions of lawmakers at the time they made a law?

_____

_____

_____

✓ Reading Check

Bracket the text that tells what the Warren Court was known for.

✓ Reading Check

Underline the sentence that describes the power the President has over the Supreme Court.

1. In a civil case, a court
   A. accuses a person of breaking the law.
   B. interprets the Constitution.
   C. settles a dispute.
   D. decides on a person's punishment.

2. A court of original jurisdiction is also known as
   A. a court of appeals.
   B. a trial court.
   C. a final court.
   D. a state court.

3. The Court of Claims is an example of
   A. a court of appeals.
   B. a special federal court.
   C. a state supreme court.
   D. all of the above

4. Which of the following gave the Supreme Court the power of judicial review?
   A. Congress
   B. the Constitution
   C. the Judiciary Act
   D. *Marbury* v. *Madison*

5. A brief is
   A. a majority opinion.
   B. a minority opinion.
   C. a written argument.
   D. an oral argument.

Short Answer Question

Identify the lower courts of the federal court system. What is the main job of each?

_____

_____

_____

_____

Reading Preview

Section 1 Federalism: One Nation and Fifty States

Objectives

1. Understand that public policy is a major concern of all levels of government.
2. Understand how federalism involves state powers and shared powers.
3. Explore the concept of federalism in action.

Target Reading Skill

Identify Main Ideas Identifying the main idea can help you remember what you read. The main idea is the most important point in a paragraph. The first sentence of a paragraph often states the main idea directly. Read this paragraph and look for its main idea.

Governments at all levels make public policy to help solve public problems. Public problems are situations that affect many people. Policies set by state and local governments affect people's lives most directly. They often aim to solve problems in communities.

Note that the main idea of the paragraph is stated directly in the first sentence. All the other information in the paragraph supports this idea.

Vocabulary Strategy

Using Context Clues Have you ever come across a word you know that is being used in a new way? You can figure out the new meaning of the word by looking at its context. The words and sentences around a word are the context. Consider the underlined word in this sentence.

Working together is the <u>key</u> to finding solutions to public problems.

You may understand the word *key* to mean "a shaped piece of metal that opens a lock on something." Look at other words in the sentence to figure out the meaning of *key* here. *Key* connects the phrases *working together* and *finding solutions*. Working together can lead to finding solutions. Here, *key* means "something that leads to something else."

Target Reading Skill

Identify Main Ideas
Bracket the sentence that states the main idea of the second paragraph under *Public Policy.*

✓ Reading Check

Underline the sentence that tells how public policy relates to public problems.

Vocabulary Strategy

Using Context Clues
What does the underlined word mean here? Circle words that give clues to its meaning.

_____

_____

_____

✓ Reading Check

Put a check mark next to the sentence that explains how the Tenth Amendment gives powers to the states.

¹ State governments meet our needs in many ways. These governments take most of the responsibility for schools, highways, health, and safety.

Public Policy

Governments at all levels make **public policy** to help ⁵ solve public problems. Public problems affect many people. Policies set by state and local governments affect people's lives most directly.

Government, communities, and individuals need to work together to find and carry out answers to public ¹⁰ problems. People who work for the government make choices when making public policy. Citizens also make choices about which solutions to support.

Federalism

Some delegates at the Constitutional Convention wanted a strong national government. Others wanted the ¹⁵ states to keep most of the power. The Framers tried to bring these two points of view together by choosing federalism. The Constitution lists the powers of the national government. It does not <u>cover</u> the powers of the states. States get their powers from the Tenth ²⁰ Amendment. This amendment gives states all powers not given to the national government or denied to the states. The national government and state governments also share many powers.

Our system of federalism is unusual. The **unitary** ²⁵ **system** is more common. The unitary system would not work well in the United States, however. Our country is too large and diverse for that system.

Key Terms

public policy (PUB lik POL uh see) *n.* the goals the government sets for meeting the country's needs

unitary system (YOO nuh tehr ee SIS tem) *n.* a type of government in which a central government holds most of the power

Federalism in Action

The powers of national government and state governments mix and overlap. There is no set way for them to
30 do this. Some people <u>press</u> to keep national government out of what they think is states' business. Other people argue that the national government should have more power over the states.

Some people think state governments can serve
35 people better than the national government. They want state governments to fit laws and programs to the needs of their states.

People who favor a strong national government point out that opportunities in different states are not
40 always equal. They say the national government needs to make sure that there is equal opportunity in all states. They also point out that some problems cost too much for states to solve. Other problems are too big. Some problems involve several states. The federal gov-
45 ernment can help with these problems.

Review Questions

1. What type of policies affect people's lives most directly?

_____

_____

2. How do the powers of the national government and state governments really work in federalism?

_____

_____

Target Reading Skill

Identify Main Ideas Underline the sentence that states the main idea in the first paragraph under the heading *Federalism in Action.*

Vocabulary Strategy

Using Context Clues What is the meaning of the underlined word in context?

_____

_____

✓ Reading Check

Number two sentences that explain why some people argue for less federal power over states' decisions.

Reading Preview

Section 2 State Legislatures

Objectives

1. Learn who state legislators are.
2. Discuss the organization of state legislatures.
3. Find out how states make laws.
4. Learn about financing state governments.

Target Reading Skill

Identify Implied Main Ideas The main idea of a paragraph is not always stated directly. Sometimes it is only implied, or hinted at. You have to put together the details in the paragraph to find out the main idea. Read this paragraph. What main idea do the details in the paragraph suggest?

> Most state legislatures have an upper house. This house is called the senate. They also have a lower house. The lower house is usually called the house of representatives. In some states, the lower house is known as an assembly or a general assembly.

All the details in the paragraph are about the two houses in most state legislatures. You could state the implied main idea in this way: *Most state legislatures have two houses.*

Vocabulary Strategy

Using Context Clues The context of a word you do not know can make the word's meaning clear. Context includes words, phrases, and sentences around the word. The context sometimes restates the meaning of the word. Look at the underlined word in this sentence. Does the context give clues to its meaning?

> Most state legislatures have the power to <u>impeach</u> officials in the executive and judicial branches. Members bring charges against a judge, governor, or President because of something they think the person has done wrong.

The words following *impeach* restate its meaning. *Impeach* means "bring charges against."

Section 2 Summary

1 State legislators make most of the laws that affect daily life. These lawmakers do their work in state legislatures. State legislatures are set up like Congress.

Who Are State Legislators?

There were fewer demands on state governments in
5 our nation's early years than there are today. They had other jobs, such as farmers, lawyers, or businesspeople. State governments took on new responsibilities over time. It became hard for state legislators to carry out their government duties and do their other jobs. Many
10 state legislators are full-time lawmakers today.

All states except Nebraska have a two-house legislature. The upper house is called a senate. The lower house is usually the house of representatives.

State governments divide the time the legislature
15 meets into sessions. Most state legislatures meet every year. The sessions may be from 20 days to 6 months long. The governor of a state can call special sessions.

Seats in state legislatures are **apportioned** based on equal representation. That means legislators represent
20 areas with about the same number of people. Seats used to be based on geography. One legislator might have represented a <u>rural</u> part of the state. The voters in his or her district lived in the country. Another legislator might have represented a city. In 1964 the Supreme
25 Court said that each district in a state must have about the same number of people in it.

Making Laws

A state legislator's main job is to make laws. State legislatures follow the same steps as Congress to make laws. Legislators introduce bills. They discuss them in
30 committees. They debate them. Both houses must agree on the final bill. The governor must approve it.

Lawmaking in state legislatures differs in one way from Congress. Citizens can be more involved.

Key Term

apportioned (uh POR shund) v. divided among districts

Identify Implied Main Ideas In one sentence, state the main idea of the first paragraph under *Who Are State Legislators?* Underline two sentences that point to this main idea.

Mark the Text

✓ **Reading Check**

Bracket the text that explains why more state legislators are full-time lawmakers today than in the early years of the United States.

Mark the Text

Vocabulary Strategy

Using Context Clues Circle the word or words that tell the meaning of *rural*.

Mark the Text

✓ **Reading Check**

Underline the sentence that describes the issue that the Supreme Court decided in 1964.

Mark the Text

Target Reading Skill

Identify Implied Main Ideas State the main idea of the second paragraph under *Making Laws* in one sentence.

_____

_____

_____

Vocabulary Strategy

Using Context Clues Circle the word or words that help you understand the meaning of *budget*.

✓ **Reading Check**

In the text, number ways state legislatures check the executive branch.

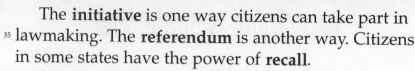

⟳ **Target Reading Skill**

Identify Implied Main Ideas What is the main idea of the second paragraph under *Financing State Government*?

_____

_____

_____

✓ **Reading Check**

In the text, circle seven ways a state can raise money.

The **initiative** is one way citizens can take part in 35 lawmaking. The **referendum** is another way. Citizens in some states have the power of **recall**.

State legislatures have the power to check the activities of the executive and the judicial branches. The legislature in many states must approve officials and judges 40 chosen by the governor. State legislatures also must approve the governor's budget, or spending plan. They check how executive agencies do their jobs. State legislators also look at how federal money is spent in their state. Legislatures in most states have the power to 45 impeach officials in the executive and judicial branches.

Financing State Government

State governments need money to provide services to citizens. States raise more than half of their **revenue** from taxes. Most tax revenue comes from sales tax and income tax. Most states have two kinds of **sales taxes.** 50 They charge a general sales tax on almost all goods sold. They charge another kind of sales tax called an **excise tax.** Most states have an **income tax**, too.

States also get money through **bonds** and lotteries. State and local governments can turn to Congress 55 for money. This money comes to states as categorical grants or block grants.

Review Questions

1. How are state legislatures organized?

_____

2. What is a state legislator's main job?

_____

Key Terms

initiative (ih NISH uh tiv) *n.* a way for people to propose laws
referendum (reh fuh REN dum) *n.* in this case, a law is given to the voters to approve or reject
recall *v.* an election that is held when people think that a government worker is not doing their job
revenue (REV uh noo) *n.* income
sales taxes (SAYLZ TAK suz) *n.* extra money added to the price of goods and services
excise tax (EK sīz TAKS) *n.* a charge on certain goods, such as gasoline and tobacco
income tax (IN kum TAKS) *n.* a tax on what people and businesses earn
bonds (BONDS) *n.* certificates that people buy from the government

Objectives

1. Discuss the roles of the governor.
2. Learn about other state executive officials.
3. Learn about state executive agencies.

Target Reading Skill

Identify Supporting Details The main idea of a paragraph is supported by details. Supporting details give more information about the main idea. They help explain it. They may give examples or reasons to support it. Read this paragraph.

> The governor has the power to make a budget for the state. The legislature must approve the budget. No state money may be spent without the legislature's approval. The governor usually writes the budget, though. That gives him or her a lot of control over how much money goes to different groups and programs.

The main idea is underlined. Note that the other information in the paragraph supports the main idea. Each sentence gives at least one supporting detail.

Vocabulary Strategy

Using Context Clues There are many places to look for clues to the meaning of a word you do not recognize. You may find context clues in the same sentence as the word. Or you may have to look farther. Check words and phrases in nearby sentences. Look beyond those sentences to other sentences and even to other paragraphs.

You may not know the meaning of the word *documents* in the first paragraph under the heading *Other Executive Officials*. Note the word *records* in the same sentence. Maybe you know that records are written reports about different things. That gives you a clue that documents also might be papers containing information.

Now look at the underlined word *supervises* in the same paragraph. What clues do you find to its meaning in nearby sentences?

Section 3 Summary

Vocabulary Strategy

Using Context Clues What is another name for the state militia? Circle it.

✓ **Reading Check**

Circle the words that describe the governor's greatest source of executive power.

Target Reading Skill

Identify Supporting Details The main idea in the second paragraph under *State Executive Agencies* is underlined. Circle examples that support this main idea.

Target Reading Skill

Identify Supporting Details The main idea in the second paragraph under *The Roles of the Governor* is underlined. Number the details that support this main idea.

✓ **Reading Check**

What executive agency is usually one of the largest in state government? Bracket its name in the text.

---

¹ A governor and a group of officials lead the executive branch of state government. The responsibilities of state government have grown. Governors have been given more power to handle them. The officials in the execu-
⁵ tive branch help carry out the state's laws and programs.

The Roles of the Governor

The governor is chief executive, like the President. That means he or she is head of the executive branch. The governor makes sure laws are carried out. The governor is also commander in chief of the state militia, or
¹⁰ National Guard. The governor chooses officials to help carry out the state's work. Making a state budget is the governor's greatest source of executive power.

The governor also has legislative powers, like the President. The governor can give ideas for laws in the
¹⁵ form of bills, budgets, or speeches. The governor can get the support of legislators or the public for his or her ideas. The governor can also veto laws. Governors in 43 states have the **item veto**.

The governor, like the President, also has some judi-
²⁰ cial powers. Governors can choose certain state judges, for example. Governors can also shorten or overturn the sentences of people convicted of crimes.

State Executive Agencies

State executive agencies do the daily work of the executive branch. They include the departments of health,
²⁵ revenue, and natural resources.

The state education agency is usually one of the largest executive agencies. It makes sure that the state's education laws are carried out. State laws set the number of school days per year. They decide which subjects
³⁰ you have to study. They also decide how many classes you must pass to graduate. This agency works with local school districts to carry out education laws. It also sets standards for teachers.

> **Key Term**
> **item veto** (ī tum VEE tō) *n.* the power to say no to certain parts of a bill

Other Executive Officials

A group of executive officials helps the governor. The
35 group includes the lieutenant governor. The lieutenant
governor's job is like the Vice President's job. The secretary of state, attorney general, and state treasurer
also help the governor. The secretary of state is in
charge of official records and <u>documents</u>. He or she
40 also <u>supervises</u> elections. The attorney general is the
state's chief lawyer. The state treasurer oversees the
state's money matters.

Some people compare these state executive officials
to the President's Cabinet. However, the governor does
45 not choose them like the President chooses members of
the Cabinet. The voters of the state elect many executive officials.

Review Questions

1. Describe the governor's role as chief executive.

_____

_____

_____

2. How do state executive officials differ from members of the President's Cabinet?

_____

_____

© Pearson Education, Inc., Publishing as Pearson Prentice Hall. All rights reserved.

Key Term

lieutenant governor (loo TEN unt GUV er ner) *n.* the state official
who is second in rank to the governor

Reading Preview

Section 4 State Courts

Objectives

1. Learn what state courts do.

2. Learn about judges in state courts.

3. Discuss a case study in federalism and the courts.

Target Reading Skill

Identify Supporting Details Chapters, sections, subsections, and paragraphs all have main ideas. Each of these parts also has details that support the main ideas. Supporting details explain the main idea. They help make the main idea more meaningful to the reader.

Look at this diagram. It shows the main idea of a subsection of Chapter 11. It also shows some details that support the main idea.

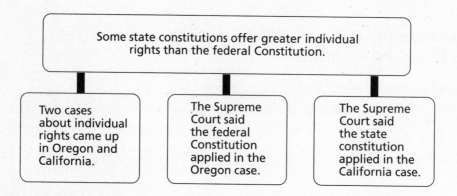

Some state constitutions offer greater individual rights than the federal Constitution.

| Two cases about individual rights came up in Oregon and California. | The Supreme Court said the federal Constitution applied in the Oregon case. | The Supreme Court said the state constitution applied in the California case. |

Vocabulary Strategy

Using Context Clues Always look at context when you find a word you do not know. Surrounding words, sentences, and paragraphs may offer clues to the meaning of the word.

Look at the context of the word *advantages* in the second paragraph under *Judges in State Courts*. Do surrounding words or sentences hint at the meaning of *advantages*?

Section 4 Summary

1 There are two levels of law: state law and federal law. Federal courts interpret the United States Constitution. State court systems interpret state constitutions. State courts handle cases that have to do with people's
5 everyday lives.

The organization and names of state courts vary. Most state judicial systems have three levels. The first is the state trial courts. They hear civil cases and criminal cases. The second is the state appeals courts. They
10 review cases from the trial courts. The third is the state supreme court. This is the highest level. It deals with cases that go beyond the appeals courts.

What State Courts Do

State courts check the two other branches of state government. For example, a state court may decide that a
15 law passed by the state legislature goes against the state constitution. State courts also protect the rights of citizens. But hearing civil and criminal cases is probably the best-known job of state courts.

Judges in State Courts

Judges play an important part in the state court sys-
20 tem. State court judges have many of the same duties as federal judges.

The way state court judges are selected varies. It depends on the state and the level of the court. Judges run for election in some states. There are advantages to
25 this. An elected judge is responsible to the public. The election of judges checks the power of a governor. The governor might want to choose friends and supporters to be judges.

Some people do not think judges should be elected.
30 They think that judges must make decisions based on the law and the facts. They do not want judges to do only what might please voters. These people think that judges should be chosen based on merit, or ability.

Some states use the **Missouri Plan**. Under this plan,
35 the governor chooses a judge from a list. Voters vote

Key Terms
Missouri Plan (muh ZER ee PLAN) n. one way to choose judges

✓ Reading Check

In the text, number the three levels of a state court system.

⟳ Target Reading Skill

Identify Supporting Details
The main idea of several paragraphs in the section *Judges in State Courts* is underlined. Circle two supporting details in the paragraph.

Vocabulary Strategy

Using Context Clues What is the meaning of *advantages*?

_____

_____

_____

✓ Reading Check

Number the sentences that describe the Missouri Plan for selecting judges.

"yes" or "no" in the next election to have the judge stay in office for twelve years.

The length of time judges spend in office depends on the state and the level of court. Most serve from 4 to
40 15 years. Judges in Rhode Island hold office for life.

Most states have **judicial action commissions**. These groups look into complaints against judges.

Case Study: Federalism and the Courts

It is not easy to draw a line between federal power and state power. The judicial branch plays an important role
45 in deciding questions of federalism.

Two U.S. Supreme Court cases help answer this question. The cases are from Oregon and California. In each case, owners of a shopping mall took members of citizens' groups to court. The groups had passed out
50 leaflets and gathered signatures at the mall. The owners said it was their right to stop such activity on their property. The citizens' groups said they were using their right to freedom of speech.

In the Oregon case, the Supreme Court said the
55 owners of the mall had the right to use their property as they wanted. In the California case, the Court took the side of the citizens' groups. It pointed out that California's constitution offers greater protection of free speech than does the federal Constitution. The fed-
60 eral Constitution was used in the Oregon case. The state constitution was <u>applied</u> in California.

Review Questions

1. What is the best-known job of the state courts?

_____

2. Some people do not think judges should be elected. How do these people want judges to be chosen?

_____

Key Terms

judicial action commissions (joo DISH ul AK shun kuh MISH unz)
n. groups that look into complaints against judges

1. States get their powers from the
   A. Constitution.
   B. Tenth Amendment.
   C. Bill of Rights.
   D. state constitutions.

2. States raise revenue from
   A. taxes.
   B. lotteries.
   C. bonds.
   D. all of the above

3. What does the governor oversee as commander in chief?
   A. the state budget
   B. the state legislature
   C. the state militia
   D. the state constitution

4. The lieutenant governor is
   A. second in rank to the governor.
   B. in charge of the state legislature.
   C. head of the executive branch.
   D. chosen by the attorney general.

5. Which is the highest state court?
   A. state supreme court
   B. state appeals court
   C. state trial court
   D. U.S. Supreme Court

Short Answer Question

How can citizens be involved in lawmaking at the state level?

_____

_____

_____

_____

Reading Preview

Section 1
Types of Local Government

Objectives

1. Describe counties and townships.

2. Explain how New England towns are run.

3. Learn about special districts.

4. Describe the different types of city government.

Target Reading Skill

Compare and Contrast Comparing and contrasting can help you understand information. When you compare, you look at how two or more things are alike. When you contrast things, you look at how they differ.

Think about the types of local governments as you read this section. How are they alike? How are they different? Make notes in a diagram like this.

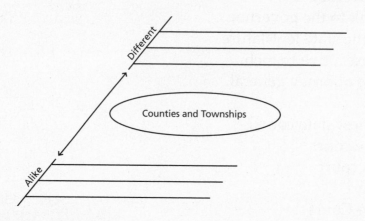

Vocabulary Strategy

Using Word Parts Prefixes, roots, and suffixes are all word parts. You can use what you know about word parts to understand the meaning of words.

Suffixes come after the root of a word. They often change the word's part of speech and meaning. The suffix *-ship* means "state, condition, or quality." It can also mean "something showing a state or quality." Think about the meaning of the words below. Each has the suffix *-ship*.

friend + ship = friendship   leader + ship = leadership
"the state of being friends"   "showing qualities of a leader"

Section 1 Summary

¹ States create local governments. They also give local governments their powers. Local governments include counties, cities, and towns. They use their powers to help meet the needs of communities.

⁵ Local government is the level of government that is closest to you. Teachers, police officers, and others work for local governments. Services such as road repair and water supply come from local governments.

Counties and Townships

Counties are the oldest type of local government.
¹⁰ English settlers divided colonies into counties. They did this to carry out laws in rural areas. Most counties today help state governments keep law and order. They collect taxes, too. Counties also may offer services, from libraries to health care.

¹⁵ Most counties are governed by a county **board**. County boards are also called commissions. Board members set up county programs and pass **ordinances**.

Counties are often broken into townships in the Middle Atlantic states and the Midwest. At first, town-
²⁰ ships were needed to help carry out certain jobs. They set up schools and repaired roads in rural areas far from county government. County and city governments have now taken over most of the jobs that townships used to do.

New England Towns

²⁵ The town was another type of rural government in New England. Town citizens were busy with local government. Voters met once a year at town meetings. They passed laws and set taxes. They also decided how money should be spent. Some small New England
³⁰ towns still have yearly town meetings. They are the closest thing we have to direct democracy.

Target Reading Skill

Compare and Contrast
Circle ways that counties and townships are alike.

Vocabulary Strategy

Using Word Parts Use what you know about the suffix -ship to explain the meaning of township.

_____

_____

_____

✓ Reading Check

Bracket the sentence that tells the difference between a county and a township.

✓ Reading Check

Circle the text that shows how town meetings are similar to direct democracy.

Key Terms

board (BORD) n. group of people who run an organization

ordinances (ORD nun siz) n. local laws

Compare and Contrast Write *A* next to sentences that tell how special districts and counties are alike. Write *D* next to sentences that tell how they differ.

✓ **Reading Check**

List two things a special district can do that an individual community cannot.

_____

_____

✓ **Reading Check**

Put a plus sign next to the sentence that tells a strength of the commission plan. Put a minus sign next to the sentence that tells a weakness of the plan.

At the yearly town meeting, the people elect a board. It has three to five members. It carries on town business during the year. Towns in New England have most of the duties that counties have in other regions.

Special Districts

A special district is another type of local government. It usually provides a single service. Special districts do things that are too much work or cost too much for one community to do. They can serve one community or cover parts or all of several communities. A school district is a special district. Most special districts are run by a board.

Cities

A city is a **municipality** where a lot of people live. Towns and villages are municipalities where fewer people live. Most municipalities today are cities.

The state sets the borders and powers of a municipality. Some communities write **charters**. Charters must be approved by the state. State laws set the plan of government in other communities.

The governments of most municipalities follow one of three plans. These are mayor-council, council-manager, or commission. The mayor in the mayor-council plan is the executive. The council is the legislative branch. It makes laws.

The council in the council-manager plan makes laws. It hires a city manager to handle city business.

The commissioners in the commission plan make ordinances together. Each also directs one of the city's departments. The commission plan does not have a single leader. This can cause problems. Most cities that have tried the commission plan do not use it any more.

Review Questions

1. How are New England towns run?

_____

2. What are the three types of city government?

_____

Key Terms

municipality (myoo ni suh PA luh tee) *n.* city government
charters (CHAR terz) *n.* plans of government

CHAPTER
12

Reading Preview

Section 2 Local Government Services and Revenue

Objectives

1. Examine how local governments provide education, health, and public safety services.
2. Discuss how local governments provide utilities.
3. Understand how local governments control land use.
4. Learn how local governments collect revenue to pay for services.

Target Reading Skill

Use Signal Words Signal words point out relationships among ideas or events. Words such as *like, similarly,* and *also* make a comparison. Words such as *unlike, in contrast to,* and *however* show a contrast.

Vocabulary Strategy

Using Word Parts Prefixes are word parts added before the root of a word. They have their own meanings. They change a word's meaning. Look at the prefixes *inter-* and *intra-*, for example.

Prefix	inter-	intra-
Meaning	between, among	within
Example	interstate	intrastate
Use	The interstate highway connects cities across the nation.	The intrastate road system joins cities and towns within the state.

Use what you know about these prefixes to figure out the meaning of words as you read.

Target Reading Skill

Use Signal Words Circle the signal word under the heading *Education, Health, and Public Safety* that shows contrast.

✓ Reading Check

Circle the text that describes the role local government plays in community health.

1 Local governments help us in many ways. They provide **utilities**. They build parks, schools, and roads. They plan for town growth.

Education, Health, and Public Safety

Local governments offer many services. These include 5 education, health and welfare services, and public safety.

Local governments spend the most money on education. Counties, cities, and school districts provide public education. State governments pay about one third or more of school costs. The federal government 10 helps to pay for buildings and special programs. Local and state governments often disagree about money for state education, however.

Local governments look after public health and welfare. Local officials make sure health laws are obeyed. 15 They inspect restaurants, hotels, and water. They make sure state and federal pollution laws are obeyed. Local officials carry out public assistance, or welfare, programs. These programs help the needy. Federal, state, and local governments often share the cost of these 20 programs.

Local governments take care of public safety. Police and firefighters help keep us safe. The police and fire departments teach people how to stop crime and fires. Local governments also hire people to make sure safety 25 rules, called codes, are followed.

Utilities

Local government services also include utilities. These are water, gas, electricity, sewage treatment, and garbage pick-up. Local governments often own and run water and sewage treatment plants. Towns often 30 arrange for private companies to help, too. These companies may supply gas and electricity and pick up garbage. Utilities are best provided at the local level. That way they can better fit local needs.

Key Term

utilities (yoo TI luh teez) *n.* services people need, such as water, gas, and electricity

Land Use

Local governments use **zoning** to plan and control
35 growth. Zoning keeps homes and businesses separate.

People who plan communities ask questions about
land use. How will use of the land affect people? Are
there enough low-cost apartments and houses? Will a
new factory control pollution?

40 The planning process has many steps. A local government chooses a planning commission. The commission presents a proposal to the city council or county
board. This group makes the final decision.

Revenue: Paying for Services

Taxes are one way to raise money. About 25 percent of
45 local government funds come from **property tax**. Some
communities bring in money with a local sales tax. Some
city governments tax people who work there. The idea is
to collect money from people who use city services.

Communities also get money from bridge tolls and
50 parking meters. Utilities owned by the government, such
as electric companies, also bring in money. Local governments also can borrow money. <u>Intergovernmental
revenue</u> is another source of money. A community may
get a **grant**. Grants help provide services of national or
55 state importance at the local level.

Most communities face problems in paying for services. The demand for services is often greater than the
money available.

Review Questions

1. Who pays for public education?

_____

2. Why do local governments use zoning?

_____

Key Terms

zoning (ZŌ ning) *n.* local rules that divide a community into areas
and tell how the land in each area can be used

property tax (PROP er tee TAKS) *n.* a tax on land and buildings

intergovernmental revenue (in ter guh ver MEN tul REV uh noo) *n.*
money given by one level of government to another

grant (GRANT) *n.* money given by federal and state governments
to local communities

✓ Reading Check

Number important ques-
tions people might ask
when deciding on
land use.

↻ Target Reading Skill

Use Signal Words Circle
the word under
*Revenue: Paying for
Services* that shows
comparison.

Vocabulary Strategy

Using Word Parts Circle
the prefix in the under-
lined word. Use the
prefix to explain the
word's meaning.

_____

_____

_____

✓ Reading Check

Bracket the sentence that
explains why cities tax
people who work
there.

Reading Preview

Section 3 Conflict and Cooperation Between Governments

Objectives

1. Describe relations between local governments and between local and state governments.
2. Examine relations among local, state, and federal governments.

Target Reading Skill

Make Comparisons Comparing two or more things helps you remember how they relate to one another. As you read, compare the responsibilities of local, state, and federal government.

Vocabulary Strategy

Using Word Parts The prefixes *co-, col-, com-, con-,* and *cor-* all have the same meaning. They mean "with or together." These prefixes are added to various roots. Look at the chart to see some examples. Note that the words bring together the meaning of the prefix and the meaning of the root.

Prefix	Root and Its Meaning	Meaning of Word
co-	-operate "work"	cooperate: "work together"
col-	-lect "choose, gather"	collect: "gather together"
com-	-pare "bring forth"	compare: "bring together"
con-	-nect "bind, tie"	connect: "bind together"
cor-	-respond "respond, agree"	correspond: "agree with"

Section 3 Summary

¹ Local governments work together to serve citizens. They also work with state and federal governments. Governments cooperate and come into <u>conflict</u> as they work to get things done.

Relations Between Local Governments

⁵ Local governments connect with each other in various ways to meet citizens' needs. They form **councils of governments**. They meet in other kinds of groups, such as the Conference of Mayors. They talk about matters that affect them all. They work together to find
¹⁰ answers to problems.

Conflicts can occur between local governments. Money matters can cause conflicts. Towns often compete with each other for new businesses. They also compete for federal money. Another cause of conflict is how one
¹⁵ community's policies affect nearby communities.

Problems also lead to cooperation between local governments. Communities may work together to provide services that cost too much for one community. Townships team up to answer emergency calls, for
²⁰ example. Small communities sometimes turn to counties for help. A county can build a jail or hospital to serve several small towns.

Local and State Governments

Many states play a large part in deciding how local governments are set up. Other states have given cities
²⁵ and some counties **home rule**.

Conflict can develop between local and state governments. They may not agree about what is a local matter and what is a state matter. Local and state laws sometimes come into conflict. State law is usually car-
³⁰ ried out when that happens.

Key Terms
councils of governments (KOUN sulz UV GUV ern muntz) *n.* local groups that join forces to help meet people's needs

home rule (HŌM ROOL) *n.* when cities and counties run their own affairs

---

Vocabulary Strategy

Using Word Parts The root -*flict* means "strike." Underline the prefix and circle the root in *conflict* in the text. Then use what you know about its prefix and root to explain its meaning.

_____

_____

_____

Target Reading Skill

Make Comparisons Read the first paragraph under *Local and State Governments*. Compare how states decide how local governments are set up.

_____

_____

_____

✓ Reading Check

In the text, number four ways that citizens benefit when local governments work together.

Read and think about the underlined text. Then answer this question. Why do you think a state government usually wins any conflict with a local government?

_____

_____

_____

_____

 **Target Reading Skill**

Make Comparisons Underline the sentence under *Local, State, and Federal Governments* that shows what all levels of government have in common.

✓ **Reading Check**

How might people in one community benefit from a faraway community's relationship with the federal government?

_____

_____

_____

Many state governments work with local governments. They do this to help solve local problems. They do this to carry out state programs, too. They also help local programs run well. State officials help local offi-
35 cials in finance, health, and education. States also give licenses to town and city workers.

Local, State, and Federal Governments

The federal government gives money to local governments for many uses. It might pay for job-training programs. States decide how to share the money among
40 local governments. Towns and cities then run the programs. The federal government also gives aid directly to local governments.

Local officials may not agree with federal and state officials about how to spend money. States often have
45 the power to decide who gets federal money. Most federal money for local governments can be used only in certain ways. Towns and cities may have to do without federal money if they want to set their own policies. But most of them cannot pay for big projects without
50 some federal help.

Many problems affect all levels of government. Cooperation is the best way to solve them. All levels of government work together to stop pollution, for example. They work together to solve crimes like bank rob-
55 bery and kidnapping. Cooperation is a good way to deal with national issues.

Review Questions

1. What do local governments do when they meet in groups such as councils of governments?

_____

_____

2. In what ways do state governments work with local governments?

_____

_____

1. Special districts can
   A. provide subways and parks.
   B. serve one or more communities.
   C. take care of county business.
   D. set boundaries and powers of cities.

2. Who oversees the executive branch in the council-manager plan of city government?
   A. council
   B. mayor
   C. commissioners
   D. manager

3. Local governments get revenue from
   A. grants.
   B. parking meters.
   C. property tax.
   D. all of the above

4. Local governments come into conflict when they compete for
   A. new businesses.
   B. neighboring communities.
   C. bridge tolls.
   D. all of the above

5. Most communities cannot pay for big projects without
   A. federal help.
   B. state lotteries.
   C. national goals.
   D. job training.

Short Answer Question

What level of government has the biggest effect on your daily life? Give examples of how it affects you.

_____

_____

_____

_____

Reading Preview

Section 1
Why Societies Have Economies

Objectives

1. Describe the characteristics of people's many wants and how resources satisfy wants.
2. Explain the steps of production to consumption.
3. Determine how choices are made to satisfy wants.
4. Discuss how scarcity affects economic choices.

Target Reading Skill

Recognize Words That Signal Sequence Certain words signal sequence. Sequence is the order of ideas or events. Ideas may appear in order of importance. Events are often presented in time order. Read this paragraph about the production process for pasta.

First, farmers use soil, water, seeds, farm machinery, and labor to produce wheat. Next, they sell the wheat to a grain-milling company. The company combines labor and machinery to turn the wheat into flour. Then it sells the flour to a pasta maker. After buying the flour, the pasta maker adds other ingredients to it. The pasta maker then uses labor and machines to mix, roll, and cut the dough. Finally, the pasta is ready to be packaged and distributed.

The underlined words signal sequence. As you read, look for these and other words that signal the order of ideas or events.

Vocabulary Strategy

Using Context Clues One way to figure out the meaning of a word you do not recognize is to use context clues. Context is the surrounding words and sentences. These words and sentences may contain clues to the meaning of the word. Read the sentence below:

The truck that delivers food to the supermarket is part of the distribution process.

The sentence includes a context clue to the meaning of *distribution*. The clue is the word *delivers*. Distribution is making goods and services available to people.

Section 1 Summary

¹ In every society, people choose how to use resources to produce goods and services. Goods and services meet people's wants.

People's Many Wants

Everyone has wants. Food, clothing, and <u>shelter</u> are
⁵ basic wants. But people want more than just basics. They want to be entertained, for example. They want to be educated. And they want health care.

Various factors affect people's wants. One is environment. If you live in Alaska, you want warm clothes.
¹⁰ Societies or cultures also affect wants. Most Americans want to live in a house or apartment. But tents best fit life for some people in Mongolia. People's wants also change. Some wants can be met only for a short time. For example, clothes from last year may not fit
¹⁵ you now.

Using Resources

The resources people use to produce goods and services are called **factors of production**. Economists—people who study economies—identify three basic factors of production. These are labor, land, and capital.
²⁰ • Labor includes time and energy. It also includes the knowledge and skills people use in their jobs.

• Land includes the many natural resources used to produce goods. Soil, water, wildlife, and timber are some examples.

²⁵ • **Capital** includes tools, machines, or buildings used to produce goods. Tools and factories are called capital goods when they are used as capital. Money is not a factor of production. But money that is available for investing or spending is sometimes called
³⁰ financial capital.

Key Terms

factors of production (FAK terz UV pruh DUK shun) *n.* the labor, land, and capital people use to make goods and provide services

capital (KAP ih tul) *n.* anything used to produce goods and services, such as tools and machines

---

© Pearson Education, Inc., Publishing as Pearson Prentice Hall. All rights reserved.

Vocabulary Strategy

Using Context Clues What does the underlined word mean? Explain what context clues you used to figure out its meaning.

_____

_____

_____

✓ Reading Check

In the text, number the factors that affect people's wants.

✓ Reading Check

Bracket the sentence that tells how land affects a society's economy.

Vocabulary Strategy

Using Context Clues
Bracket context clues to the meaning of the underlined word.

✓ Reading Check

How are production, distribution, and consumption of goods and services related?

_____

_____

Target Reading Skill

Recognize Words That Signal Sequence In the second paragraph, underline words that signal sequence.

✓ Reading Check

Circle the factors that people must balance when they want two things that are in conflict.

✓ Reading Check

Underline the text that explains why both rich and poor nations face the problem of scarcity.

Production to Consumption

Labor, land, and capital are <u>combined</u> in a process called production. Farmers make food by bringing together soil, water, and sunlight (land) with seeds and machinery (capital). They use their ideas, skills, time, 35 and energy (labor).

Production is followed by **distribution**. Trucks that deliver food help distribution. After distribution, goods and services are ready for **consumption**.

Making Choices

There are never enough resources to produce all the 40 goods people want. So people must choose which wants will be met and which will not. These choices are economic choices. One part of choosing is looking at the benefits you will receive from each choice. A second part involves the cost of each choice. The major 45 cost of any choice is giving up the benefits you would have received from a different choice. Every economic decision has an **opportunity cost**.

Scarcity

Scarcity is a problem in rich and poor nations. Scarcity is not based on the resources a nation has. It is based 50 on the relationship between wants and the resources available to meet them. Individuals, businesses, and governments must make choices about resources. These choices involve deciding how to use limited resources to produce goods and services to meet peo- 55 ple's unlimited wants.

Review Questions

1. Why must people choose which wants will be met and which will not?
2. How does scarcity affect economic choices?

Key Terms

distribution (dis truh BYOO shun) *n.* how goods and services are brought to people
consumption (kun SUMP shun) *n.* buying or using goods and services
opportunity cost (op er TOO nih tee KOST) *n.* what you give up when you use resources for one thing instead of another
scarcity (SKAYR suh tee) *n.* when resources are limited compared with how much people want

---

Reading Preview

Section 2
Basic Economic Decisions

Objectives

1. Understand that determining what and how much to produce is a basic economic choice.
2. Explain why deciding how to produce goods and services is a second basic economic question.
3. Understand that deciding who will get goods and services is a third basic economic decision.

Target Reading Skill

Understand Sequence Noting the sequence of events can help you understand and remember them. Sequence is the order in which events happen. Events often follow each other in a cause-and-effect relationship.

   You can use a numbered list like the one below to track the order of events.

   1. Researchers develop robots.
   2. The robots are used for factory work.
   3. Some people lose their jobs to the robots.

Vocabulary Strategy

Using Context Clues Context can clarify the meaning of words you do not recognize. Context is the surrounding words, phrases, and sentences. Sometimes the context will restate the word:

   Economists—*people who study how economies work*—have identified three basic factors of production.

As you read, look at context to see if a word is restated.

Section 2 Summary

Vocabulary Strategy

Using Context Clues
Underline the context clue that restates the meaning of *quantity*.

✓ Reading Check

Circle the text that describes who decides what to produce.

↻ Target Reading Skill

Understand Sequence Complete this numbered list with the sequence of events related to new technology in the clothmaking industry.

1. _____

2. _____

3. _____

✓ Reading Check

Bracket the sentence that explains the relationship between production and technology.

¹ Basic economic decisions are made every day. The three most basic decisions are

- What goods and services should be produced? How much of them should be produced?
- ⁵ How should these goods and services be produced?
- Who will get the goods and services?

What and How Much?

People in every economy must decide what to produce. They base their decisions on their resources. A farmer who owns land and machinery may decide to ¹⁰ grow wheat. You might decide to mow lawns. Owners of resources decide what to produce based on a prediction of what people will want.

The owner of the resources also decides the **quantity**, or amount, to produce. The amount produced ¹⁵ depends on the land, labor, and capital available. It is also based on the amount that the owner thinks he or she can sell.

How to Produce Goods and Services

The second major economic decision is how to combine land, labor, and capital to produce goods and ²⁰ services. People usually choose the combination of resources that will cost the least.

The desire for less costly ways to make goods led to new **technology**. Technology had its beginnings in the early 1800s. At the time, cloth makers began using ²⁵ power looms. These new looms cost a lot. But they made cloth much faster than old handlooms. The cost of making cloth soon dropped.

Key Terms

quantity (KWAN tuh tee) *n.* how much of something

technology (tek NOL uh gee) *n.* the use of science to help commerce or industry

Technology is still important in deciding how to produce goods. For example, researchers have developed seeds that grow larger crops. <u>Advances</u>, or improvements, in electronics have given us robots to use in factories. Computers speed up many jobs. The Internet allows businesses to sell to many people.

Who Gets What?

Who gets the goods that are produced is the third basic economic decision. People must decide how goods and services will be divided. Wants are always greater than resources. That makes this decision important and sometimes difficult.

Various questions are part of this decision. Should goods be shared equally among everyone? Should people receive goods based on what they say they want? Should a small group decide who gets what? Or should people who own more resources and make more products get more?

Societies have solved this problem in different ways. They have based decisions on their goals and values. A society that wants equality might have a system for sharing products equally. A society that values freedom might let citizens compete freely for goods. Goals and values affect how a society makes all three basic economic decisions.

Review Questions

1. How does an owner of resources decide how much of a good or service to produce?

_____

_____

2. How do people usually choose how to produce goods?

_____

_____

Vocabulary Strategy

Using Context Clues
Circle a context clue that restates the underlined word.

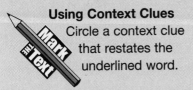

✓ **Reading Check**

Underline the sentence that explains what a society's values have to do with its economy.

Reading Preview

Section 3
Three Types of Economies

Objectives

1. Identify and discuss traditional economies.
2. Identify and discuss command economies.
3. Identify and discuss market economies.
4. Discuss modern-day economies in China and the United States.

Target Reading Skill

Recognize Words That Signal Sequence Signal words point out relationships between ideas or events. Some signal sequence, or the order of events. The chart below shows some words that signal sequence.

Words That Signal Sequence			
first	next	last	then
before	during	after	finally
second	third	later	now
when	since	as a result	because

Look for these words as you read. They will help you understand the relationships between ideas and events.

Vocabulary Strategy

Using Context Clues Synonyms and antonyms in context can help you figure out the meaning of words you do not recognize. A synonym is a word with the same meaning as another word. An antonym is a word with the opposite meaning. *Products* is a synonym of *goods,* for example. *High* is an antonym of *low.*

When you find a word you do not know, look at other words in context. You may find a synonym or antonym for the word. The synonym or antonym will help you figure out the word's meaning.

Section 3 Summary

¹ Resources are always limited when compared to people's wants. To solve this, societies have to organize production, distribution, and consumption. They use different economic systems to do this. The three basic
⁵ types are traditional, command, and market economies.

A Traditional Economy

Customs are a major part of a **traditional economy**. Customs are ways that people have acted for a long time. They are passed from <u>elders</u> to youth. Customs help decide what, how much, and how to produce.
¹⁰ They also decide who gets what is made.

People in a traditional economy often own their own resources. They have some freedom to decide when and how to use the resources. But many decisions are made by customs. That means the economy
¹⁵ changes little over time.

There are few traditional economies today. Some societies in Central and South America, Africa, and Asia still have mostly traditional economies.

A Command Economy

The government makes the basic economic choices in a
²⁰ **command economy**. It owns the factors of production. Or, it controls them. A central planning group decides how, what, and how much to make. As a result, only products that the government chooses are available to people. A government's goals and values affect choices
²⁵ about who gets what.

There have been command economies for centuries. Egyptian pharaohs and medieval lords ran the economies of their societies. Communist nations such as the Soviet Union also have had command
³⁰ economies in modern times.

Vocabulary Strategy

Using Context Clues
Underline the word or words that tell you that *elders* means "older people."

✓ Reading Check

Circle the sentences that explain the role that custom plays in a traditional economy.

↻ Target Reading Skill

Recognize Words That Signal Sequence Bracket words that point to the order of certain events in a command economy.

✓ Reading Check

How much individual freedom exists in a command economy?

_____

_____

_____

Key Terms

traditional economy (truh DISH uh nul ih KON uh mee) *n.* a system in which decisions are based on old ways of doing things

command economy (kuh MAND ih KON uh mee) *n.* a system in which the government runs the economy

Market Economies

Private citizens make decisions in a **market economy**. They decide what and how much to make. And they decide how to make it. Two other names for a market economy are **free enterprise** and **capitalism**.

35 Competition is important in a market economy. Producers compete to meet the wants of consumers. Workers compete for jobs.

No one citizen or group runs a market economy. Everyone takes part in running it by freely making 40 decisions. The possibility of making a **profit** <u>motivates</u> people to make certain decisions in a market economy. Wanting to make a profit also leads people to **invest** in a business.

Modern-Day Economies

Most nations today have a **mixed economy**. China had a 45 command economy before the late 1980s. Then the government took steps to create a more mixed economy. Now, for example, privately owned shops sell consumer goods. Our economy is a market—or free enterprise—system. It has some elements of a command economy, 50 too. Our government provides certain services. These include education, mail services, and an army.

Review Questions

1. Who owns resources in a traditional economy?

_____

2. Who takes part in running a market economy?

_____

Key Terms

market economy (MAR kit ih KON uh mee) *n.* a system in which people decide what and how much to make and who gets what
free enterprise (FREE en ter PRĪZ) *n.* a system in which there is little or no control by the government
capitalism (KAP ih tuh liz um) *n.* a system in which people decide how to use capital to make goods and provide services
profit (PROF it) *n.* how much more a buyer pays for something than the cost to make it
invest (in VEST) *v.* to use your money to help start or grow a business, with the hope of making a profit
mixed economy (MIKST ih KON uh mee) *n.* a system that mixes the three basic economic systems

1. Which of the following is *not* one of people's basic wants?
   A. education
   B. food
   C. shelter
   D. clothing

2. Money available for investing or spending is sometimes called
   A. opportunity cost.
   B. capital goods.
   C. financial capital.
   D. unlimited resources.

3. The quantity of a good or service that is produced depends on the available
   A. land.
   B. labor.
   C. capital.
   D. all of the above

4. The desire to find the least costly way to produce goods and services led to the growth of
   A. resources.
   B. technology.
   C. capital.
   D. all of the above

5. Capitalism and free enterprise are other names for a
   A. market economy.
   B. command economy.
   C. mixed economy.
   D. traditional economy.

Short Answer Question

Compare and contrast the three basic economic systems.

_____

_____

_____

_____

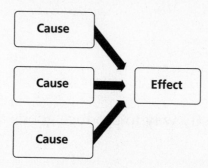

CHAPTER 14

Reading Preview

Section 1 The Principles of Our Market Economy

1. Understand the circular flow of economic activity.
2. Learn about supply and demand.

Target Reading Skill

Recognizing Multiple Causes A cause makes something happen. An effect is what happens. Sometimes an effect has more than one cause. This diagram shows more than one cause for just one effect.

As you read, notice where many causes, or factors, come together to produce one effect.

Vocabulary Strategy

Recognizing Signal Words Certain words show how ideas or events are connected. The words below signal causes and effects.

Look at how cause-and-effect signal words are used in these sentences.

> Few people wanted to buy the new product, because its price was high. As a result, the producer lowered the price.

Because signals a cause or reason why people were not buying the product. *As a result* points to an effect or what happened when people would not buy the product.

Words Signaling Causes		Words Signaling Effects	
because	since	as a result	for this reason

Section 1 Summary

¹ Our economy is based on a free enterprise, or market, system. But it mixes features of all three basic economic systems: traditional, command, and market.

The Circular Flow of Economic Activity

The diagram shows how goods, services, labor, and ⁵ money flow through the United States economy.

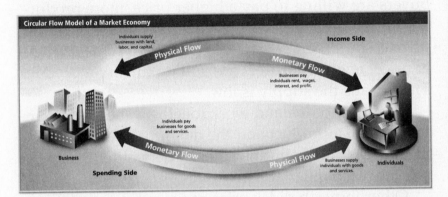

Businesses that create goods or services are called producers. Labor is just one resource that producers need to create goods. Producers need land and the raw materials found on the land. Producers also need capital.
¹⁰ Capital includes tools and machines used in production.

Producers exchange a kind of payment for the use of land and capital. They pay rent for the use of land. They pay **interest** for the use of capital. And they pay wages for the use of people's labor.

Supply and Demand

¹⁵ Buyers and sellers exchange goods and services through a market. Producers and individuals act as buyers. They also act as sellers. Markets decide how much will be made in a free enterprise economy. Markets also determine prices. Individuals in our free ²⁰ enterprise system are free to make choices in a market. <u>For this reason</u>, producers compete to sell goods and services to them.

Key Term

interest (IN trist) *n.* an amount of money charged for borrowing money

Vocabulary Strategy

Recognizing Signal Words
Do the underlined words signal a cause or an effect?

_____

✓ Reading Check

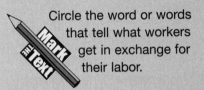

Circle the word or words that tell what workers get in exchange for their labor.

Laws of supply and demand describe what happens when people make choices in a market. **Demand** is the amount of a product buyers are willing and able to buy at different prices. More people will buy an item at a low price. That means that the quantity, or amount, demanded by buyers will be high. Fewer people will buy an item at a high price. That means that the demand will be low.

Supply is the amount of a product that producers are willing and able to offer at different prices. When buyers are willing to pay a higher price, more producers are willing to offer a product. As a result, the supply is high. When buyers are not willing to pay a higher price, fewer producers are willing to offer a product. That means the supply is low.

Supply and demand work together. They determine the price of a product and the quantity offered. The amount supplied and the amount demanded will tend to equal each other at the **market price**.

Other things besides price can affect demand. For example, the demand for basics, such as milk, does not change much when the price changes. That is because people believe they need milk at almost any price. Advertising and fashion can also affect demand. For example, you might decide to buy higher-priced jeans <u>because</u> the brand is more popular.

Review Questions

1. What determines the price of a product and the quantity offered?

_____

_____

2. What three resources do producers need to create goods?

_____

_____

Key Terms

demand (dih MAND) *n.* the amount of a product or service buyers are willing and able to buy at different prices

market price (MAR kit PRĪS) *n.* the price at which buyers and sellers agree to trade

Reading Preview

Section 2 The Role of Business in the American Economy

Objectives

1. Learn about the role of the entrepreneur.
2. Discuss how factors of production are used.
3. Identify three models for owning a business.
4. Learn about the rise of big business.

Target Reading Skill

Understanding Effects An effect is what happens as the result of a cause or factor. Sometimes a cause can produce several effects. The diagram below shows this.

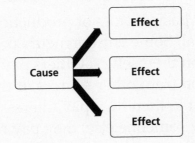

As you read, look for effects.

Vocabulary Strategy

Recognizing Signal Words *As a result* and *for this reason* are two ways to signal an effect. Various other words also point to effects. Some of these are shown in the chart.

Effect Signal Words		
therefore He worked a full day. Therefore, they paid him for eight hours of work.	so She ran her own business, so she was very busy.	if . . . then If he needs money for his new business, <u>then</u> he may have to borrow it.

Look for these signal words as you read. Use them to identify effects in the text.

Vocabulary Strategy

Recognizing Signal Words Put a checkmark next to a word that signals an effect in the first paragraph under *The Role of the Entrepreneur*.

Target Reading Skill

Understanding Effects Underline what happens to an entrepreneur if his or her business fails.

✓ Reading Check

Bracket the text that explains what motivates people in a capitalist economy to start a business.

Vocabulary Strategy

Recognizing Signal Words What effects does *if . . . then* signal in the first paragraph under *Using the Factors of Production*?

_____

_____

¹ In a market economy, privately owned businesses carry out production. A business is any organization that uses labor, land, and capital to produce goods or services.

The Role of the Entrepreneur

Businesses are important to our economy. Therefore, ⁵ people who start businesses play a major role. An **entrepreneur** begins with an idea. The idea may be a new product. Or it may be a new way of making something. The entrepreneur then raises money to begin.

Starting a business involves risk. If the business ¹⁰ fails, the entrepreneur could lose the money put into it. If the business does well, he or she will make a **profit**. The hope of earning a profit leads people to start and run businesses. This is called the profit motive.

Using the Factors of Production

The three basic factors of production are labor, land, ¹⁵ and capital. Some entrepreneurs provide the factors of production themselves. Others pay to get the factors of production from other sources. If they borrow money from a bank, then they pay interest. If they use land owned by someone else, they pay rent. If they hire ²⁰ workers, they pay them, too.

Some people who study economics believe that an entrepreneur is the fourth factor of production. They say that entrepreneurs provide ideas. Entrepreneurs also take risks in exchange for profit.

How Businesses Are Owned

²⁵ In the United States, there are three basic types of business ownership. A **sole proprietorship** is the most common. Most are small. They include restaurants and repair shops. The owner decides how to run the busi-

Key Terms

entrepreneur (ahn truh preh NOOR) *n.* a person who starts a business

profit (PROF it) *n.* the money made by a business, minus its costs

sole proprietorship (SŌL pruh PRĪ uh ter ship) *n.* a business owned by one person

ness. The profits belong to the owner alone. But the
30 owner is also responsible for paying off all debts. As a
business grows, it becomes more difficult to run it. It
also can be hard to borrow money to grow the business.

A **partnership** is another type. Many law firms and
medical groups are partnerships. The advantages and
35 disadvantages are like those of a sole proprietorship.
The main difference is that more than one person
shares risks and benefits.

A **corporation** differs from the other two in an
important way. The owners are not personally respon-
40 sible for the business. Many corporations sell stock to
the public. Stock is a share of the ownership. It raises
the money needed to start, run, and expand the business. People who buy stock are called stockholders
They make money from stock by sharing the profits.

45 A corporation costs more to start than other businesses. And it is more limited by government rules.
Still, corporations create most of the products, profits,
and jobs in our economy.

The Rise of Big Business

In our country's early years, most businesses were sole
50 proprietorships. Then, in the 1800s, new inventions
and ways of manufacturing helped industry grow.
Successful sole proprietors turned their businesses
into corporations in order to grow.

In the past 100 years, large corporations have
55 become a major force. Today, they play a major part in
our economy. They can make goods and provide services better than smaller businesses. For this reason,
they will probably still grow in importance.

Review Questions

1. What are the three basic forms of business ownership in the United States?

_____

2. What helped industry to grow in the 1800s?

_____

Key Terms

partnership (PART ner ship) _n._ a business owned by two or more
corporation (kor puh RAY shun) _n._ a business that is separate
from the people who own it

Understanding Effects
Underline the text that describes what happens when a sole proprietorship grows.

✓ **Reading Check**
Underline the most common form of business ownership in the United States.

Vocabulary Strategy

Recognizing Signal Words Put a checkmark next to the word that signals the effect of large corporations working more efficiently than smaller corporations.

✓ **Reading Check**
Circle the text that tells why large corporations have grown in importance.

Section 3
Labor in the American Economy

Objectives

1. Describe the growth of wage labor.
2. Discuss the rise of labor unions and learn about their history.
3. Discuss today's labor force.

Target Reading Skill

Identify Causes and Effects Identifying causes and effects helps you understand the relationship between events. Read this paragraph.

It is easy to understand why conflict develops between workers and business owners. Business owners want to keep costs low and profits high. They often do this by keeping wages low. Workers want to earn the highest possible wages.

Conflict between workers and business owners is an effect. When you ask why conflict develops, you are asking about its causes. The causes of conflict are the following:

1. Business owners want to keep costs low and profits high. They often do this by keeping wages low.
2. Workers want to earn the highest possible wages.

As you read this section, ask: Is this situation an effect? Does this event cause another event?

Vocabulary Strategy

Recognizing Signal Words Some words connect causes and effects. Look at these cause-and-effect signal words in the sentences below.

Cause	Signal Words	Effect
The new machines	caused	many accidents.
The factory closing	resulted in	the loss of many jobs.

Look for words that connect causes and effects as you read this section.

Section 3 Summary

1 Labor is different from the other factors of production. People provide it. They care about working conditions and wages. Owners want to keep costs low and profits high. One way to do this is to keep wages low.
5 Workers want to earn the highest possible wages. This creates a conflict between workers and owners.

The Growth of Wage Labor

Most Americans had control over their working conditions when our country was young. Many were farmers. They produced most of what they needed. They
10 could do this because they owned land. Other Americans were craftspeople. They worked for themselves or someone they knew.

Great changes came in the 1800s. Better farm machines meant that farms needed fewer workers.
15 Machines produced more goods more cheaply than people could by hand. These changes led craftspeople, farm workers, and others to wage labor. They worked in mines, factories, and workshops. Business owners paid low wages. Wage laborers worked long hours.
20 And most of the jobs were boring and dangerous.

The Rise of Labor Unions

<u>Workers had little power over wages and working conditions on their own.</u> So the workers formed **labor unions.** By the 1880s, there were many small unions. One goal of unions was to force business owners to
25 take part in **collective bargaining.**

Unions used various methods to get their demands met. They would stay on the job but work very slowly. They got people to **boycott** products. But their main weapon was the **strike.**

Vocabulary Strategy

Recognizing Signal Words Write *C* next to the cause and *E* next to the effect connected by the word *because* in the first paragraph under *The Growth of Wage Labor.*

✓ Reading Check

Circle the sentences that tell what changes came in the 1800s.

◎ Target Reading Skill

Identify Causes and Effects Bracket the effect of the underlined cause and circle the signal word.

Key Terms

labor unions (LAY ber YOON yunz) *n.* groups of workers that try to improve pay and protect members' rights
collective bargaining (kuh LEK tiv BAR gih ning) *n.* when union members and owners try to agree about wages and conditions
boycott (BOY kot) *v.* refuse to buy
strike (STRĪK) *n.* when workers refuse to work

30   Owners did different things when workers went on strike. They hired "scabs," or strikebreakers. These non-union workers replaced striking workers. Owners used lockouts to keep union members from going into a factory. Some forced workers to sign "yellow-dog
35 contracts." These contracts said the worker would never join a union. Owners also made "blacklists." As a result, employers would not hire people whose names were on this list.

Labor Unions Since 1930

By the 1930s, the government began to accept the right
40 of unions to exist and to strike. Congress passed the Wagner Act in 1935. It said employers had to bargain with unions. It also made illegal some of the things that owners did to stop unions.

   In the 1930s, industrial unions began. They were a
45 new kind of union. They included skilled and unskilled workers in one industry, such as steel. In 1935, some industrial unions formed the Committee of Industrial Organizations (CIO). They became independent in 1938. In 1955, the CIO and the AFL joined
50 forces. They formed the AFL-CIO.

Today's Labor Force

The labor force is the number of people working at each type of job. It has changed a lot. More women are part of the labor force now. Farmers are a smaller part of it. Fewer workers have manufacturing jobs.
55 Businesses that offer services have grown. These include banks and restaurants.

   The change from an industrial economy to a service economy has caused problems. Workers lose their jobs when factories close. They do not always have the
60 training to find new jobs. This has caused many people to face major changes in their lives.

Review Questions

1. What is wage labor?

_____

_____

2. Conflict between which two groups has had an important effect on our economic system?

_____

_____

1. A market economy needs a flow of
   A. goods.
   B. services.
   C. resources.
   D. all of the above

2. The amount supplied and the amount demanded tend to equal each other at the
   A. higher price.
   B. market price.
   C. lower price.
   D. all of the above

3. Which of the following is not a factor of production?
   A. land
   B. labor
   C. profit
   D. capital

4. Which was a goal of the American Federation of Labor (AFL)?
   A. collective bargaining
   B. higher profits
   C. sit-down strikes
   D. industrial unions

5. Which of these groups is a larger part of the labor force today than in the past?
   A. farmers
   B. women
   C. factory workers
   D. none of the above

Short Answer Question

List the advantages and disadvantages of a sole proprietorship.

_____

_____

_____

_____

Reading Preview

Section 1 Managing Your Money

Objectives

1. Learn to understand your income by knowing what you have.
2. Discuss how to make financial choices.

Target Reading Skill

Read Ahead Try reading ahead when you come across passages you do not understand. You may be able to gather more information as you read ahead. You may also find charts or other images that help explain the text.

Read the first paragraph of the section summary, for instance. You may not fully understand what income and expenses are when you first see them mentioned. If you read ahead, however, you find examples and explanations of both. You can find more information about income in the text. You can find more information about expenses in both the text and the illustration.

Vocabulary Strategy

Using Context Clues Context can give clues to the meaning of a word you do not know. Context is the words, phrases, and sentences surrounding a word. Context clues take many forms. Sometimes they are examples that help explain a word's meaning. Read this paragraph.

> You can earn income directly by working. Earned income comes in several forms. These are salary, wage, commission, and bonus.

You may never have seen the underlined term before. The first sentence gives the clue that it can be money made by working. The third sentence also gives clues to the meaning of *earned income*. It gives four examples of this type of income.

Section 1 Summary

¹ It is important to learn how to manage money. First, you need to know your expenses. You need to know your goals and values. Finally, you need to make a budget. A budget is a plan for spending and saving. It ⁵ can help you set goals and reach them.

Income: Knowing What You Have

There are many forms of income. The pay that people receive for work is called *earned income*. It comes in several forms. These are salary, wage, commission, and bonus. A salary is a fixed amount that someone receives ¹⁰ for work. It is paid at regular times, such as every week. A wage is an amount paid per hour of work. A commission is a percentage of money based on sales. A bonus is extra income given as a reward. People also often receive **fringe benefits**. Fringe benefits include ¹⁵ medical care, sick leave, and paid vacation days.

People receive income from other sources, too. People earn interest on a bank account. People who own stock receive **dividends**. People can also receive income from selling or renting property. They can receive it as ²⁰ gifts. They can also inherit it when someone dies.

You can follow these steps to understand income. Add all sources of income. Then subtract what is paid in taxes. The result is called **disposable income**.

Making Financial Choices

People choose how to use money based on their goals ²⁵ and values. Some carefully plan to stay out of debt. Some save for a goal. The goal might be buying a house or going to college. Many people give money to people in need.

Key Terms

fringe benefits (FRINJ BEN uh fitz) *n.* payments other than money that you receive for work

dividends (DIV ih denz) *n.* money from the profits of companies paid to people who own stock

disposable income (dih SPŌ zuh bul IN kum) *n.* the amount of money left after taxes are paid

---

Target Reading Skill

Read Ahead Look ahead to find where you can learn about making a budget. Circle text and illustrations you find.

Vocabulary Strategy

Using Context Clues Number examples that help you understand the meaning of *fringe benefits*.

✓ Reading Check

Underline the sentence that explains why it is important to budget your money.

Target Reading Skill

Read Ahead The word *include* suggests that rent and car payments are not Kathy's only fixed expenses. Look ahead at the text and illustration to find another. Write *FE* next to any you find.

Vocabulary Strategy

Using Context Clues Circle examples that help you understand what variable expenses are.

✓ Reading Check

Circle Kathy's most important monthly expenses. Circle her least important expenses.

Kathy spent her money on consumer goods. She
30 bought clothes, a TV, and luggage. Kathy's spending led to credit card troubles. These problems made her think about her values and goals. She learned that good spending and saving habits are important.

Kathy decided to make a budget. Making a budget
35 is a way to decide what to spend and save. It helps you set aside enough money for the things you need. It also helps you not buy what you cannot afford.

Kathy decides that her first budget will cover one month. Her disposable income is $1,800 a month. She
40 looks at her expenses. Some are **fixed expenses.** These include rent and car payments. Kathy also has **variable expenses.** These include food, clothes, and telephone. Cutting back on variable expenses is one way to help save money. Kathy figures how much she can save
45 each month. She also decides how much of her credit card debt she can pay.

She makes this budget for the month:

MONTHLY BUDGET	
rent	$750
car payment	$220
car insurance	$50
food	$180
personal (clothes, entertainment, etc.)	$120
utilities (electricity, gas, water)	$50
gasoline/transportation	$50
telephone	$50
savings	$125
credit card debt	$205
TOTAL	$1,800

Review Questions

1. How do you know what your disposable income is?

_____

_____

2. How can a budget help you save money? How can it help you with spending?

_____

_____

Key Terms

fixed expenses (FIXT ek SPEN suhs) *n.* costs or bills that have to be paid regularly, such as every month

variable expenses (VAYR ee uh bul ek SPEN suhs) *n.* costs or bills that change from month to month

Objectives

1. Learn about making spending decisions.
2. Discuss how to make savings decisions.
3. Learn about insurance.

Target Reading Skill

Paraphrase Paraphrasing helps you understand what you read. When you paraphrase, you restate, or say again, information in your own words. You could paraphrase the first paragraph on the next page like this:

> Having a budget doesn't mean you don't have to make money decisions. You still have to choose what to buy and how to save. Your goals and values can help you.

Try paraphrasing as you read parts of this section. Saying the information in your own words will help you understand it better.

Vocabulary Strategy

Using Context Clues Nearby words, sentences, and paragraphs can give you clues to the meaning of a word you do not recognize. Sometimes the context will restate the meaning of a word. Look at this example:

> People buy insurance to protect themselves from injury or loss. In return, they pay premiums to the insurance company. These <u>regular payments</u> keep their insurance coverage going.

Note that the underlined words restate what premiums are. As you read, pay attention to the context of words you do not know. You may find the meanings of words restated in the surrounding words, sentences, and paragraphs.

Section 2 Summary

© Pearson Education, Inc., Publishing as Pearson Prentice Hall. All rights reserved.

Target Reading Skill

Paraphrase Paraphrase the bracketed paragraph.

_____

_____

_____

_____

Vocabulary Strategy

Using Context Clues
Circle a context clue for the term *use credit*.

✓ Reading Check

Identify possible advantages and disadvantages to buying a more expensive item. Write a plus sign (+) next to one advantage. Write a minus sign (–) next to one disadvantage.

[1] You have to make decisions about money even if you have a budget. You have to choose which goods and services to buy. You have to choose a savings plan. Your goals and values help you make these decisions.

Making Spending Decisions

[5] People's values affect their buying decisions. Other factors also affect decisions about spending. Friends, salespeople, and advertisements may influence you.

Wise shoppers consider various factors before deciding what to buy.

Factors Affecting Spending Decisions	Questions to Ask
Price	Do I have the money to buy this? Is its price about the same as the prices of other models of similar quality?
Quality	Will the product last? Is it well made? Does its quality match its price?
Features	Does the product have the features I need? Will I be paying for features I don't need?
Warranty and Service	Does the product have a **warranty**? Will the store repair or replace the product or give me my money back if it breaks down?
Sales and Discounts	Can I buy the same product at a lower price at a discount store or a special sale?

[10] Shoppers sometimes decide to buy a more expensive item. They may want to get high quality or special features. They may use credit to do this. That means they do not pay the whole price at once. They usually make a down payment. Then they borrow the rest.

[15] It is important to pay attention to the real cost of an item when borrowing money. The real cost is the purchase price plus interest. Shoppers using credit must pay interest on the money they borrow. The item costs more than if the shopper pays the whole price at once.

Key Term

warranty (WOR un tee) *n.* promise by the maker of a product to repair the product if it breaks within a certain time period

Making Savings Decisions

20 There are many ways to save money. Three factors can help you decide which is best for you.

The first factor is **liquidity**. How quickly can you get the money you have saved?

The second factor is income. How much will you 25 earn from the money you save? Banks offer savings plans that earn interest. Banks often pay higher interest on a **time deposit**. People also may buy stocks or bonds. Bonds pay a fixed rate of interest. Stockholders receive income from a company's profits in the form of 30 dividends. Other investment choices are mutual funds and real estate. A mutual fund is a collection of money from many investors. You can earn income from land you own by renting or selling it.

[When you save or invest, you usually make a trade- 35 off between income and liquidity. The interest rate on your savings account may be high. But if you must leave your money on deposit longer, it is less liquid. Stock and real estate can be hard to turn back into cash.

The third factor is safety. There is a trade-off 40 between safety and income. Savings accounts and bonds are fairly safe. But both pay low interest. Stocks can provide more income. But they also carry more risk.

Insurance

Most people cannot save enough to cover an emergency. They buy **insurance** for protection. People buy life 45 insurance to protect their families from loss of income. Property insurance protects houses, cars, and other property. Health insurance helps pay for medical care.

Review Questions

1. What factors help people to decide what to buy?
2. What factors can help people decide how to save?

Key Terms

liquidity (lih KWIH duh tee) *n.* turning savings back into cash
time deposit (TĪM dih POZ it) *n.* a savings plan with a set length of time that you must keep your money in the account
insurance (in SHER uns) *n.* a paid plan that protects a person from the cost of injury or loss

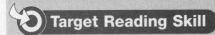

Target Reading Skill

Paraphrase What is one way to restate the sentence in brackets?

_____

_____

_____

_____

Vocabulary Strategy

Using Context Clues In the third paragraph, find and underline a context clue for *real estate.*

✓ Reading Check

Write *For* next to reasons to invest in stocks. Write *Against* next to reasons not to invest in stocks.

✓ Reading Check

Underline the sentences that tell the purpose of insurance.

Reading Preview

Section 3 Careers: Planning for the Future

Objectives

1. Think about careers and how to choose the best one for you.
2. Learn to research careers that interest you.
3. Learn about satisfying employers' expectations.

Target Reading Skill

Summarize When you summarize, you state the main ideas of what you have read. You also may include important supporting details. Summarizing helps you understand what you read. A summary can be used to study what you have read. It is shorter than the original text. It is also more to the point. Be sure to pause from time to time to summarize as you read.

Vocabulary Strategy

Using Context Clues There are many kinds of context clues. You can find clues in surrounding words, sentences, or paragraphs. Some clues define, or give the meaning of, unfamiliar words. Other clues only hint at the meaning. Here is an example of a context clue that defines a word:

There are thousands of careers. The occupation you choose to follow as your life's work is up to you.

Note that the second sentence defines the word *career*. A career is an occupation a person chooses to follow as his or her life's work.

Section 3 Summary

1 Planning your **career** may be the most important planning you do. How you choose to make a living will affect other economic decisions you make in your life.

Thinking About Careers

There are thousands of careers. Various factors will help 5 you to choose one. They include the economy, your education and training, and your interests and abilities. Your goals and values will affect your choice, too.

Career choices change as the economy changes. In the past, most Americans had farming or factory jobs. 10 Now most have service jobs. Computers and new technology have replaced some jobs. But they also create new jobs. Many new jobs demand special training. These include engineering, law, and medicine.

Your interests and abilities can help you pick a 15 career. What subjects are you good at? What you enjoy outside school can also help you. Your goals and values are important, too. Do you like a fast <u>pace</u>? Do you want to live in the country? Do you enjoy travel? Your answers can help you identify possible careers.

Career Research

20 You can research career fields. Most libraries have information. The *Occupational Outlook Handbook* is one good source. It tells about hundreds of jobs. It describes the education, training, and other skills needed.

Talking with someone in a career is another way to 25 get information. You can ask questions such as:

- What do you actually do in this job?
- What training and education are needed?
- What do you like most about your job? What do you like least?
30 - What jobs are available in this field now? In the future?

Key Terms

career (kuh REER) *n.* a job which you do as your life's work

Occupational Outlook Handbook (ah kyoo PAY shuh nul OUT luk HAND buk) *n.* a career guide published by the Department of Labor

---

Target Reading Skill

Summarize Write MI next to the main idea of *Career Research.* Find two important supporting details and write D next to each.

✓ Reading Check

In the text, number important factors to consider when selecting a career.

Vocabulary Strategy

Using Context Clues What does the underlined word mean? Circle the word or words that give hints to its meaning.

_____

_____

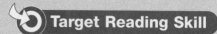

On-the-job experience also gives you information. You might get a part-time or summer job in a field that interests you. For example, you might work in an office
35 to see what happens each day. Many students volunteer in hospitals and day-care centers. This helps them to see what careers in medicine and teaching are like.

Satisfying Employers

Understanding what an employer expects can help a worker to be successful. Employers look for people
40 with basic skills. They want workers who are willing to learn. They want workers who care about what they do. Many employers want people with a <u>positive</u> outlook. They also like employees with a "can do" approach and who do not give up. This persistence is
45 an important quality.

Career decisions are never final. Most people change careers—or jobs within a career field—more than once. Career planning does not stop. Your interests, goals, skills, and experience continue to change.

Review Questions

1. How does the economy affect career choices?

_____

_____

2. Name three ways to get information about a career field.

_____

_____

_____

Chapter 15 Assessment

1. Salaries and wages are examples of
   A. fringe benefits.
   B. earned income.
   C. sick leave.
   D. disposable income.

2. Which of the following change from month to month?
   A. fixed expenses
   B. car payments
   C. variable expenses
   D. none of the above

3. The real cost of an item bought with borrowed money includes
   A. credit.
   B. interest.
   C. quality.
   D. discounts.

4. Which of these are ways that can help people to save their money?
   A. mutual funds
   B. savings accounts
   C. stocks
   D. all of the above

5. Which of the following can people buy for protection?
   A. insurance
   B. training
   C. real estate
   D. all of the above

Short Answer Question

How do you make a budget?

_____

_____

_____

_____

_____

Reading Preview

Section 1
Government Intervention in the Economy

Objectives

1. Discuss American values and economic goals.
2. Identify the limits of free enterprise.
3. Explain how governments correct and prevent economic problems.
4. Explain the debate over government intervention in the economy.

 **Target Reading Skill**

Ask Questions It is a good idea to look through a section before reading it. Look at headings and photos in the section. As you do, you will probably have questions. Write down questions that occur to you. Then read to find answers to your questions.

Look at the heading *The Need for Reform,* for example. You may have these questions about this section of the text: What is reform? Why is it needed? Where is it needed? Asking questions such as these gives you a purpose for reading. You can read to find answers to your questions.

Vocabulary Strategy

Using Roots and Prefixes Roots and prefixes can help you understand the meaning of words you have not seen before. Remember:

- A root is the base of a word. A root has meaning by itself.
- A prefix goes in front of the root. A prefix changes the meaning of the root.

You will come across the words *inhumane* and *intervention* in this section. Break each into a prefix and root to try to learn its meaning.

Prefix +	Root =	Word
in-	humane	inhumane
"not"	?	?
inter-	ven	intervention
"between"	"come"	?

Section 1 Summary

¹ The government plays many roles in our economy. It makes rules for business. It spends about $2 trillion each year. It collects taxes. The federal government is the biggest consumer in our economy. It is also the
⁵ biggest employer.

American Values and Economic Goals

Our government is based on several basic values. The Framers of the Constitution believed that **economic freedom** is a basic right of citizens. They wanted a new nation with an economy based on a market system. They
¹⁰ wanted the economy to be strong and able to grow.

Article 1, Section 8 of the Constitution gives Congress power to support a market economy. Congress can issue money. It can collect taxes and borrow money. It can also set up a mail service and build roads. In the
¹⁵ early years of our country, most people expected the government to play a small role in the economy.

The Need for Reform

The free-enterprise system has made our nation rich. But our economy also has some problems. Many people believe these problems are not fixed by letting the mar-
²⁰ ket system work on its own. This chart shows some economic problems the government has had to face.

Reasons Why Government Has Become Involved in Our Economy
1. Businesses have sometimes earned profits unfairly.
2. Working conditions have sometimes been unsafe and <u>inhumane</u>.
3. Unsafe products have harmed consumers.
4. Not all Americans have had economic security.
5. The economy has been unstable.
6. The environment has been damaged.

Key Term

economic freedom (ek uh NOM ik FREE dum) *n.* being able to own property, make money, and decide what to make, buy, and sell

Target Reading Skill

Ask Questions What question comes to mind when you look at the heading *American Values and Economic Goals*?

_____

_____

Circle the text that answers your question.

✓ Reading Check

Underline the sentence(s) that tell(s) what the Framers wanted to ensure for the new nation.

Vocabulary Strategy

Using Roots and Prefixes Draw a line between the prefix and root of *inhumane* in the chart. What do you think the root means? What does *inhumane* mean?

_____

_____

✓ Reading Check

Circle the text that tells why the government has become involved in the economy.

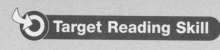

Ask Questions What question would you ask based on the heading *Methods Governments Use*?

_____

_____

_____

✓ **Reading Check**

Bracket the sentence under *Methods Governments Use* that describes the relationship between taxes and the economy.

Vocabulary Strategy

Using Roots and Prefixes
What does *intervention* mean?

_____

_____

✓ **Reading Check**

Number three disadvantages and three advantages of government involvement in the economy.

Methods Governments Use

Local, state, and federal governments use various methods to change how the economy works.

1. *Governments set rules for businesses.* They limit workers' hours. They set safety rules. And they set up agencies to carry out laws.

2. *Governments give money to people who need help.* The money pays for food, shelter, and medical care.

3. *Governments own resources and produce goods and services.* They run businesses that help many people.

4. *Governments give money to private businesses.* That helps to create important products or services.

5. *Governments control the amount of money they spend and the amount they get in taxes.* Taxes take money from the economy. Spending puts money back.

6. *Governments make tax rules and collect special taxes.* They change the tax rates. They reward certain economic activities and punish others.

Government Intervention

There is a bad side to government being involved in the economy. Government rules can limit our freedom to make profits and to do what we want with our property. Government's part in the economy can cost a lot, too. The taxes that pay for programs take large parts of people's incomes. Also, people often say the government uses more time, money, and paperwork than needed.

Government <u>intervention</u> often creates conflict. Freedom clashes with equality and justice. It also clashes with the health of the public and the environment. People disagree about which values are more important.

Review Questions

1. What methods do governments use to solve economic problems?

_____

_____

_____

2. Why does government involvement in the economy create conflict?

_____

_____

CHAPTER 16

Reading Preview

Section 2 Government's Efforts to Solve Economic Problems

Objectives

1. Discuss how the government ensures fair business practices.
2. Describe how government regulations protect workers and consumers.
3. Explain how government provides economic security, helps to maintain economic stability, and works to protect the environment.

Target Reading Skill

Use Prior Knowledge Your prior knowledge is what you already know about something. Follow these steps to use prior knowledge:

1. Look at headings and illustrations before beginning to read. Also look at features and vocabulary words.

2. Think about what you already know about the topic of what you have previewed.

3. Correct what you already know with new information as you read.

Vocabulary Strategy

Using Roots and Prefixes Breaking a word into parts can help you understand its meaning. It helps to know the meaning of common prefixes. Review the meaning of these prefixes.

Prefix	Meaning
anti-	against
syn-, sym-, syl-, sys-	together, with
in-	not
inter-	between
re-	back, again
un-	not

Target Reading Skill

Use Prior Knowledge What do you already know about labor unions that helps you understand this section?

_____

_____

_____

✓ Reading Check

Underline the sentences that explain what the Sherman and Clayton Antitrust Acts accomplished.

✓ Reading Check

Circle the sentences that explain how the government protects work-place safety.

1 People want freedom, equality, and justice. People expect the government to solve problems while balancing freedom and fairness.

Ensuring Fair Business Practices

Competition is meant to keep prices fair. In the 1800s, 5 many business owners thought of ways to get rid of competition. Some industries were run by a **trust**. A trust is a corporation that controls a market. It has monopoly power. That is the power to control prices. A business with this power is often called a **monopoly**.

10 Citizens got angry about monopolies. In 1890, Congress passed the Sherman Antitrust Act. It outlaws deals that limit competition. The Clayton Antitrust Act was passed in 1914. It outlaws many practices of monopolies and trusts.

Protecting Workers and Consumers

15 Our government has often protected workers. It passed the Fair Labor Standards Act of 1938. It passed laws to limit work hours. And it set minimum wages. Other laws said employers must bargain with unions.

The government also guarded workers from danger. 20 Labor unions argued that work conditions must be safe. All companies did not want to pay for safer machines. In 1971, the government began the Occupational Safety and Health Administration (OSHA). OSHA sets safety and health standards at work.

25 The government also guards us from harmful foods and drugs. It set up the Food and Drug Administration (FDA) in 1927. The FDA sees that food, make-up, and drugs are safe. New drugs are tested before they are sold. The government created the Consumer Product 30 Safety Commission (CPSC) in 1972. The CPSC makes rules for toys, tools, and other goods.

Key Terms

trust (TRUST) *n.* a group of several companies that are helped by the high prices they all agree to charge

monopoly (muh NOP uh lee) *n.* a single business with the power to control prices in a market

Providing Economic Security

In 1929, hard times began for our nation. This time is called the Great Depression. In 1932, President Franklin D. Roosevelt began programs called the New Deal. The
35 programs were meant to help the economy. They were meant to help people in need.

In 1935, the Social Security Act was passed. It replaces the income lost when a person retires, is injured, or dies. The act also created unemployment
40 insurance. That gives money to people who lose jobs.

Maintaining Economic Stability

The economy goes through a **business cycle**. Companies make more goods during a growth time. New jobs are created. A recession follows each time of growth. A recession is a time of slowdown. Fewer
45 goods are made. Unemployment goes up.

Citizens want a stable economy. So the government tries to lessen the ups and downs. **Monetary policy** is control of the money supply. **Fiscal policy** is the government's plan for spending money and gathering taxes. It
50 affects the economy, too. That is because our government is an important spender and collector of taxes.

Protecting the Environment

The government also protects the environment. The government passed the Environmental Protection Act in 1970. This important law created the Environmental
55 Protection Agency (EPA). <u>The EPA controls pollution. It decides what and how much can be dumped into our air, water, and soil.</u>

Review Questions

1. What government agencies help protect consumers?
2. How does government maintain economic stability?

✓ Reading Check

Bracket text that explains the purpose of the New Deal programs.

✓ Reading Check

What is the difference between monetary policy and fiscal policy?

_____

_____

_____

_____

Target Reading Skill

Use Prior Knowledge What do you know about the environment that helps you better understand the underlined information?

_____

_____

_____

Key Terms

business cycle (BIZ nis sī kul) *n.* a repeated series of "ups" of growth and "downs" of recession

monetary policy (MON ih tayr ee POL uh see) *n.* control of the money supply by the Federal Reserve System

fiscal policy (FIS kul POL uh see) *n.* a government's decisions about how much it spends and how much it collects in taxes

Objectives

1. Discuss how the nation maintains its economic health.

2. Understand how the federal budget works.

3. Identify sources of federal income.

Target Reading Skill

Predict Making predictions helps you set a purpose for reading. Having a purpose for reading helps you understand and remember what you read. To make a prediction, follow these steps:

1. Look at the headings, images, and anything else that stands out in the text.

2. Predict what the text might discuss.

3. Connect what you read to your prediction.

4. Change your prediction if what you read does not support it.

Vocabulary Strategy

Using Roots and Prefixes Always look closely at words you do not recognize while reading. You may be able to break them into word parts such as prefixes and roots. Then you can use what you know about the prefixes and roots to figure out the meaning of the words.

You will come across the words *inflation* and *imports* in this section. Figure out their meanings by breaking them into a prefix and root. The information in the chart will help you.

Word	Prefix	Root
inflation	in- "in, into"	flat "blow"
imports	im- "in, into"	port "carry"

Section 3 Summary

[1] The federal government is now the main manager of the economy. It has three major jobs. It tracks the economy's health. It adjusts the economy's performance. And it takes care of a huge sum of public money.

The Nation's Economic Health

[5] Our government keeps track of how many people are out of work. It counts new jobs. These and other numbers help to measure the economy's health. Then the government decides how to improve the economy.

The rate of **inflation** is one major sign of the econo-[10] my's health. Money loses its buying power during inflation. That makes inflation a worry for the government, companies, and consumers.

Inflation is hard to control. As prices rise, workers want higher pay. Companies then spend more on labor. [15] They have to raise prices even higher to make a profit.

The **gross domestic product (GDP)** is another sign of the economy's health. A major goal of government is to help the economy grow. A rising GDP, without rising prices, usually means the economy is growing. A [20] falling GDP means the economy needs help. To help, the government may increase its spending.

The Federal Budget

The government pays for things like unemployment, medical care, and retirement. It also spends money on national defense and federal highways.

[25] Federal spending is planned ahead of time. The **federal budget** decides in detail how much will be spent in a year. The budget also estimates how much will be received from taxes.

Key Terms

inflation (in FLAY shun) *n.* a general rise in the price of goods and services

gross domestic product (GDP) (GRŌS duh MES tik PROD ukt) *n.* the total dollar value of all goods and services made in the country in a year

federal budget (FED rul BUJ it) *n.* the government's plan for how it will raise and spend money

---

Target Reading Skill

Predict What can you predict about the text under *The Nation's Economic Health?*

_____

_____

_____

Vocabulary Strategy

Using Roots and Prefixes Use the prefix and the root of *inflation* to explain what it means.

_____

_____

✓ Reading Check

Underline the sentences that explain what causes inflation.

✓ Reading Check

List five things the federal government spends its money on.

1. _____

2. _____

3. _____

4. _____

5. _____

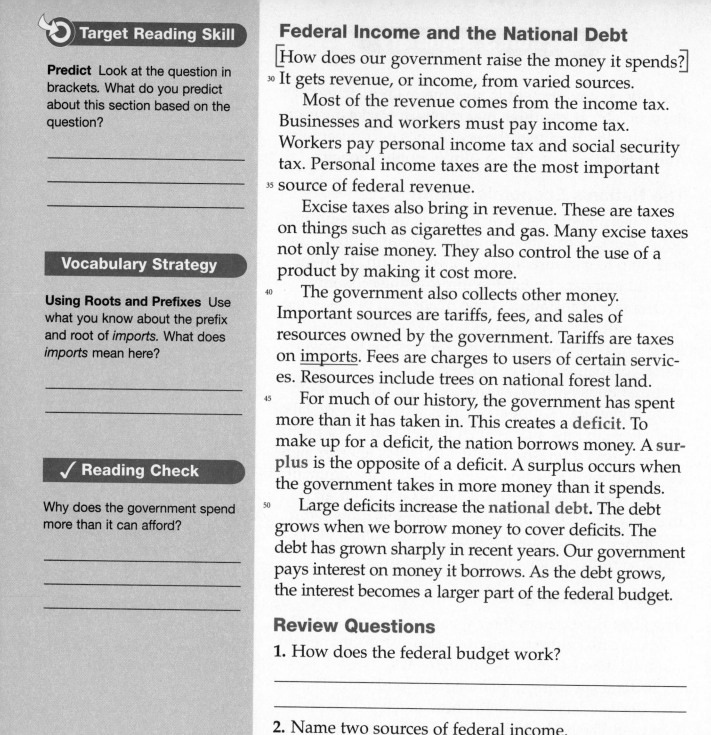

Target Reading Skill

Predict Look at the question in brackets. What do you predict about this section based on the question?

_____

_____

_____

Vocabulary Strategy

Using Roots and Prefixes Use what you know about the prefix and root of *imports*. What does *imports* mean here?

_____

_____

✓ Reading Check

Why does the government spend more than it can afford?

_____

_____

_____

Federal Income and the National Debt

[How does our government raise the money it spends?]
30 It gets revenue, or income, from varied sources.

Most of the revenue comes from the income tax. Businesses and workers must pay income tax. Workers pay personal income tax and social security tax. Personal income taxes are the most important
35 source of federal revenue.

Excise taxes also bring in revenue. These are taxes on things such as cigarettes and gas. Many excise taxes not only raise money. They also control the use of a product by making it cost more.
40 The government also collects other money. Important sources are tariffs, fees, and sales of resources owned by the government. Tariffs are taxes on <u>imports</u>. Fees are charges to users of certain services. Resources include trees on national forest land.
45 For much of our history, the government has spent more than it has taken in. This creates a **deficit**. To make up for a deficit, the nation borrows money. A **surplus** is the opposite of a deficit. A surplus occurs when the government takes in more money than it spends.
50 Large deficits increase the **national debt**. The debt grows when we borrow money to cover deficits. The debt has grown sharply in recent years. Our government pays interest on money it borrows. As the debt grows, the interest becomes a larger part of the federal budget.

Review Questions

1. How does the federal budget work?

_____

_____

2. Name two sources of federal income.

_____

_____

Key Terms

deficit (DEH fuh sut) *n.* how much more the government spends than it takes in

surplus (SER plus) *n.* how much more the government takes in than it spends

national debt (NASH uh nul DET) *n.* the total amount of money the government owes

1. Which of the following is *not* a power given to Congress?
   A. to collect taxes
   B. to borrow money
   C. to sell bonds
   D. to build roads

2. Government involvement in the economy
   A. is expensive.
   B. limits our freedom to make profits.
   C. affects our freedom to buy and sell.
   D. all of the above

3. Monopoly power is the power
   A. to control prices.
   B. to control products.
   C. to control businesses.
   D. none of the above

4. Which agency sets safety and health standards in the workplace?
   A. FDA
   B. OSHA
   C. GDP
   D. EPA

5. What does the government often do when inflation gets too high?
   A. It raises Social Security tax.
   B. It lowers Social Security tax.
   C. It raises interest rates.
   D. all of the above

Short Answer Question

List some of the ways that the government works to solve economic problems.

_____

_____

_____

_____

_____

Objectives

1. Examine the different functions of money.

2. Explore the many characteristics of our money.

3. Discuss the value of our currency.

 **Target Reading Skill**

Use Context Clues Looking at context can sometimes help you figure out the meaning of a word you do not know. Context includes the words and sentences around a word. Read this paragraph:

> Our market economy could not work without money. <u>Without money,</u> we would have to rely on **bartering**. Such <u>trading</u> would not be easy in today's economy.

You may not know the meaning of the word in bold. But nearby words give clues to its meaning. The underlined context clues tell you that *bartering* means "trading without money."

Vocabulary Strategy

Recognizing Word Origins A word's origin is where the word comes from. The words *ideal* and *legal* in this section contain the Greek suffix *-al.* This suffix means "having to do with, belonging to." The word *ideal* contains the Greek root *ide-,* meaning "thought or idea." The word *legal* contains the Latin root *leg-,* meaning "law."

Knowing the origins of words can help you understand their meanings. As you read, use your knowledge of the roots and suffix in *ideal* and *legal* to figure out what the words mean.

Section 1 Summary

¹ Our market economy could not work without money. Without money, we would have to rely on **bartering**. Such trading would not be easy in today's economy.

The [Functions] of Money

Money has three basic uses. Most important, it is used ⁵ for exchange. People give and take money in exchange for goods. Second, money is a standard of value. Prices stated in money terms allow you to compare values. All prices are given in dollars and cents. Third, money is a store of value. You can put money aside to use ¹⁰ later.

The Characteristics of Our Money

There are various kinds of money. An economy may use **currency** as money. In the past, other objects were used as money. These include salt, furs, grains, and gold. These kinds of money worked well in the ¹⁵ economies in which they were used. None would work well in our economy today. Each is missing one or more of six characteristics. These characteristics make our currency <u>ideal</u> for our economy.

Target Reading Skill

Use Context Clues Circle the context clue that explains the meaning of the bracketed word.

✓ **Reading Check**

Circle the text that tells how money allows consumers to compare the values of goods and services.

Vocabulary Strategy

Recognizing Word Origins
What do you think *ideal* means?

_____

_____

Key Terms
bartering (BAR ter ing) *v.* trading goods and services
currency (KER un see) *n.* the coins and paper bills used as money

✓ Reading Check

Underline the sentence that explains why gold and silver are not ideal currency today.

Vocabulary Strategy

Recognizing Word Origins
What do you think *legal* means?

_____

_____

✓ Reading Check

Why is the metal used to make coins worth less than their face value?

_____

_____

_____

The chart shows six characteristics of our money.

CHARACTERISTICS OF OUR MONEY
1. Our money is accepted by most people in our society.
2. Our money can be counted and measured accurately.
3. Our money is <u>durable</u> and not easily destroyed.
4. Our money is convenient and easy to carry and use.
5. Our money does not cost too much to produce.
6. The supply of our money is easily controlled.

20   For a long time, gold and silver were used as money around the world. Standard-weight coins were made from these metals. Gold and silver coins are durable. They can be counted and measured accurately. But large amounts of gold and silver are heavy and 25 hard to carry. For that reason, they are not ideal today. But gold and silver still have value. That is because it is expensive to find them and dig them from the ground.

The Value of Our Currency

Our coins are generally a mixture of copper and nickel. The metal in each coin is worth less than the coin's face 30 value. Our bills are just paper. These words appear on them: "This note is <u>legal</u> tender for all debts, public and private." Our currency has value because the government says it does. The government stands behind our money.

Review Questions

1. What are the three basic uses of money?

_____

_____

2. Name four characteristics of our money.

_____

_____

_____

Objectives

1. Analyze the beginnings of banking.
2. Discover the many different kinds of money used.
3. Understand how bank services provide access to money.
4. Discuss how the business of banking functions in our national economy.

Target Reading Skill

Interpret Nonliteral Meanings The literal meanings of words are exactly what the words mean. Nonliteral meanings usually involve images or comparisons. These strongly communicate an idea to the reader. Read this sentence.

They were hoping to <u>strike</u> gold near Gemstone City.

The literal meaning of *strike* is "hit." In this sentence, *strike* has a nonliteral meaning. It means "find or discover suddenly." *Strike* is a more vivid word than *find*.

Be aware of nonliteral meanings as you read. A word may not mean exactly what it says.

Vocabulary Strategy

Recognizing Word Origins The words *receipt* and *fraction* appear in this section. Each contains a Latin root.

Word	Root	Meaning
receipt	ceipt- (cept-, ceiv-)	take, seize
fraction	fract-	break

Knowing these roots can help you figure out the meanings of words as you read. You probably know that *receive* means "take, accept." Maybe you know that *fragile* means "breakable." As you read, use your knowledge of these roots to try to determine the meanings of *receipt* and *fraction*.

Target Reading Skill

Interpret Nonliteral Meanings
Restate the underlined sentence in your own words.

_____

_____

_____

Vocabulary Strategy

Recognizing Word Origins
Explain the meaning of *receipt* based on its root.

_____

_____

✓ Reading Check

How does the story of Hiram Wakefield show how banks developed?

_____

_____

_____

_____

¹Societies created banks to help businesses and individuals. Banks help people exchange money safely and easily. Banks also help people save money.

The Beginnings of Banking

Merchants and goldsmiths in Europe first created
⁵banks during the Middle Ages. More goods were being exchanged. Larger amounts of money were used.

Banks also were needed in the young United States. The following story is not true. But it shows how banks formed.

¹⁰Hiram Wakefield was a goldsmith in Colorado. He heard that gold was found near Gemstone City. He moved there and set up a shop. <u>Soon Hiram's business was booming.</u> Miners brought in gold to be weighed and stored. When a miner wanted to store gold, Hiram
¹⁵gave him a <u>receipt</u> that showed the gold's value.

Miners could give any shopkeeper one of Hiram's receipts. In exchange, the shopkeeper gave them what they wanted. Business owners could exchange receipts for gold. The receipts became a form of money.

²⁰Miners only rarely exchanged their receipts for all the gold they had in Hiram's safe. Hiram decided that he could lend some gold to miners who needed it. Miners who received these loans signed a note. The note said they would pay back the gold plus a fee for borrowing it.

²⁵Hiram had become the Gemstone City banker. His system of holding money and giving blank receipts and loans is similar to what banks do today.

The Kinds of Money

Currency is one kind of money. Checks are another. Checks are accepted in exchange for goods and servic-
³⁰es. Checks are not as durable as currency. Checks can only exist in an economy if there are banks. A person deposits money in a bank. That money is known as a **demand deposit**. The person can withdraw that money "on demand" by writing a check.

Key Term

demand deposit (dih MAND dih POZ it) *n.* the money in a checking account

35 Traveler's checks are a third kind of money. The exact amount of the traveler's check is printed on it. Traveler's checks, demand deposits, and currency make up the **money supply**.

Bank Services

Our banks offer three main services: checking accounts, 40 saving accounts, and loans. Checking accounts make doing business easy. Checks can be used instead of cash to pay for goods.

When people put money in savings accounts, the bank pays them interest. This is because the bank can 45 use the money from customers' savings to make a **loan** to another individual or business. The borrower agrees to pay back the amount borrowed. The borrower also pays a certain amount of interest.

The Business of Banking

The largest source of profit for most banks is interest 50 on loans. The interest paid on savings accounts is less than the interest the bank receives on loans. The difference between the amount paid and the interest received is a major part of a bank's income.

Modern banking works on the principle of **fraction-** 55 **al reserve banking**. Banks keep only a fraction of people's deposits <u>on hand</u>. The money deposited in banks helps those who need to borrow money. It helps the economy grow.

Review Questions

1. What are three kinds of money people use?

_____

2. Explain the idea of fractional reserve banking.

_____

_____

Key Terms

money supply (MUN ee suh PLĪ) *n.* the total amount of money available

loan (Lōn) *n.* an amount of money borrowed for a certain time

fractional reserve banking (FRAK shun ul ri ZERV BANGK ing) *n.* banking that holds back a certain portion of the money deposited by customers and uses the rest for loans and investments

---

✓ **Reading Check**

Bracket the sentence that explains how checks differ from currency.

Vocabulary Strategy

Recognizing Word Origins If the Latin root *fract-* means "break," what does *fraction* mean?

_____

_____

Target Reading Skill

Interpret Nonliteral Meanings What does the underlined phrase mean?

_____

_____

✓ **Reading Check**

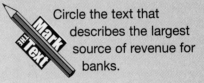

Underline the text that explains why banks pay customers who keep their money in savings accounts.

✓ **Reading Check**

Circle the text that describes the largest source of revenue for banks.

Reading Preview

Section 3
The Federal Reserve System

Objectives

1. Learn about the beginning of the Federal Reserve System.
2. Understand the organization of the Federal Reserve System.
3. Learn about the functions of the Federal Reserve System.
4. Explore the delicate balance between money and the economy.

Target Reading Skill

Use Context Sometimes the meaning of a word makes sense only in its context. Context is the words, phrases, or sentences that surround the word. You can make sense of a word you do not know by thinking about the meanings of nearby words and phrases.

Read the first sentence. To understand the meaning of the word *panic*, think about the meaning of the underlined word in the second sentence.

> People with money in banks began to panic. They <u>feared</u> that the banks would go out of business.

The context of *panic* helps you understand that it means "feel great fear."

Vocabulary Strategy

Recognizing Word Origins You will find the words *regulate* and *recession* in this section. Both have Latin roots. The word *regulate* contains the root *regula-*, meaning "rule." The word *recession* contains the root *cess-*, meaning "go." Each word also has other Latin word parts. As you read, think about what you know about the meanings of the parts of each word. Use your knowledge to figure out the meaning of the whole word.

Section 3 Summary

¹ The federal government <u>regulates</u> banks and the nation's money supply. It does this through the Federal Reserve System.

The Federal Reserve System

The economy stopped growing in the late 1800s and
⁵ early 1900s. Businesses closed. Workers lost their jobs. People with money in banks feared that banks would go out of business, too. They wanted all their money in cash. Many banks did not have enough money on hand to meet the demand. Some banks had to close
¹⁰ down. Many customers lost their money.

The public finally asked the government to step in. People wanted the government to make rules for how banks worked. They also wanted the government to <u>assist</u> banks when they needed help.

¹⁵ Congress created the **Federal Reserve System**, or "the Fed" in 1913. This system became the central bank of the United States.

Organization of the Fed

The Fed is an independent agency of the federal government. It is not influenced by politics. Lawmakers
²⁰ who created the Fed wanted it to keep in touch with the country's business needs.

Congress divided the country into twelve geographic regions. These are called Federal Reserve districts. There is one Federal Reserve Bank in each district. It
²⁵ oversees banking there. It also pays attention to the economic problems of that area.

The most powerful people in the Fed are the seven members of the Board of Governors. The President appoints them for 14-year terms. The **Board of**
³⁰ **Governors** runs the Federal Reserve System.

Key Terms

Federal Reserve System (FED rul rih ZERV SIS tum) *n.* central bank that offers services to banks and oversees their activities

Board of Governors (BORD UV GUV er nerz) *n.* group of seven people who run the Federal Reserve System

---

Vocabulary Strategy

Recognizing Word Origins
What does *regulate* mean?

_____

_____

Target Reading Skill

Use Context Bracket any words or phrases that help you to understand the meaning of *assist*.

✓ Reading Check

Circle the paragraph that explains how and when the Federal Reserve System was created.

✓ Reading Check

Underline the text that tells how the Federal Reserve keeps in touch with the business needs of the country.

Functions of the Fed

The Fed's many jobs are shown in the chart below.

FUNCTIONS OF THE FEDERAL RESERVE
1. Supplying currency. Each bill in our currency is a Federal Reserve note. Each Federal Reserve note comes from one of the twelve Federal Reserve Banks.
2. Serving as the government's bank. The Fed keeps the federal government's checking accounts. It also keeps track of the federal government's debts.
3. Providing services. Checks you write for purchases pass from the seller's bank through the Fed before returning to your bank.
4. Regulating banks. The Fed sets rules for banks. Then it makes sure they are followed.
5. Making loans to banks. The Fed will make loans to banks. Banks pay the Fed a special low rate of interest called the discount rate.
6. Controlling the money supply. This is the most powerful job of the Fed. The size of the money supply has a great effect on the health of the economy.

Money and the Economy

In a healthy economy, spending is about equal to the economy's ability to produce goods. Greater demand for goods and services makes prices rise. A rise in
35 prices throughout the economy is called inflation.

Sometimes there is less money than there are goods to spend it on. Businesses may cut back on production. The result is a **recession**.

Controlling the money supply is difficult. When
40 prices rise, the Fed may make it harder for people to get loans. Spending slows when less money is being loaned. And prices are less likely to continue to rise. In a recession, the Fed often makes it easier for banks to make loans. Increased lending encourages spending.

Review Questions

1. Describe the organization of the Fed.

_____

_____

2. Why is controlling the money supply the Fed's most important job?

_____

_____

Key Term
recession (rih SESH un) *n.* a slowdown in the economy

✓ **Reading Check**

Underline the sentence in the chart that describes the Federal Reserve's involvement with checks.

Vocabulary Strategy

Recognizing Word Origins If the Latin root *cess-* means "go," what does *recession* mean?

_____

_____

Target Reading Skill

Use Context Circle any words in the chart that help you understand the meaning of <u>note</u> in this context.

✓ **Reading Check**

Number two sentences that explain why the Fed makes it harder to get loans when prices rise.

1. Which of the following is a function of money?
   A. standard of value
   B. store of value
   C. used for exchange
   D. all of the above

2. Our money has value because it is
   A. made of gold and silver.
   B. easily destroyed.
   C. backed by the government.
   D. all of the above

3. A demand deposit is money a person
   A. puts in a checking account.
   B. puts in a savings account.
   C. borrows from a bank.
   D. all of the above

4. Which is a type of savings institution?
   A. credit union
   B. savings and loan association
   C. mutual savings bank
   D. all of the above

5. How many Federal Reserve districts are there?
   A. 50
   B. 12
   C. 1
   D. 3

Short Answer Question

What is the Federal Reserve System, and what are its functions?

_____

_____

_____

_____

_____

Reading Preview

Section 1
Government and Economic Goals

Objectives

1. Discuss the relationship between full employment and price stability.

2. Study the government's role in the circular flow of economic activity.

3. Investigate the process of national income accounting.

Target Reading Skill

Recognize Word Origins Words have come into the English language from various languages. Many English words can be traced to Latin or Greek. The words *promote* and *domestic* in this section both have Latin origins. *Promote* comes from the Latin word *promotus,* meaning "move forward or ahead." *Domestic* comes from the Latin word *domus,* meaning "house or home." This information about word origins will help you to understand the meanings of *promote* and *domestic* as you read.

Vocabulary Strategy

Recognizing Signal Words Signal words point out relationships between ideas or events. Words can signal time, sequence, importance, comparisons, contrasts, causes, effects, and examples. The chart below shows words that signal examples.

Words That Signal Examples		
for example	for instance	such as
like	specifically	as

Look for these signal words as you read. They will point to specific examples of ideas or things.

Section 1 Summary

¹ The government is important to the economy. It tries to improve the economy in difficult times.

Full Employment and Price Stability

People are happy when prices don't change and there are jobs. They are not happy when prices go up and ⁵ down and people can't find jobs.

Americans worried about the lack of jobs after World War II. People feared there might be another economic downturn <u>like</u> the Great Depression. Then Congress passed the Employment Act of 1946.

¹⁰ This act was based on three ideas.

- *General Welfare* The Constitution's preamble says the government should <u>promote</u> the general welfare. This means the government should serve the best interests of citizens. The Employment Act of 1946 ¹⁵ did this. Its goal was for everyone to have a job and for prices to hold steady.

- *Full Employment* This means that no person who wants work should be out of a job.

- *Price Stability* This means keeping prices even. ²⁰ People have the greatest buying power when prices don't change. When prices go up, buying power drops.

Government and the Circular Flow

Since World War II, the government has become a big part of the economy. The diagram shows this.

²⁵ A **mixed economy** includes government, businesses, and people. Government can tax businesses and people. In exchange for taxes, the government provides services.

Key Terms

full employment (FUL em PLOY munt) *n.* when every person who wants to work has a job

mixed economy (MIKST ih KON uh mee) *n.* a system that includes the government, companies, and people

---

Recognizing Signal Words
What does the underlined word signal?

_____

_____

_____

Target Reading Skill

Recognize Word Origins What does *promote* mean under *General Welfare*?

_____

_____

✓ Reading Check

Underline the text that tells the chief goal of the Employment Act of 1946.

✓ Reading Check

Circle the text that explains what role the government plays in the flow of economic activity.

Target Reading Skill

Recognize Word Origins Use the root of the word *domestic* to help you explain its meaning in this context.

_____

_____

Vocabulary Strategy

Recognizing Signal Words What does *For example* signal here?

_____

_____

_____

✓ Reading Check

Bracket the sentence that tells why economic growth is important.

National Income Accounting

National income accounting helps us to see changes in
30 the economy. It tracks spending, and it tracks income.
It helps voters and government leaders make decisions
about government spending and taxes, too.

National income accounting includes the gross
<u>domestic</u> product (GDP). The GDP is the value of
35 goods and services made and sold in a year. Services
that do not involve production are not counted. <u>For
example</u>, Social Security payments are not included.

In an economy, total spending must equal total
income. Spending is all the money used to buy goods
40 and services. It includes money spent by people, businesses, and the government. Income includes wages,
rents, interest, and profits.

There is **economic growth** if the GDP goes up and
prices stay about the same. Citizens enjoy a higher stan-
45 dard of living. Growth is one goal of the economy.
Other goals are full employment and price stability.
Policy makers want jobs for all, and they do not want
large increases or decreases in the overall price level.
Inflation happens if the price level increases. **Deflation**
50 happens if the price level decreases.

Review Questions

1. What role does national income accounting play in
the economy?

_____

_____

2. What are three goals of our economy?

_____

_____

Key Terms

national income accounting (NASH uh nul IN kum uh KOWN ting)
n. how our nation keeps track of income and spending

economic growth (ek uh NOM ik GRŌTH) *n.* a time when more
goods and services are produced

inflation (in FLAY shun) *n.* a rise in overall price level

deflation (dih FLAY shun) *n.* a fall in overall price level

Reading Preview

Section 2
Paying for Government

Objectives

1. Discuss tax fairness.
2. Identify different types of income taxes.
3. Examine the effects of taxes on individuals and the economy.

Target Reading Skill

Analyze Word Parts When you come across a word you do not know, try breaking it into parts. What you know about the parts of the word may help you understand its meaning. The root is the basic part of a word. It gives the basic meaning. Prefixes and/or suffixes added to the root may change the meaning.

The words *impose* and *impact* in this section have the same prefix, *im-*. The prefix *im-* can mean "in, into, against." The two words have different roots. The root *pos-* means "place, put." The root *pact-* means "push." Use what you know about the word parts to understand the meaning of *impose* and *impact* as you read.

Vocabulary Strategy

Recognizing Signal Words Certain words signal the order of ideas or events. Some of these words are used in groups.

Word Groups That Signal Order		
first, second, third (and so on)	first, next, last	first, then, finally

Look for these signal word groups as you read. They will point to ideas or events that are listed in a certain order.

Section 2 Summary

Analyze Word Parts What do you think the word *impose* means here?

_____

_____

✓ **Reading Check**

Circle the detail that tells who should receive the benefits of a fair tax.

Vocabulary Strategy

Recognizing Signal Words Circle signal words in the second-to-last paragraph. What do they signal?

_____

_____

[1] Federal, state, and local governments tax citizens. The government must <u>impose</u> taxes fairly. It also must think about how taxes affect those who pay them.

Tax Fairness

As citizens, we expect to receive goods and services from our government. We pay for those goods and services through taxes. It is the duty of both citizens and government leaders to understand what makes a good tax.

A good tax must be:

- necessary—a tax should pay for something that citizens want.
- fair—people in the same situations should be treated alike when it comes to paying taxes.
- certain—the government must know how much money people will have to pay and how much a tax is likely to raise.
- convenient—if taxpayers find it hard to pay, it is not convenient; if government finds it hard to collect, it is not convenient.
- economical—the cost of collecting the tax must be small compared to the amount of money collected.

There are two important ideas about tax fairness. The first is the benefits-received principle. The benefits should go to people who pay the tax. Think about the tax on gasoline. It is fair. The more gas a driver buys, the more miles he or she travels on government-built roads. The more gas taxes a driver pays, the more benefit he or she receives from using roads.

The second idea is the ability-to-pay principle. In other words, a citizen should pay taxes in relation to his or her ability to pay. Ability-to-pay usually relates to how much a person earns.

Types of Income Taxes

There are three types of income taxes:

- *Proportional Tax* Each taxpayer pays the same proportion of his or her income in taxes.
35 - *Progressive Tax* A person with a higher income pays a higher percentage of taxes.
- *Regressive Tax* A person with a lower income pays a larger percentage of tax. Sales tax on food and clothing is a regressive tax. That's because people with
40 lower income spend a higher percentage of that income on everyday items.

Effects of Taxes

A tax on income is called a **direct tax**. The person who pays it has no choice. An **indirect tax** generally ends up as part of the price a consumer pays for a product.
45 A sales tax is an indirect tax.

The impact of a tax is the financial burden on the payer. The tax impact is great on people who *must* buy a product. Some people must take certain drugs to stay alive. They have no choice but to pay higher prices,
50 even if taxes on the drugs increase.

Review Questions

1. Explain the ability-to-pay principle.

_____

_____

2. What are the three types of income-tax systems?

_____

_____

✓ Reading Check

Number the three types of income taxes in the text.

↻ Target Reading Skill

Analyze Word Parts Use its parts to help you explain the meaning of *impact*.

_____

_____

✓ Reading Check

Bracket the sentences that explain the difference between a direct tax and an indirect tax.

Key Terms

proportional tax (pruh POR shuh nul TAKS) *n.* a system in which people pay equal parts of their income as taxes

progressive tax (pruh GREH siv TAKS) *n.* a system that takes a larger percent of tax from people with higher incomes

regressive tax (rih GREH siv TAKS) *n.* a system that takes a larger percent of tax from people with lower incomes

direct tax (duh REKT TAKS) *n.* a tax on income

indirect tax (in duh REKT TAKS) *n.* a tax that is usually part of the price people pay for a product

Reading Preview

Section 3
Government Policy and Spending

Objectives

1. Discuss spending policy goals.
2. Identify and describe the types of government budgets.
3. Explore the patterns of federal government spending.
4. Explore the patterns of state and local government spending.

 **Target Reading Skill**

Recognize Word Origins Remember that recognizing where a word comes from can help you understand what it means. The Greek words *polis* and *polites* mean "city" and "citizens." The root of both words is *pol-*, meaning "city, state." Many words in English contain this root. *Politics, politician, cosmopolitan,* and *metropolis* are examples.

Use what you know about the Greek root *pol-* to understand the origins and meanings of words you find in this section.

Vocabulary Strategy

Recognizing Signal Words Some words signal generalizations. A generalization is a general statement. Read this sentence:

Many citizens become upset when programs are cut back.

This sentence is a generalization. It makes a general statement about how citizens react to program cutbacks. The word *many* limits the general statement. The chart shows other limiting words that often appear in generalizations.

Words That Signal Generalizations		
some	many	most
sometimes	often	usually
probably	are likely to	may

Look for these signal words as you read. They may point to a generalization.

Section 3 Summary

[1] The government must have goals for spending. It also must create budgets that explain its spending.

Spending-Policy Goals

Policy decisions made by the government are based on public goals. Public goals are often set when we elect
[5] leaders. Our government wants a strong and stable economy. So it sets an economic stabilization <u>policy</u>. The policy has three main goals:

- *Economic Growth* The government promotes economic growth to develop a higher standard of living.
[10] - *Stable Prices* The government keeps prices stable to avoid inflation and deflation.
- *Full Employment* The government wants all citizens who are able to work to have jobs.

Types of Government Budgets

There are three types of federal government budgets:
[15] - With a **balanced budget,** a government does not spend more than the tax revenues it receives.
- With a **deficit budget**, a government spends more than the tax revenue it receives. To do so, it must borrow money.
[20] - With a **surplus budget,** a government spends less than it receives in tax revenues.

   The business cycle shows repeated "ups" and "downs" in the GDP (gross domestic product) over time. The government can use its budget policy to con-
[25] trol these "ups" and "downs." In a "down" time, our nation may have a deficit budget. More government spending will create economic growth and jobs.

Target Reading Skill

Recognize Word Origins Use what you know about the root of *policy* to explain its meaning.

_____

_____

Vocabulary Strategy

Recognizing Signal Words Circle a word under *Spending-Policy Goals* that limits a general statement. What is the statement about?

_____

_____

_____

✓ Reading Check

In the text, number the three main goals of an economic stabilization policy.

✓ Reading Check

Underline the sentence that explains how the government can control the GDP.

Key Terms

balanced budget (BAL unst BUJ it) *n.* a plan in which a nation does not spend more than the tax money it receives

deficit budget (DEH fuh sut BUJ it) *n.* a plan in which a nation spends more than the tax money it receives

surplus budget (SER plus BUJ it) *n.* a plan in which a nation spends less than the tax money it receives

Vocabulary Strategy

Recognizing Signal Words What is the signal word in the underlined statement? How does it limit the meaning of the statement?

_____

_____

_____

✓ Reading Check

Bracket the name of the largest entitlement program.

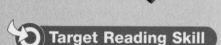

↻ Target Reading Skill

Recognize Word Origins
Underline a word in one of the last two paragraphs that contains the Greek root *pol-*. Then use the root to explain its meaning.

_____

_____

✓ Reading Check

List a situation in which state and local governments might ask for outside assistance.

_____

_____

Federal Government Spending

The federal budget explains spending by the government. It is divided into two kinds of spending. Direct
30 expenditures are for the purchase of goods and services. Transfer payments do not involve the production of any goods or services.

Most transfer payments are for **entitlement programs**. The largest of these programs is Social Security.
35 Other transfer payments are for Medicaid, Medicare, and unemployment help.

A deficit happens when the nation spends more than it receives in tax money. The national debt is the amount of money the government owes to lenders.
40 Many people worry about the size of the national debt. Interest rises as the debt rises. Interest payments mean that there is less money in the budget for other spending choices.

State and Local Government Spending

State and local government money comes from several
45 kinds of taxes. These include sales, property, and income taxes. Some governments also charge tax on personal property, gasoline, and other things.

State and local governments spend a third of their money on education. Other spending includes welfare
50 assistance and highways. Local governments also pay for police, fire protection, water, and sewage.

Often states need federal help, and local governments want state help to pay for these services.

Review Questions

1. List the three types of federal budgets.

_____

_____

2. What are the two kinds of spending in the federal budget? How do they differ?

_____

_____

Key Term

entitlement programs (in TĪ tul munt PRŌ gramz) *n.* programs that give help to people because the law says they must

---

1. Economic growth takes place when the GDP increases without increases in
   A. prices.
   B. employment.
   C. deflation.
   D. all of the above

2. A good tax is
   A. fair.
   B. convenient.
   C. certain.
   D. all of the above

3. A regressive tax takes a larger percentage of tax from people with
   A. higher incomes.
   B. varying incomes.
   C. lower incomes.
   D. moderate incomes.

4. With a surplus budget, a government spends
   A. more than the tax revenue it receives.
   B. the same amount as the tax revenue it receives.
   C. less than the tax revenue it receives.
   D. none of the above

5. Which does not involve transfer payments?
   A. Medicare
   B. Social Security
   C. unemployment assistance
   D. government bonds

Short Answer Question

Which of the five characteristics of a good tax do you think is the most important? Explain your reasoning.

_____

_____

_____

_____

_____

Objectives

1. Discuss the need for order.
2. Learn about the need to protect people's safety and property.
3. Consider the need to protect individual freedoms and promote the common good.
4. Discuss laws and morals.

 **Target Reading Skill**

Identify Contrasts One way to understand a group of ideas is to look at how they differ. When you look at differences among ideas, you are contrasting them.

Read the first paragraph in this section summary. Now look at how rules and laws differ:

Rules	Laws
Everyone does not have to follow all rules.	Everyone must follow all laws.

Identifying differences, or contrasts, between rules and laws helps you understand these ideas. Use contrasting to help you understand other ideas as you read.

Vocabulary Strategy

Using Context Clues Context can help you understand the meanings of words you do not recognize. Context is the words and sentences around a word. Sometimes the context will give a clue to a word's meaning. Read this paragraph.

> Property also includes ideas. Ideas for a new cereal, game, or skateboard are the property of the person or company who thought of them. The idea belongs to that person.

You may not be sure of the meaning of *property* in the first sentence. The examples in the second sentence help to make clear the meaning of *property*.

Section 1 Summary

¹ Rules set standards. They also set punishments for not meeting standards. Society has rules that it expects all people to follow. These rules are called **laws**. Laws are the only rules that everyone has to follow.

The Need for Order

⁵ One purpose of laws is to bring order to society. Laws do this in the following ways:

1. Laws tell people what they may or may not do. Traffic laws are one example.

2. Laws set standards in many areas. Standards for
¹⁰ education are one example. Standards for <u>measuring devices</u> such as supermarket scales are another.

3. Laws tell people how something should be done. They might tell how public officials should be elected, for example.

¹⁵ **4.** Laws help settle serious conflicts. For example, laws provide peaceful ways of settling conflicts in court.

Protecting Safety and Property

Another purpose of laws is to protect people's safety and property. Laws keep people safe by protecting their lives. Physical attacks such as murder are against
²⁰ the law. These actions are punished by prison or even death. Laws also keep people safe by protecting the quality of their lives. Laws especially look after people who are less able to protect themselves. These include children and the elderly.

²⁵ Laws against stealing are one way the government protects your property. Laws also give you rights if your property is damaged. Property is more than just a person's belongings. Any creation can be protected by law. Books, CDs, and games display the copyright
³⁰ symbol ©. Brand names have the ® symbol. That stands for "registered trademark." Copyrights and trademarks are warnings. They say it is against the law to copy something without permission.

Key Term

laws (LOZ) *n.* government rules that all people must follow

© Pearson Education, Inc., Publishing as Pearson Prentice Hall. All rights reserved.

Vocabulary Strategy

Using Context Clues What is a *measuring device*? Put a checkmark next to the word or words that gave a clue to the term's meaning.

_____

_____

✓ Reading Check

Bracket the text that tells how laws bring order to society.

↻ Target Reading Skill

Identify Contrasts CDs and brand-name products are examples of property protected by law. How do they differ?

_____

_____

_____

✓ Reading Check

Underline the word that tells what is protected by laws against stealing.

Target Reading Skill

Identify Contrasts Contrast the two purposes of laws named in the Constitution.

_____

_____

_____

✓ Reading Check

Bracket the sentence that tells how the Constitution protects basic rights and freedoms.

Vocabulary Strategy

Using Context Clues Underline any sentences that give clues to the meaning of *civil disobedience*.

✓ Reading Check

How do people's morals influence their regard for laws?

_____

_____

_____

Protecting Freedom and Society

The Constitution names two other purposes of laws.
35 One is to protect freedom. The other is to protect society.

The Constitution is the land's highest law. It protects basic rights and freedoms by limiting the government's power. The Fourteenth Amendment also guarantees that laws will be applied fairly and equally to everyone.

40 The Constitution's Preamble says that one goal of our government is to promote the general welfare. This means that laws protect not only safety, property, and freedom. They also protect society as a whole.

Laws and Morals

Laws reflect many of our basic values and beliefs. It is
45 our values and **morals**, however, not laws, that hold our nation together.

Most Americans obey laws because they want to do so. Stealing and murder are against the law. But most people believe those actions are wrong anyway. Laws
50 are needed so the government can act against people who act wrongly.

Some people disobey the law if it goes against their beliefs. Breaking a law this way is called <u>civil disobedience</u>. Someone might refuse to pay income tax
55 if they oppose government spending on nuclear weapons. People who take part in civil disobedience accept their punishment. They understand the need for order in society.

Review Questions

1. Describe two ways that laws bring order to society.

_____

_____

2. When do people take part in civil disobedience?

_____

_____

Key Terms

morals (MOR ulz) *n.* beliefs about what is fair and what is right or wrong

civil disobedience (SIV ul dis uh BEE dee uns) *n.* breaking a law without using violence because the law goes against one's beliefs

Reading Preview

Section 2
Where Our Laws Come From

Objectives

1. Learn about laws made by legislatures.
2. Discuss how judges' decisions and agency regulations affect laws.
3. Understand how laws are organized.
4. Learn how laws are changed.

Target Reading Skill

Compare and Contrast Comparing and contrasting is a way to analyze information and understand it better. When you compare, you look at how two or more things are alike. When you contrast, you look at how they differ. As you read this section, compare and contrast different kinds of laws. Use a diagram like this to organize the similarities and differences.

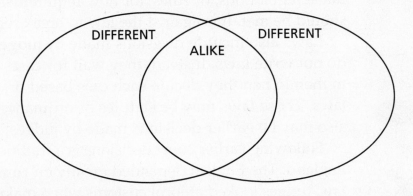

Vocabulary Strategy

Using Context Clues Words and phrases do not always mean exactly what they say. Look at the underlined phrase in this example.

Our laws grow out of common values and beliefs.

You can tell right away that the phrase does not mean that our laws actually grow. Context helps you understand what the phrase means here. The whole sentence suggests that the phrase means "develop from" or "are based on." The image of growing makes the idea more vivid, or colorful.

Section 2 Summary

Target Reading Skill

Compare and Contrast
Write *A* next to text that tells how federal and state laws are alike. Write *D* next to text that tells how they differ.

✓ Reading Check

Underline the sentences that tell the meaning of *statutes* and *ordinances*.

Vocabulary Strategy

Using Context Clues What does *spell out* mean in context?

_____

_____

✓ Reading Check

Bracket the text that tells what common law is.

[1] Our laws have several sources. Some are written by legislatures. Others come from the decisions of judges. Government agencies set others.

Laws Made by Legislatures

Written laws made by legislatures are called **statutes**. [5] *Statute* usually refers to laws made by Congress or by state legislatures. Laws made by city or town councils are often called ordinances.

We all must obey federal laws or statutes. Only people within a state or town must obey laws passed by a [10] state or local government. Laws may differ in different states or towns. That is because one state or community's customs may differ from another's.

Other Effects on Law

Regulations made by government agencies are laws, too. Government agencies <u>spell out</u> the requirements of [15] laws made by Congress and state legislatures. They make regulations, or rules, for how requirements should be met. It is against the law to break regulations.

Laws also include decisions made by judges. Judges do not write laws. Instead, they wait for cases to come [20] to them. Then they decide each case based on existing laws. Those laws may be statutes or ordinances. They also may be earlier decisions made by judges.

Following earlier court decisions is a tradition from England. The English depended greatly on **common** [25] **law**. Judges looked at local customs when making decisions. They also looked at written records of how other judges decided similar cases. Judges followed a decision if it was like the beliefs of their community. Sometimes judges made new decisions based on current customs. [30] These rulings then became examples for future cases.

Key Terms

statutes (STACH ootz) *n.* written laws made by legislatures

common law (KOM un LO) *n.* a body of law based on judges' decisions

How Laws Are Organized

Laws are organized in different ways. Some are organized into a **legal code**. A legal code is a collection of laws. The laws deal with one subject. Traffic laws, for example, are collected in a state's motor vehicle code.
35 A legal code organizes laws so they are current and easy to find.

Legal codes have a long history. The Code of Hammurabi, for example, was made almost 4,000 years ago by the Babylonian king Hammurabi. It contained
40 almost 300 laws. We share some ideas about family laws and criminal laws with this ancient legal code.

Other laws are organized in a constitution. A constitution is a collection of basic rules of government. The United States Constitution is one example. Constitutions
45 say how laws may be made. They say what the government can and cannot do. And they list citizens' rights.

Changing the Law

In our country, citizens <u>have the final word</u> on all laws. We can add, change, or remove a law with the help of our elected representatives. We can make major changes,
50 such as amending the Constitution. We can make minor changes, such as doing away with a local ordinance.

Sometimes laws become out of date. People may also change their ideas about what is fair. The government will usually change a law if most people disagree
55 with it.

Review Questions

1. Where do our laws come from?

_____

_____

2. Whose help do citizens need to change a law?

_____

_____

Key Term
legal code (LEE gul KŌD) *n.* a written collection of laws, often organized by subject

Target Reading Skill

Compare and Contrast Write *SIM* above details that tell how legal codes and constitutions are similar. Write *DIFF* above details that tell how they differ.

✓ Reading Check

Circle the text that tells how constitutions affect laws.

Vocabulary Strategy

Using Context Clues What does the underlined phrase mean?

_____

_____

✓ Reading Check

Underline the text that explains what happens when a law becomes out of date.

Objectives

1. Learn about criminal law.

2. Explore civil law.

3. Discuss where criminal law and civil law meet.

 **Target Reading Skill**

Make Comparisons Comparing two or more situations helps you to see how they are alike. You can compare different kinds of law as you read this section. Use a chart like the one below. List the characteristics of each kind of law. Then look at the two lists. What characteristics do the two kinds of law share?

Characteristics of Criminal Law	Shared Characteristics	Characteristics of Civil Law

Vocabulary Strategy

Using Context Clues Nearby words, phrases, and sentences often give clues to the meanings of words you do not recognize. Sometimes the clue is a synonym. A synonym is a word with the same meaning as another word. Read this passage.

> Rulings in civil cases may also be based on statutes. Most civil statutes sum up the unwritten laws on which judges have based their decisions over the years.

You may not know the word *rulings* in the first sentence. The word *decision* in the next sentence is a synonym for *ruling*. It helps you to understand that rulings are judges' decisions. As you read, try looking for synonyms in context. They can help you understand words you do not know.

Section 3 Summary

¹ Laws affect your life in many ways. Criminal law and civil law are the two main types of laws.

Criminal Law

Criminal law is the group of laws that deal with crimes. A **crime** may be an act, such as stealing. A
⁵ crime may also be failing to do something that the law says people must do. One example is refusing to pay income tax. The main purpose of criminal law is to protect society.

Criminal laws must set fair <u>penalties</u>. Some crimes
¹⁰ deserve bigger penalties than others do. This means that people guilty of the same crime may not get the same punishment. For example, a person who commits a crime for the first time often gets a lighter penalty.

There are two types of crimes:

¹⁵ • A **felony** is a more serious crime. The penalty can be more than one year in prison. Felonies include kidnapping and murder.

• A **misdemeanor** is a less serious crime. The penalty is often a fine. Littering and driving without a
²⁰ license are misdemeanors.

Congress, state legislatures, and local lawmakers can make criminal laws. But no single government leader can make a law that says a certain act is a crime.

Congress decides which types of behavior are
²⁵ crimes anywhere in the United States. Each state legislature can make its own criminal laws. But state laws must not go against federal statutes or the Constitution. Some acts may be against the law in one state but not in another.

Vocabulary Strategy

Using Context Clues
Circle the word that is a synonym for *penalties*.

Target Reading Skill

Make Comparisons How are felonies and misdemeanors alike?

_____

_____

_____

✓ Reading Check

Bracket the text that explains the difference between a felony and a misdemeanor.

Key Terms

criminal law (KRIM uh nul LO) *n.* group of laws that tells which acts are crimes, what happens in court, and how crimes are punished

crime (KRĪM) *n.* an act that is against the law because the government considers it harmful to society

felony (FEL uh nee) *n.* a serious crime, such as murder

misdemeanor (mis dih MEE nuhr) *n.* a less serious crime, such as littering

Vocabulary Strategy

Using Context Clues
Circle the word that is a synonym for *disputes*.

✓ Reading Check

Underline the text that describes the purpose of civil law.

⟳ Target Reading Skill

Make Comparisons
Put a checkmark next to two sentences that tell how criminal law and civil law are alike.

✓ Reading Check

Bracket the text that explains the role of civil law in a case of injury from drunk driving.

Civil Law

30 Civil law is the group of laws that help settle disagreements between people. Civil law offers a way for people to settle <u>disputes</u> in court. An individual or group involved in the conflict must first ask for help. This is done by suing, or taking the matter to court.

35 What happens in court is different in civil cases and criminal cases. The main question in criminal cases is, "Did the accused person commit a crime?" Judges and juries compare the facts of the case with the statute that defines the crime. The main question in civil cases is, 40 "What is a fair way to settle this disagreement?" To decide, judges and juries often look at earlier decisions in similar cases.

Where Criminal Law and Civil Law Meet

Both criminal law and civil law help bring order to society. Both protect people's rights. Criminal law gives 45 government the power to protect society. It takes action against people who commit crimes. Civil law provides a way for individuals or groups to settle conflicts in an orderly manner.

Sometimes a situation involves both criminal and 50 civil law. Suppose a drunk driver who has no insurance injures someone. Criminal law protects society by punishing the driver. But it does not say that the driver must pay the injured person's medical bills. That is where civil law comes in. The injured person can sue. 55 A civil court can make the driver pay the injured person's medical bills.

Review Questions

1. Who has the power to make criminal laws?

_____

_____

2. How do judges and juries make decisions in civil cases?

_____

_____

Key Term
civil law (SIV ul LO) *n.* the group of laws that help to solve disagreements between people

1. Which of the following is *not* a purpose of laws?
   A. to bring order to society
   B. to protest government actions
   C. to protect people's safety
   D. all of the above

2. Which explains why laws may differ in different states?
   A. Congress makes other laws.
   B. Customs may differ.
   C. Laws reflect basic values.
   D. Local laws are called ordinances.

3. Which of the following is involved in making laws?
   A. legislatures
   B. judges
   C. government agencies
   D. all of the above

4. Which of the following is *true*?
   A. People guilty of the same crime always receive the same punishment.
   B. All crimes have maximum and minimum penalties.
   C. Someone who commits a crime for the first time often receives a lighter penalty.
   D. none of the above

5. An individual or group can use civil law to settle a disagreement by
   A. suing.
   B. accusing.
   C. punishing.
   D. ruling.

Short Answer Question

Compare and contrast the ways that laws are organized.

_____

_____

_____

_____

_____

Reading Preview

Section 1
Crime in American Society

Objectives

1. Examine the problem of crime in the United States.
2. Identify and describe the types of crimes.
3. Discuss the causes of crime.

Target Reading Skill

Understand Sequence Understanding the sequence, or order, of events can help you remember them. Some events follow each other in a cause-and-effect chain. One event causes, or leads to, another. Look at this diagram.

Some people cannot earn enough money to support themselves.	They feel that society does not work well for them.	They commit a crime.

As you read, look for causes and effects that show a sequence of events.

Vocabulary Strategy

Using Roots and Suffixes Breaking a word into parts can help you understand its meaning. Roots and suffixes are word parts.

- A root is the base of a word. It has meaning by itself.
- A suffix comes after the root. It changes the root's meaning. It also changes the part of speech of the word.

You will find the words *worsen* and *victimless* in this section. Break each into a root and a suffix to try to learn its meaning.

Root +	Suffix =	Word
worse	-en "become"	worsen
victim	-less "without"	victimless

¹ Crimes and their causes vary. Americans' ideas about what should be done about crime also vary.

The Problem of Crime

In general, there is more crime in cities than in suburbs or rural areas. Poor neighborhoods also often have
⁵ more crime than wealthy ones.

Crime costs people, businesses, and governments billions of dollars each year. Crime makes people afraid. Everyone in society suffers as the problems caused by crime worsen.

The Types of Crimes

¹⁰ There are several major kinds of serious crimes. These are crimes against people or property.

Crimes against people threaten, hurt, or end a person's life. **Assault** is placing someone in fear without making physical contact. This is called **battery** if physi-
¹⁵ cal contact occurs. Killing someone is called homicide. A killing that is done on purpose is called murder.

Crimes against property happen more often than other crimes. Most involve stealing. There are three kinds of stealing:

²⁰ • Larceny is taking anything of value that belongs to another person without using violence.

• Robbery is taking something from another person by force or by threat of violence. Robbery is both a crime against property and a crime against a person.

²⁵ • **Burglary** is when someone breaks into a building and plans to do something against the law inside.

Other kinds of crimes against property include arson and vandalism. Arson is the act of setting fire to

✓ Reading Check

Circle the parts of the country that tend to have higher crime rates.

⟳ Target Reading Skill

Understand Sequence
In the text, mark the effect that happens when crime comes to a neighborhood.

Vocabulary Strategy

Using Roots and Suffixes
Draw a line between the root and the suffix in *worsen.* What does the word mean?

_____

_____

Key Terms

assault (uh SOLT) *n.* making someone afraid without touching them in any way

battery (BAT uh ree) *n.* making someone afraid using physical contact, such as with a weapon

burglary (BER gluh ree) *n.* breaking into a building and planning to do something against the law inside

Vocabulary Strategy

Using Roots and Suffixes
What does *victimless* mean?

_____

_____

✓ Reading Check

Underline the text that tells who the victims of "victimless" crimes are.

Target Reading Skill

Understand Sequence
In the chart, circle what many people think happens as a result of watching violent acts.

✓ Reading Check

Bracket the text in the chart that explains the connection between crime and poverty.

someone's property on purpose. Vandalism is damag-
30 ing property on purpose.

White-collar crimes are nonviolent crimes by office workers for personal or business gain. Fraud is taking someone else's property or money by cheating or lying. **Embezzlement** is stealing money that is in your care.

35 Drug use and gambling are known as "victimless crimes." These are acts that hurt no one except those who commit them.

Crimes against the government include treason and terrorism. **Treason** is going against one's country by
40 helping its enemies or by making war against it. **Terrorism** is a crime in which people or groups of people use violence to get what they want.

The Causes of Crime

Poverty	Some people cannot earn enough money. They may feel society does not work well for them.
Social Change and Changing Values	New technology and changes in the economy bring about changes in society. Values change, too. Some people lose their sense of right and wrong.
Poor Parenting	Children whose parents did not care for them properly may find it hard to control their behavior as adults.
Drug Abuse	People may steal to support a drug habit.
Permissive Courts	Some people say too few criminals are sent to prison. Some say criminals are let out of prison too soon.
Too Few Police	Some say police departments need more money to hire police. They believe that more police will help stop crime.
Violence in the Media	Violence on television, in movies, and in computer games may cause people to become more violent.

Review Questions

1. What is the economic effect of crime?

2. Explain what a white-collar crime is.

Key Terms
embezzlement (im BEH zul munt) *n.* stealing money that has been trusted to your care
treason (TREE zun) *n.* going against your country by helping its enemies or by making war against it
terrorism (TER er ih sum) *n.* using, or saying you will use, violence in order to get what you want

Objectives

1. Describe the arrest and pre-trial process.
2. Learn about going to trial.
3. Learn about correctional institutions.
4. Discuss challenges facing the criminal justice system.
5. Analyze proposals for fighting crime.

Target Reading Skill

Recognize Words That Signal Sequence Signal words point out relationships between ideas or events. Some words that signal sequence include *before, during, after, when, then,* and *at this time.*

Look for words that signal sequence as you read. These words will help you understand the order of events. When you know the order of events, you can write them in a chart like this.

Vocabulary Strategy

Using Roots and Suffixes A suffix added to a root changes its meaning. It also often changes the word's part of speech. Parts of speech include nouns, pronouns, verbs, adjectives, and adverbs. Consider the suffix *-ant*, which means "person who." It is often added to a root that is a verb. The root and the suffix make up a word that is a noun. Here are some examples.

Verb		Suffix		Noun
serve	+	ant	=	servant
attend	+	ant	=	attendant
defend	+	ant	=	defendant

You will find the word *defendant* in this section. Use what you know about its root and suffix to figure out its meaning.

Section 2 Summary

Target Reading Skill

Recognize Words That Signal Sequence Underline words that signal the order of events in the first two paragraphs under *The Arrest and Pre-Trial Process.*

Vocabulary Strategy

Using Roots and Suffixes What does *defendant* mean?

_____

_____

✓ Reading Check

Underline the sentence that explains why a defendant would agree to engage in plea bargaining.

[1] The criminal justice system protects society against those who break the law. It also protects the rights of people accused of crimes.

The Arrest and Pre-Trial Process

To arrest a person, the police must have **probable**
[5] **cause**. A person can also be arrested if the police have a **warrant**. During the arrest, police must give the Miranda warning. After the arrest, the person has the right to call a lawyer. Then he or she is placed in a jail cell. The case is given to a prosecutor.

[10] Soon after the arrest, the person appears in court. The person is now called the <u>defendant</u>. The defendant's lawyer is called the defense attorney.

At the first appearance in court, the judge may set **bail.** The defendant can remain in jail without bail if
[15] the judge decides he or she is dangerous to society.

The Constitution says that a grand jury must review cases involving serious federal crimes. The grand jury decides if there is probable cause. The grand jury may either return an **indictment** or refuse to indict. A defen-
[20] dant who is indicted must appear in court for a felony **arraignment**.

Most criminal cases never go to trial because the defendant pleads guilty. When a defendant knows that the evidence is strong, he or she might make a deal
[25] with the prosecutor. This is called **plea bargaining**. It gives the defendant a milder punishment.

Key Terms

probable cause (PROB uh bul KOZ) *n.* a good reason to believe that a suspect has been involved in a crime

warrrant (WOR unt) *n.* a legal paper, issued by a court, allowing police to make an arrest or search

bail (BAYL) *n.* money that a defendant gives the court as a kind of promise that he or she will return for the trial

indictment (in DĪT munt) *n.* a charge against a person accused of a crime

arraignment (uh RAYN munt) *n.* a court hearing in which the defendant is charged with a crime and pleads guilty, not guilty, or no contest

plea bargaining (PLEE BAR gih ning) *n.* agreeing to plead guilty in exchange for a lesser charge or a lighter sentence

Going to Trial

Jury selection is the first step in a trial. Rights granted by the Constitution tell how a trial is run. The trial must be speedy and public. Its purpose is to decide if
30 the defendant is innocent or guilty.

Statements made by witnesses are usually the most important evidence in a trial. A witness may be a person who saw the crime, the defendant or victim, or anyone who knows something about the defendant,
35 victim, or crime.

At the end, attorneys for each side make closing arguments. The judge gives directions to the jury. A jury must decide if the defendant is guilty beyond a reasonable doubt.

Correctional Institutions

40 A person convicted of a crime enters the corrections system. He or she may go to a treatment program, jail, or prison. People convicted of serious crimes are usually sent to prisons. In prison, they are called inmates. With good behavior, an inmate may get **parole**.

Challenges Facing the System

45 Our criminal justice system must deal with a huge number of people. There are not enough judges and other employees in many courts to handle all those waiting for trial. Prisons are overcrowded, too.

Proposals for Fighting Crime

Many people suggest attacking causes of crime such as
50 poverty. Others want to be harder on criminals. Many people want the death penalty for serious crimes. Others fear that innocent people might be put to death.

Review Questions

1. Name the three types of correctional institutions.

_____

2. What are two ideas for fighting crime?

_____

Key Term

parole (puh RŌL) *n.* letting an inmate go free to serve the rest of his or her sentence outside of prison

---

✓ **Reading Check**

In the text, number the different people attorneys call as witnesses in a trial.

↻ **Target Reading Skill**

Recognize Words That Signal Sequence Put a check mark above the words that signal the beginning and the ending of a trial in which the defendant is found guilty.

✓ **Reading Check**

Circle the reason why the criminal justice system would parole a criminal.

✓ **Reading Check**

Underline the sentences that tell what problems face the prison system.

✓ **Reading Check**

What are the arguments for and against the death penalty?

_____

_____

_____

Objectives

1. Discuss the history of juvenile courts.

2. Describe juvenile court procedure.

3. Consider possibilities for strengthening juvenile justice.

Target Reading Skill

Recognize Words That Signal Sequence Various words signal the order of steps in a process. These groups of signal words often appear in descriptions of processes.

first, second, third   first, next, last

first, then, finally   before, during, after

This section describes steps in the court process for young people who have committed crimes. Look for words that signal the order of steps in the process. These words may appear separately or in groups.

Vocabulary Strategy

Using Roots and Suffixes Certain suffixes make words adjectives. An adjective is a word that describes something. The suffixes *-ile, -il* and *-al, -ial* form adjectives, for example. These suffixes have the meaning "having to do with."

You will find the words *juvenile* and *initial* in this section. Try to figure out their meanings based on what you know about their roots and suffixes.

Word =	Root +	Suffix
juvenile	juven- "young person"	-ile "having to do with"
initial	init- "beginning"	-ial "having to do with"

Section 3 Summary

Children accused of crimes were treated like adults until the late 1800s. Then a separate justice system was created for young people.

Juvenile Courts

Juvenile courts are state courts set aside for young people, or juveniles. Their goal is to help juveniles in trouble, not to punish them. Most states say that a juvenile is a person under the age of 18.

A youth thought to have broken a criminal law goes before a juvenile court. A juvenile found guilty of a crime is called a **delinquent**. Children may also go to court on other charges. These include running away, disobeying, or truancy. Truancy is skipping school without permission. These are not crimes. They are illegal only for young people. A youth found guilty of one of them is a **status offender**. That is a youth judged to be beyond the control of parents or a guardian.

Juvenile Court Procedure

Jenna Williams is 16 years old. Suppose she is arrested for shoplifting. First, the police must decide what to do with Jenna. They might return her to her parents. They might give her case to a social service agency. That is a group that helps children and families. Jenna has shoplifted before. She also has run away from home before. For these reasons, the police take her to a county detention home, or juvenile hall.

Next, Jenna goes through an informal court process called "intake." A social worker questions Jenna. The social worker also looks at her past record and family situation. The case may be dismissed. Then the juvenile is sent home or directed to a social service agency. Jenna has a past record. So the social worker sends her case to the next step in juvenile court.

Key Terms

delinquent (dih LIN kwunt) *n.* a young person found guilty of a crime

status offender (STAT us uh FEN der) *n.* a young person found guilty of running away, disobeying, or skipping school

---

Vocabulary Strategy

Using Roots and Suffixes What does *juvenile* mean in the underlined phrase?

_____

_____

✓ **Reading Check**

Underline the text that explains why the juvenile court system was created.

↻ **Target Reading Skill**

Recognize Words That Signal Sequence Underline words that signal the order of steps in juvenile court procedure.

Using Roots and Suffixes
What does *initial* mean?

_____

_____

✓ Reading Check

In the first two paragraphs on this page, number the steps that Jenna goes through during this part of the juvenile justice system.

✓ Reading Check

Circle the text that describes the flaws people have found in the juvenile justice system.

The <u>initial</u> hearing is next. A judge makes sure that a law was broken. He or she makes sure there is good evidence that the youth did it. The judge decides that
35 there is probable cause to believe that Jenna stole makeup. The judge sends her back to juvenile hall.

Then the adjudicatory hearing is held. It takes the place of a trial. It is not public. After the hearing, the judge makes a decision. The judge finds Jenna to be a
40 delinquent under the juvenile law of her state.

The dispositional hearing is next. First, the judge considers the youth's school situation, family, and past behavior. Then the judge decides on a sentence. The young person might go to a state institution. He or she
45 might go to a group home or treatment program. Probation is also possible. Probation lets a person go free. But he or she is supervised by a court official called a probation officer.

Aftercare is the last step. Each juvenile is given a
50 parole officer. The parole officer gives the young person advice and information about school, jobs, and other needed services.

Strengthening Juvenile Justice

Some people think the juvenile system does not work well. They say judges are overworked. They say judges
55 make quick decisions without knowing much about children. Others say the system is too easy on juveniles. Some argue that juvenile courts should be done away with. They say it is in the best interests of a youth to go to trial in a criminal court. A defendant's
60 rights are better protected there.

There are many successful programs for delinquents. Residential treatment centers are community-based programs. Juveniles live in small group homes instead of large state institutions. Psychologists and
65 social workers help them change their behavior.

Review Questions

1. What is a juvenile court?

_____

_____

2. Why does Jenna go to juvenile court?

_____

_____

Chapter 20 Assessment

1. Which is *not* a crime against property?
   A. larceny
   B. arson
   C. homicide
   D. all of the above

2. Which is considered a cause of crime in the United States?
   A. poor parenting
   B. drug abuse
   C. poverty
   D. all of the above

3. A grand jury decides whether
   A. there is probable cause for the crime.
   B. the defendant is innocent or guilty.
   C. the defendant will go to prison.
   D. to set bail or hold the defendant in jail.

4. What is usually the most important evidence in a trial?
   A. answers given by the defendant
   B. statements made by witnesses
   C. arguments made by attorneys
   D. directions given to the jury

5. A juvenile who is found guilty of a crime is a
   A. runaway.
   B. delinquent.
   C. guardian.
   D. misdemeanor.

Short Answer Question

Describe what a jury does in a trial.

_____

_____

_____

_____

_____

Objectives

1. Learn about the principles of civil law.

2. Discuss some types of civil cases.

3. Explore the wide range of civil cases.

Target Reading Skill

Recognizing Multiple Causes A cause makes something happen. An effect is what happens. Some events have more than one cause. Consider some of the causes of civil court cases, for example.

Use a diagram like this to list multiple causes as you read.

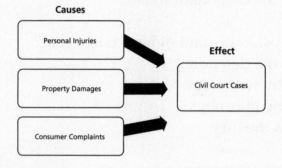

Vocabulary Strategy

Recognizing Word Origins Many English words come from other languages. The words *equity* and *mental* in this section come from Latin. The words *typical* and *physical* come from Greek. The chart shows the meaning of the roots of these words:

Root	Meaning
equ-	equal, even
ment-	mind
typ-	having the characteristics of
physi-	nature, growth

As you read, use your knowledge of these roots and the context to understand what the words mean.

Section 1 Summary

In a <u>typical year</u>, Americans file more than a million **lawsuits**. A civil case, like a criminal case, always has a plaintiff and a defendant. In a criminal case, the plaintiff is always the government. The defendant is the person
5 or persons accused of a crime. In a civil case, the plaintiff is usually an individual. The defendant may be an individual, group, business, or even a government body.

Principles of Civil Law

The main purpose of civil law is to settle disagreements fairly. Civil courts depend on the principles of
10 compensation and equity.

Under civil law, a person has a right to **compensation**. Suppose someone damages your bicycle. You have to pay $45 to fix it. The person refuses to pay you. So you take him or her to court. The judge rules that the
15 person must pay $45. This money is called **damages**.

Not every problem can be settled by money. Sometimes courts turn to **equity**. Suppose that fumes come from a nearby factory. Making the factory owners pay money to everyone in town will not stop the smell.
20 The case has to be settled in a different way. Under the rules of equity, a court may issue an **injunction**. For instance, a court might order the factory to stop the fumes. Damages make up for past injuries. An injunction prevents future harm.

© Pearson Education, Inc., Publishing as Pearson Prentice Hall. All rights reserved.

Vocabulary Strategy

Recognizing Word Origins Is a typical year like or unlike other years?

_____

_____

✓ Reading Check

Underline the text that tells the main purpose of civil law.

Key Terms

lawsuits (LO soots) *n.* cases in which a court is asked to settle a disagreement

compensation (kahm pun SAY shun) *n.* money that makes up for harm caused by another person's acts

damages (DAM ih juz) *n.* money paid to try to make up for a loss

equity (EH kwuh tee) *n.* the use of general rules of fairness to settle conflicts

injunction (in JUNK shun) *n.* an order to do or not do a certain act

Vocabulary Strategy

Recognizing Word Origins
Which of the underlined words describes suffering of the body? Which describes suffering of the mind?

_____

_____

Target Reading Skill

Recognizing Multiple Causes In the text, number two causes of probate cases.

✓ Reading Check

Circle the name of the type of civil case that might involve someone who died.

✓ Reading Check

Bracket the sentence that describes the goal of the settlement of all civil law cases.

Some Types of Civil Cases

25 • Personal injury cases can involve both <u>physical</u> and <u>mental</u> suffering. For example, relatives of someone killed in an accident may want compensation for their mental suffering.

• Property cases often involve damage. The plaintiff
30 must prove that the defendant did the damage on purpose or was careless.

• Consumer cases involve buyers and sellers. Many laws set basic rules for **contracts**. Conflicts happen if a buyer or seller does not follow the contract.

35 • Housing cases involve landlords and tenants. A tenant usually signs a lease. This agreement states rights and responsibilities. Civil law allows a tenant or a landlord to take steps if the other does not follow the lease.

40 • Domestic cases involve families. Most of them relate to divorce.

• Probate cases involve the property of a person who has died. Sometimes there is no will. Or there are questions about whether a will can be trusted.

The Wide Range of Civil Cases

45 Civil courts find ways to settle any disagreement. For some cases, the courts use compensation. For others, the courts use equity. Sometimes the courts combine the two. All civil cases have something in common. Their goal is to make a fair settlement and to place
50 responsibility where it belongs.

Review Questions

1. Name the two main principles that civil courts use to settle conflicts.

_____

2. What different relationships are involved in consumer and housing cases?

_____

_____

Key Term

contract (KĂN trakt) *n.* agreements between buyers and sellers

---

Objectives

1. Learn about preparing for a civil trial
2. Discuss juries and verdicts in civil trials
3. Understand problems in the civil courts
4. Appreciate the need for alternatives

Target Reading Skill

Understand Effects An effect is what happens as a result of a specific cause or factor. Read this paragraph.

> Court delays are the result of various factors. There are not enough judges to handle the growing number of cases. Time is needed to gather evidence. Selecting a jury can take a long time because both sides have to approve jury members. Court rules make it possible for lawyers to delay trials in ways that will help their side.

This paragraph explains that court delays are a result of various factors. These factors make court delays happen. Court delays are an effect of the factors listed. As you read, note what happens as the result of other causes or factors.

Vocabulary Strategy

Recognizing Word Origins Knowing a word's origins can help you understand its meaning. You will come across the words *subpoena* and *verdict* in this section. Both have Latin origins. The Latin phrase *sub poena* means "under penalty or punishment." *Verdict* can be traced to the Latin word *verus*. The word *verus* means "true." This information will help you understand these words when you find them in your reading.

¹ Civil procedure is the process that takes a case through the civil justice system. The federal and state courts have rules about how a disagreement must be brought to trial. The purpose of these rules is to settle disputes ⁵ in a fair and orderly way.

Preparing for a Civil Trial

A civil lawsuit begins with a **complaint** filed with a court. The complaint describes the problem. It also suggests a solution. This may be damages, equity, or both. The person who files the complaint becomes the ¹⁰ plaintiff. The defendant learns about the lawsuit by receiving a copy of the complaint and a **summons**. The defendant files an **answer**. In the answer, the defendant either admits or denies responsibility.

The next step is for the parties to gather evidence. ¹⁵ The parties are the two sides of the case. Information is gathered through **discovery**. Discovery makes sure that the plaintiff, defendant, and lawyers know of any evidence that might be presented at the trial.

One method of discovery is a <u>subpoena</u>. ²⁰ Information may also be gathered by asking questions in a **deposition**. A court reporter writes down what is said. Lawyers use depositions to find out what witnesses will say in court. Questions can also be mailed to people. They must answer them in writing. Both ²⁵ depositions and written answers must be truthful.

Vocabulary Strategy

Recognizing Word Origins Think about what you know about the origins of the word *subpoena*. Why does someone who receives a subpoena take it seriously?

_____

_____

_____

✓ Reading Check

Underline the sentence in the first paragraph that explains what civil procedure is.

Target Reading Skill

Understand Effects Put a checkmark next to an effect of the defendant's receiving a summons.

Key Terms

complaint (kum PLAYNT) *n.* a legal document that charges someone with having caused harm

summons (SUM unz) *n.* an order to appear in court

answer (AN ser) *n.* a written response to a complaint

discovery (dis KUV uh ree) *n.* the process of gathering evidence before a trial

subpoena (suh PEE nuh) *n.* a court order to produce a witness or document

deposition (dep uh ZISH un) *n.* the record of answers to questions asked before a trial

Juries and Verdicts in Civil Trials

Civil and criminal trials are alike in some ways. There are also important differences. The chart shows some of these.

Differences Between Criminal and Civil Trials	
Criminal Trials	**Civil Trials**
More risk is involved for the defendant, since sentences are more serious.	Less risk is involved for the parties.
The defendant has the right to a jury.	Parties may have a jury when federal cases involve more than $20 and state and local cases involve usually more than $2,000.
The verdict is based on a unanimous vote	The verdict is not always a unanimous decision.
The government must prove the defendant s guilt beyond a reasonable doubt.	The judge or jury decides which side has presented the more convincing and reasonable evidence.

Problems in the Civil Courts

There are problems with the civil court system.

30 • Delays are one problem. There are not enough judges to handle the number of cases. Selecting a jury can take a long time. Court rules make it possible for lawyers to delay trials in ways that help their side.

• The cost of trials is another problem. Costs include
35 lawyers' fees, filing fees for court papers, and payments for expert witnesses.

Most lawsuits never go to trial. Plaintiffs often drop cases if they have little chance of winning. Sometimes the high cost of a trial causes parties to settle the mat-
40 ter out of court.

Review Questions

1. In a civil case, what is the purpose of discovery?

2. In a civil case, how does the judge or jury make a decision?

Vocabulary Strategy

Recognizing Word Origins If *ver-* means "true," what is a verdict?

_____

_____

_____

✓ Reading Check

In the chart, circle the amount of money that usually needs to be involved to have a jury trial in state and local courts.

✓ Reading Check

Underline the text that tells why plaintiffs sometimes drop cases before trial.

Section 3
Choices in Civil Justice

Objectives

1. Discuss avoiding civil trials.
2. Learn about cutting the cost of civil trials.
3. Understand the debate over large awards.
4. Appreciate the decision to sue or not to sue.

 **Target Reading Skill**

Identify Cause and Effect A cause makes something happen. An effect is what happens. Identifying causes and effects can help you understand relationships between events or situations. Read this sentence.

> The high cost of civil trials leads some people to settle conflicts out of court.

The high cost of trials is the cause. It makes something happen. What happens is that some people settle conflicts out of court. That is an effect of the high cost.

Look for causes and effects as you read this section. Identifying them will help you understand how situations or events are connected.

Vocabulary Strategy

Recognizing Word Origins Knowing something about a word's origins often helps you understand its meaning. You will find the words *arbitrator* and *mediator* in this section. Both have Latin roots. Both have the same Latin suffix. Look at their meanings

Root +	Suffix =	Word
arbitrat- "hear, judge, decide"	-or "someone who does"	arbitrator
mediat- "middle"		mediator

Use this information to help you understand these words as you read.

Section 3 Summary

1 There are ways to settle disagreements without a civil trial. There are also ways to save time and money in a trial.

Avoiding Civil Trials

There are various ways to keep from going to trial.
5 One way is for people to come to an agreement on their own. Sometimes they can bring in a third person to help. Mediation, arbitration, and "rent-a-judge" programs all use a third person to avoid a trial.

Mediation brings people together to settle their dis-
10 agreement. The third party is a <u>mediator</u>. The mediator does not make a decision. He or she listens to both sides and helps them reach a compromise.

In **arbitration,** a person listens to both sides. This person—called an arbitrator—makes a decision. He or
15 she is usually an expert on the subject of the case. So it takes less time to decide. The federal government and more than 40 states require that such decisions be obeyed.

People can also settle conflicts through private judges.
20 The two sides hire a person to hear and decide the case. This process is sometimes called "rent-a-judge."

Referees and mock trials may also settle conflicts.

- A judge can appoint a referee. The referee listens to both sides. Then he or she makes recommendations
25 to the judge. The judge makes the final decision.

- A mock trial shows how a case might be settled in a civil trial. Lawyers for each side summarize their case before a jury. The jury gives a verdict that is not official. The two sides do not have to follow it. A mock
30 trial often helps parties compromise.

Target Reading Skill

Identify Cause and Effect Circle an effect of mediation, arbitration, and rent-a-judge programs.

Vocabulary Strategy

Recognizing Word Origins What is a mediator? What is an arbitrator? Use what you know about the origins of these words to explain.

_____

_____

_____

✓ Reading Check

Bracket the sentence that tells what mediators do.

Key Terms

mediation (mee dee AY shun) *n.* the use of a third party to help settle a conflict

arbitration (ar buh TRAY shun) *n.* a legal decision by a third person that parties must obey

Cutting the Cost of Trials

There are good reasons for having civil trials. Sometimes one or both sides will not compromise. They may not want an arbitrator. A plaintiff may think he or she can get a better settlement by having a trial.

35   A trial does not always involve a lot of time and money. **Small claims court** can help lower the cost. People disagreeing about a small amount of money often get a quick, inexpensive decision. Both parties tell their stories to a judge.

The Debate over Large Awards

40 Some people argue that large awards are needed to make up for serious losses. Others argue that consumers end up paying these large awards. That is because businesses raise prices to cover their costs, and insurance companies raise their rates.

45   Efforts have been made to limit awards. First, judges usually have the power to reduce the amount of an award made by a jury. Laws also limit awards in certain cases.

To Sue or Not to Sue?

The civil justice system is full of cases. Civil trials are 50 often long and costly. People should think carefully about the best way to settle a conflict. Going to court may not be best. Other methods, such as mediation and arbitration, may work instead.

Review Questions

1. How does a mock trial help parties in a disagreement?

_____

_____

2. What should people involved in a conflict do before going to court?

_____

_____

Key Term

small claims court (smôl klāms kôrt) *n.* a civil court that people use when the amount of money involved is small, usually not more than $3,000

Chapter 21 Assessment

1. In a civil case, the plaintiff is usually
   A. the government.
   B. an individual.
   C. a group.
   D. a business.

2. The two sides of a case are called
   A. verdicts.
   B. referees.
   C. awards.
   D. parties.

3. Who receives a summons in a civil case?
   A. the defendant
   B. the plaintiff
   C. the jury
   D. the judge

4. In a civil case, the verdict may be
   A. a unanimous decision.
   B. the decision of three-fourths of the jury.
   C. given by the judge.
   D. any one of the above

5. Storefront law offices
   A. pay all the costs of going to court.
   B. settle small claims up to $3,000.
   C. provide legal services for low prices.
   D. all of the above

Short Answer Question

What are three ways to avoid a civil trial? How does each work?

_____

_____

_____

_____

_____

Section 1
The Role of Political Parties

Objectives

1. Learn about how political parties help government.
2. Discuss how political parties help citizens.

Target Reading Skill

Reread or Read Ahead Rereading and reading ahead can help you understand words and ideas in the text. You can reread to look for connections among words and sentences. You can read ahead to see whether a word or idea is explained further on.

Read the first paragraph under the heading *How Parties Help Government*, for example. Perhaps you do not understand the idea of candidates. You can get a clearer understanding by reading ahead. The next paragraph explains that candidates are chosen by political parties to run for various public offices.

Vocabulary Strategy

Using Context Clues The words, phrases, and sentences that surround a word are the context. Context can give clues to the meanings of words you do not know. Look at this example.

> Most offices are partisan. The candidates for these offices run as members of political parties.

You may not know the meaning of the word *partisan* in the first sentence. But the second sentence provides clues to its meaning. It mentions political parties. It also says that candidates for partisan offices are members of political parties. The second sentence gives you a clue that *partisan* means "having to do with or belonging to a political party."

Look for context clues to the meanings of words you do not recognize as you read. You may find clues in nearby words, phrases, and sentences.

Section 1 Summary

¹ People can act together to affect the government. People who think alike may form a **political party**. Political parties are important. <u>They try to get their members elected.</u> That way they can affect policies and ⁵ programs. They help at the local, state, and national levels.

How Parties Help Government

Political parties find candidates and **nominate** them. Some public offices are nonpartisan. That means people do not run as part of a political party. This is true ¹⁰ for many offices in local government. But most offices are <u>partisan</u>. People run as part of a political party. If elected, they try to carry out their party's programs.

Political parties set goals for the government. Each party takes a stand on issues in its **platform**. A platform ¹⁵ is made up of **planks**. Party members who get elected often turn these planks into government programs.

Party members in Congress choose leaders. Some are called majority and minority floor leaders. Others are called whips. These leaders help to make laws. ²⁰ Parties work in a similar way in state legislatures. They also offer leadership in the executive branch. The executive often appoints party members to high positions.

Political parties also keep an eye on each other. A party points out when the other party does not keep its ²⁵ promises. It also makes sure that members of the party in power are honest and work hard.

Target Reading Skill

Reread or Read Ahead Read the underlined sentence. Then read ahead to find the paragraph that describes how political parties do this. Put a check mark next to the paragraph.

Vocabulary Strategy

Using Context Clues Circle the context clues that help you figure out the meaning of the underlined word.

✓ Reading Check

Circle the text that explains how parties play a "watchdog" role in government.

Key Terms

political party (puh LIT ih kul PAR tee) *n.* a group that wishes to affect the government by getting its members elected

nominate (NAHM uh nayt) *v.* to name people to run for office

platform (PLAT form) *n.* a statement of a party's position on major issues

planks (PLANGKS) *n.* statements of a party's position on each specific issue

_____

_____

_____

Vocabulary Strategy

Using Context Clues What do you think pamphlets are? What words or phrases in context helped you to understand this?

_____

_____

_____

✓ Reading Check

Circle the text that tells why parties canvass and provide information to voters.

How Parties Help Citizens

Political parties help people in many ways.

- Political parties give citizens a way to be heard. They can help people to share their wants, needs, and ideas at the local level. At the state and national levels, party members help to create the party platform. They build a platform by debating and deciding issues.

- Political parties provide citizens with information. They supply facts and figures. They share party views on issues and arrange meetings with candidates. Parties inform citizens. They use the mail, newspapers, radio, and television. Party members and volunteers also **canvass**. They give information to convince people to vote for their candidate.

- Parties offer citizens ways to get involved. A party needs the help of many people to be a success. This is especially true at election time. Volunteers write letters and hand out <u>pamphlets</u>. They make phone calls. They raise money and hold events. On election day, they remind people to vote. They may even drive voters to the polls.

It is both your right and your responsibility to participate in government. Working through a party is one way to play your citizen role.

Review Questions

1. What are four ways political parties help government?

_____

_____

2. Name two ways that parties help to inform citizens.

_____

_____

_____

Key Term

canvass (KAN vus) _v._ go door-to-door handing out information and asking people which candidates they support

Reading Preview

Section 2
Our Two-Party System

Objectives

1. Discuss a brief history of political parties.

2. Understand the role of third parties.

3. Explore the characteristics of today's parties.

4. Learn about changes in party strength.

Target Reading Skill

Paraphrase Paraphrasing can help you understand what you read. When you paraphrase, you restate information in your own words. You might paraphrase the first paragraph in the section summary like this:

> There is no mention of political parties in the Constitution. Americans set up these groups on their own. We have had political parties since our country was formed.

Try paraphrasing as you read. Restate or "say back" the information in each paragraph.

Vocabulary Strategy

Using Context Clues You can usually use context to figure out the meaning of a word you do not recognize while reading. Context is the words and sentences around the word. They often give clues to the word's meaning. Use a context clue to figure out the meaning of *shifted* in this paragraph.

> The Republican Party was the major party until the Great Depression of the 1930s. Power <u>shifted</u> from one party to another in 1932. Franklin D. Roosevelt was elected president that year. Roosevelt was a Democrat.

The first sentence gives a clue. It tells you that the Republican Party was the major party until the 1930s. The last two sentences also give clues. They tell you that a Democrat was elected president in 1932. This information suggests that the meaning of shifted is "moved" or "changed." As you read, be sure to look at the context of words you do not know.

Section 2 Summary

Vocabulary Strategy

Using Context Clues What do you think *rivals* means? What clues to its meaning did you find?

_____

_____

✓ Reading Check

Who was the founder of the Democratic-Republican Party?

_____

Target Reading Skill

Paraphrase How would you paraphrase the underlined sentence?

_____

_____

_____

✓ Reading Check

Underline the text that explains how Ross Perot influenced the 1992 election.

¹ The Constitution does not talk about political parties, but Americans have formed these groups since our nation was born.

A Brief History

Alexander Hamilton led our first political party. This ⁵ was the Federalist Party. The Federalists wanted the national government to be strong. They began to lose power in the early 1800s.

Thomas Jefferson began the Democratic-Republican Party. That party did not want a strong national gov-¹⁰ ernment. Its members wanted the states to remain strong. In 1828, the party became the Democratic Party. Then the Whig party formed in 1834. They opposed the Democrats. Whigs and Democrats were <u>rivals</u> until the 1850s.

¹⁵ Today's two-party system began in 1854. The Republican Party was formed then. It replaced the Whigs. Groups that were against slavery formed it.

Republicans were the majority party for a long time. They ran the nation from the Civil War until the Great ²⁰ Depression. Then Franklin D. Roosevelt was elected President. That was in 1932. He was a Democrat. For the rest of the 20th century, power went back and forth.

The Role of Third Parties

Third parties are important, too. They are often formed in election years. They rarely win major elections. <u>Their ²⁵ candidates can change an election's outcome.</u> They can take votes away from another party. They bring up new ideas, too. For example, Ross Perot made the national debt an issue in the 1992 election. That made other candidates talk more about the problem.

Characteristics of Today's Parties

³⁰ Our two major parties have different traditions. They also see the role of government differently. The Democrats want the federal government to be in charge of many social programs. The Republicans want to reduce the power of the federal government.

³⁵ The two major parties are set up in a similar way. Both have local, state, and national groups. Each com-

munity is divided into **precincts**. Volunteers in each precinct try to get party members to vote.

Delegates to the convention write the national party
40 platform. They nominate the candidates for President and Vice President. The national committee helps the candidates for President and Vice President run their campaigns. It works to elect members of Congress. It also raises money for the party.

Supporting a Party

45 If you feel strongly about an issue, then you are likely to choose a party that shares your view. You may like certain candidates and agree with their views. That may draw you to their party. Family, friends, and teachers may also influence you.

Changes in Party Strength

50 Political parties are not as strong as they once were. There is less **patronage** now. The role of parties in campaigns has changed. Candidates used to need money from their party to run their campaigns. Party support is still a big help, but candidates today can raise their
55 own funds. Voter loyalty has changed. Only 40 percent of people now vote a **straight ticket**. Many people today vote a **split ticket**. That means candidates cannot count on the support of all their party members. And many people today are **independent voters**.

Review Questions

1. How do Democratic and Republican views of the role of government differ?

_____

2. Why do fewer people vote a straight ticket today?

_____

Key Terms

precincts (PREE singks) *n.* voting areas
patronage (PAY trun ij) *n.* system in which party leaders do favors for loyal supporters
straight ticket (STRAYT TIK it) *n.* practice of voting for candidates of only one party
split ticket (SPLIT TIK it) *n.* practice of voting for candidates of more than one party on the same ballot
independent voters (in dih PEN dunt VŌT erz) *n.* people who do not support one particular party

Vocabulary Strategy

Using Context Clues Read the two sentences that contain underlined words. How does the context show that these words have similar meanings?

_____

_____

Target Reading Skill

Paraphrase Restate the information in *Supporting a Party* in your own words.

_____

_____

_____

✓ Reading Check

Circle the sentences that tell what takes place at the national party conventions.

✓ Reading Check

Bracket the text that explains reasons why a person chooses to support a party.

✓ Reading Check

Underline the sentence that explains how split-ticket voting affects candidates for office.

Objectives

1. Discuss nominating candidates.
2. Learn about choosing presidential candidates.

Target Reading Skill

Summarize Summarizing helps you to understand what you have read. It also helps you to study it. A good summary

- includes the main points and important details.
- presents information in the correct order.
- shows connections among points and details.

As you read, stop sometimes to summarize. Review the text you have just read. Then restate the main points briefly in your own words and in the correct order.

Vocabulary Strategy

Using Context Clues Context is words and phrases around a word. It is also sentences and even paragraphs around the word. Information contained in nearby sentences and paragraphs can help make the meaning of a word clear. Look at this example.

> For some offices, a candidate may need to file a nominating petition. A number of voters must sign the petition. They say that they support the nomination by signing this document.

You may be unsure about the meaning of *petition* in the first sentence. The next sentence tells you that it is something people sign. The sentence after that tells you that it is a document. The last sentence suggests that people sign a petition to show their support for something. The sentences provide many clues to the meaning of *petition*.

Section 3 Summary

¹ The most important role of a political party is to nominate a candidate. Many candidates are chosen at party conventions.

Nominating Candidates

The nominating process may be simple. Or it may be
⁵ complex. It depends on the office. The simplest way to become a candidate is **self-nomination**. That is possible for many local offices. A **write-in candidate** is a kind of self-nominated candidate.

A few states select candidates or choose delegates at
¹⁰ a **caucus**. Caucuses used to be closed to ordinary party members. This gave great power to a few party leaders. A few state and local caucuses are still held today. But they are different. Most are open meetings.

Most candidates for state and federal office are cho-
¹⁵ sen in a direct primary. A **direct primary** is an election. During it, party members choose candidates. The person who receives the most votes is the party's nominee.

Most states use one of two kinds of direct primary. Voters in a **closed primary** must be registered as party
²⁰ members. They may vote only in that party's primary. For example, only Democrats may vote in the primary to choose a Democratic candidate. In an **open primary**, voters do not have to choose a party before voting, but they may vote in only one party's primary.

Target Reading Skill

Summarize What is the main point of the bracketed paragraph?

_____

_____

_____

Vocabulary Strategy

Using Context Clues What does the word *complex* mean? Underline any context clues that helped you understand its meaning.

_____

_____

_____

✓ Reading Check

Circle the words that describe how most candidates for state and federal office are now chosen.

Key Terms

self-nomination (self nom uh NAY shun) *n.* saying that you are running for office

write-in candidate (RĪT in KAN dih dayt) *n.* someone who asks voters to write his or her name on the ballot

caucus (KO kus) *n.* a meeting of party leaders to discuss issues or choose candidates

direct primary (dih REKT PRĪ mayr ee) *n.* an election in which party members choose candidates for their party

closed primary (KLŌZD PRĪ mayr ee) *n.* an election in which only party members may vote

open primary (Ō pun PRĪ mayr ee) *n.* an election in which voters do not need to choose a party before voting

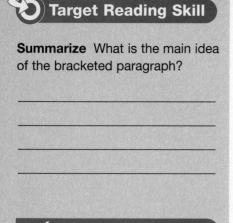

Summarize What is the main idea of the bracketed paragraph?

_____

_____

_____

_____

✓ Reading Check

Underline the sentence that explains how delegates are chosen for the national nominating conventions.

Choosing Presidential Candidates

25 To run for President, you must be over 35 years old. You must be born in the United States. A candidate must be well known. A candidate must be able to raise money. Money is needed for the campaign.

[Delegates to the national nominating convention are 30 chosen by a presidential primary election. Or they are chosen by a statewide caucus or convention. Delegates in most primary states must promise to support a certain candidate at the national convention.

The candidates begin their campaigns in the first 35 months of an election year. They campaign first in Iowa and New Hampshire. Iowa is a caucus state. New Hampshire is a primary state. If a candidate does well, he or she can raise more money. They can also attract voters in later primaries and caucuses. Some candi-40 dates drop out. Others gain strength.

The main purpose of a party's national convention is to nominate someone for President. The delegates debate and discuss the choices. Then they vote. Almost all delegates are promised to a candidate as a result of 45 the primaries or caucuses. First, a candidate for President is nominated. Then the delegates approve the candidate's choice for Vice President.

The national convention also approves the party platform. A committee writes the platform. They get 50 advice from party leaders. The delegates debate and approve a platform. The convention ends with speeches from the nominees. This is meant to bring the party together. The next step is the election campaign. The election for President is in November.

Review Questions

1. Name three ways that a candidate can be nominated.

_____

_____

2. Name three things a person must be or have to run for President.

_____

_____

Chapter 22 Assessment

1. The planks in a party platform deal with
   A. candidates.
   B. issues.
   C. offices.
   D. all of the above

2. Political parties give citizens
   A. information.
   B. ways to get involved.
   C. a way to be heard.
   D. all of the above

3. The first political party, the Federalists, wanted
   A. a strong national government.
   B. an end to slavery.
   C. more power for individual states.
   D. a two-party system.

4. Political parties
   A. are stronger today than in the past.
   B. are not as strong as they once were.
   C. are just as strong today as in the past.
   D. none of the above

5. What happened when caucuses were closed to ordinary party members?
   A. Voters had to register as members of a party.
   B. More states held primaries to select candidates.
   C. A few party leaders had great power.
   D. Delegates debated and discussed the candidates.

Short Answer Question

How and when did our two-party system develop?

_____

_____

_____

_____

_____

Reading Preview

Section 1 Being a Voter

Objectives

1. Understand general elections.
2. Explore the basics of voting.
3. Learn about becoming an informed voter.

Target Reading Skill

Set a Purpose Look at the headings and images in the text before reading. Think about what the section is about. Then set a purpose for reading. When you set a purpose for reading, you give yourself a focus. Having a focus while reading helps you to understand what you read.

Look at the first sentence in this section, for example:

Voting is the most important role of a citizen in a democracy.

This sentence can help you to set a purpose for reading. Your purpose might be to find out why voting is the most important citizen role. Now read to meet your purpose.

Vocabulary Strategy

Recognizing Signal Words There are many kinds of signal words. Signal words point to how events, ideas, or things are related. Certain words are used to signal other details or items in a list. Examples of these words are shown in the chart.

Words That Signal Other Details or Lists of Things		
also	too	in addition
and	furthermore	besides

Be aware of these words as you read. They may point to additional details. Or they may signal items in a list.

Section 1 Summary

¹ Voting is the most important role of a citizen in a democracy. Elections give citizens a voice in government.

General Elections

Voters take part in two kinds of elections. These are primary elections and general elections. People who ⁵ belong to political parties pick candidates in a primary election. Voters make final decisions about candidates and issues in a **general election**. Voters may also vote on certain questions in a general election. These questions, or ballot measures, include initiatives, referen-¹⁰ dums, and recalls. They give voters a voice.

The Basics of Voting

Voters must meet certain requirements. You must be a citizen of the United States. You must be at least 18 years old. In addition, you must live in the state where you will vote. Not everybody who meets these require-¹⁵ments can vote. People in prison and those who are mentally unable are not allowed to vote in most states.

Registration is required of voters. Local governments run the elections in most states. They set the rules for voter registration. They also run the polling ²⁰ places.

Elections take place at different times. Congress set the Tuesday after the first Monday in November as the day for federal, congressional, and presidential elections. Most elections for state offices take place then, too. ²⁵ Primary elections and elections for local governments may take place at any time. Most are in the spring. Special elections may be held at any time. In special elections, voters choose candidates to finish the terms of officeholders who have died, resigned, or been recalled.

³⁰ Voting takes place at polling places. Registered voters go to a polling place near where they live.

Target Reading Skill

Set a Purpose Read the underlined heading. Use it to set a purpose for reading. Write your purpose here.

_____

_____

_____

Vocabulary Strategy

Recognizing Signal Words
Circle a signal word in the bracketed paragraph. What sort of list is being signaled?

_____

_____

_____

✓ Reading Check

Underline the sentence that tells what happens in a primary election.

✓ Reading Check

Circle the text that tells when election day is for federal and state offices.

Key Terms

general election (JEN er ul ih LEK shun) *n.* when citizens vote to make final decisions about candidates and issues

registration (reh juh STRAY shun) *n.* signing up to be a voter

Target Reading Skill

Set a Purpose What is your purpose for reading after looking at the heading *Becoming an Informed Voter*?

_____

_____

_____

Vocabulary Strategy

Recognizing Signal Words What does the underlined word signal?

_____

_____

✓ Reading Check

Put a check mark next to the word that tells the fraction of eligible voters who vote in presidential elections.

There are different ways to vote. Some voters pull a lever on a machine. Some mark an X on paper. Some punch a hole in a card. Others make a choice on a
35 touchpad that is like an automatic teller machine. Voters who cannot get to their polling place on election day can have an absentee ballot sent to them. They mark the ballot and mail it in. States may also decide to use mail-in ballots or the Internet for voting.

Becoming an Informed Voter

40 Voters need information about the candidates to vote wisely. They can get information from many places. Public service groups have information on candidates. These groups have no ties to political parties. Newspapers and television news are other sources.
45 Voters can go to hear candidates speak. They can also watch candidates debate on television.

Voters should also learn about ballot measures. Having a complete picture of a ballot measure is important. Some states send information on ballot
50 measures to voters.

Only about half of those who could vote did vote in recent presidential elections. People sometimes think their vote cannot affect the outcome. Elections almost never are won by 1 or by even 100 votes. But voting
55 makes a difference. The 2000 presidential election was decided by only about 500 votes in Florida.

<u>Furthermore,</u> your vote still matters even if your candidate loses. By voting, you say where you stand on the issues. You state what kind of representatives you
60 want. You carry out an important civic duty. You take part in deciding who will lead our nation. You also help to decide what policies our leaders will follow.

Review Questions

1. What kinds of ballot measures do voters sometimes vote on in a general election?

_____

_____

2. What qualifications must you meet in order to vote?

_____

_____

CHAPTER 23

Reading Preview

Section 2
Influencing Your Vote

Objectives

1. Learn about messages from the candidates.
2. Understand the reasons for messages from interest groups.
3. Learn about recognizing propaganda techniques.
4. Explore how news media report the elections.

Target Reading Skill

Preview and Predict Preview the section before you begin reading. Look at the headings and images. Then predict what the subject of the section is. Use a diagram like this for your preview and prediction.

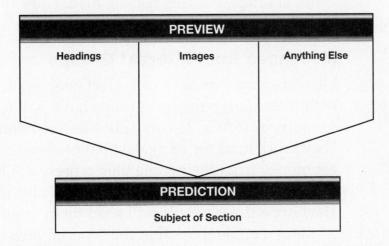

PREVIEW		
Headings	Images	Anything Else

PREDICTION
Subject of Section

Vocabulary Strategy

Recognizing Signal Words Some events are connected in cause-and-effect relationships. The words in the chart signal causes and effects.

Cause-and-Effect Signal Words		
because	since	as a result
so that	affect	lead to
therefore	for this reason	if . . . then

Vocabulary Strategy

Recognizing Signal Words Circle words that signal effects under the heading *Messages from the Candidates.*

✓ Reading Check

Underline the sentence that tells how direct mail can help candidates.

✓ Reading Check

Bracket the text that tells what PACs are.

¹ Candidates reach voters in many ways. Interest groups campaign for candidates and the issues they support. The media cover elections. All three groups influence voters.

Messages from the Candidates

⁵ Candidates try to get voters's support in many ways.

- Posters and bumper stickers make candidates' names known.
- Personal appearances help to spread a candidate's message.
¹⁰ • **Direct mail** helps candidates reach voters who have special interests.
- Candidates place ads in the **media**. Some tell voters about candidates' stands on major issues. But most focus on a candidate's personality, rather than his or ¹⁵ her abilities. For this reason, media ads are not good sources of information.

Messages from Interest Groups

Interest groups want to help elect people who agree with them. Large interest groups have political action committees (PACs) to carry out these election activities. ²⁰ They work hard for or against ballot measures. Some get money from the people they represent. Others use direct mail to find people who agree with their views. They hope these people will send them money.

Many people think that the "special interests" that ²⁵ PACs help have too much power in government. They say that interest groups stand for only a small percentage of people or care about only one issue.

Key Terms

direct mail (dih REKT MAYL) *n.* a way of sending messages to large groups of people through the mail

media (MEE dee uh) *n.* television, radio, newspapers, and magazines

Recognizing Propaganda Techniques

Candidates and interest groups want to influence how people think and act. They use **propaganda** to do this.
30 Propaganda may tell only one side of the story. It may twist the truth. It may appeal mostly to people's feelings. This chart shows six common kinds of propaganda.

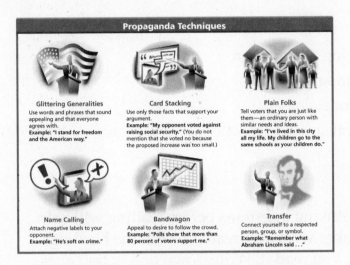

Propaganda Techniques

Glittering Generalities
Use words and phrases that sound appealing and that everyone agrees with.
Example: "I stand for freedom and the American way."

Card Stacking
Use only those facts that support your argument.
Example: "My opponent voted against raising social security." (You do not mention that she voted no because the proposed increase was too small.)

Plain Folks
Tell voters that you are just like them—an ordinary person with similar needs and ideas.
Example: "I've lived in this city all my life. My children go to the same schools as your children do."

Name Calling
Attach negative labels to your opponent.
Example: "He's soft on crime."

Bandwagon
Appeal to desire to follow the crowd.
Example: "Polls show that more than 80 percent of voters support me."

Transfer
Connect yourself to a respected person, group, or symbol.
Example: "Remember what Abraham Lincoln said . . ."

How News Media Report the Elections

News reporting is supposed to provide facts, but it sometimes shows **bias**. The news media also tell peo-
35 ple about opinion polls. A poll asks questions of a small part of a group. The answers are then taken to stand for how the whole group would answer.

Some people think that polls should not be used. Some voters choose a certain candidate mainly because
40 that candidate is leading in the polls. Others decide whether to vote or not based on opinion polls.

Many voters today receive most of their information about candidates and issues from TV. Some people say that television has made election issues seem unimpor-
45 tant. Candidates plan their messages and campaign activities to look good on TV.

Review Questions

1. How do candidates get voters to vote for them?

2. Name three ways to tell if a message is propaganda.

Key Terms

propaganda (prop uh GAN duh) *n.* a message meant to change people's ideas or actions

bias (BĪ us) *n.* giving support to one point of view

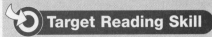
Preview and Predict Preview the section *Recognizing Propaganda Techniques*. Then make a prediction about it. Use this diagram to preview and predict.

✓ Reading Check

Underline the sentence that describes the goal of candidates and interest groups.

Vocabulary Strategy

Recognizing Signal Words
Bracket the sentence that contains a cause-and-effect signal word. Underline the word. Then write C above the cause and E above the effect.

✓ Reading Check

Circle the sentences that explain how polls influence voter behavior.

Reading Preview

Section 3
Campaigning for Office

Objectives

1. Explore planning and running a campaign.
2. Learn about financing a campaign.
3. Explain who wins an election.
4. Learn about the electoral college.

Target Reading Skill

Preview and Ask Questions Asking questions before reading will help you to understand and remember what you read. Look at the headings and images in a section before you read it. Write down one or two questions about what you see. Look for answers to your questions as you read.

You can use a chart like this for previewing and asking questions.

Preview and Ask Questions		
Headings: Images:	Questions:	Answers to Questions:

Vocabulary Strategy

Recognizing Signal Words Certain words signal a list of important ideas or details. They may also signal the importance of the ideas or details in relation to each other. These signal words are listed below.

Words That Signal Important Ideas or Details		
most important	first	above all
finally	last	least of all

Watch for these signal words as you read.

Section 3 Summary

1 All campaigns have a common goal. They want to get a candidate elected.

Planning and Running a Campaign

A winning campaign depends on the hard work of many people. Staff members help the candidate plan
5 and carry out the campaign. The campaign manager is one of the most important staff members. He or she is in charge of the campaign and guides the work of the staff.

A winning campaign finds out which issues voters think are important. Polls are used to do this. A win-
10 ning campaign also uses the media to help elect the candidate. The campaign press secretary manages the media.

[Financing a Campaign]

Candidates for major state and national offices need a lot of money. These candidates get most of their money
15 from regular people. Many also get money from political parties and PACs.

Several laws set rules for paying for campaigns for federal office. Congress set up the Federal Election Commission (FEC) to carry out these and other rules.
20 Rules for campaign funding include the following:

- No one person may give more than $2,000 to a candidate.

- Citizens may give $3 of their taxes each year to a campaign fund. Candidates cannot use money from
25 other sources if they accept these funds.

- A PAC may give up to $5,000 to a candidate for President in the primary elections. Candidates who have accepted public tax money may not take money from PACs in the general election.

✓ Reading Check

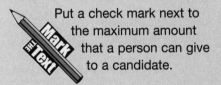

Circle the text that tells who is in charge of a political campaign.

Vocabulary Strategy

Recognizing Signal Words
Underline the words that signal the position of the campaign manager among staff members.

⟲ Target Reading Skill

Preview and Ask Questions Ask a question based on the bracketed heading.

_____

_____

_____

✓ Reading Check

Put a check mark next to the maximum amount that a person can give to a candidate.

Key Terms

campaign manager (kam PAYN MAN ih jer) *n.* the person in charge of helping a candidate run for office

campaign press secretary (kam PAYN PRES SEK ruh tayr ee) *n.* the person who helps a candidate use the media to run for office

Vocabulary Strategy

Recognizing Signal Words
Circle signal words in the section *Who Wins an Election?* Then put a check mark next to the most important detail.

✓ Reading Check

In the text, number two advantages an incumbent has over a challenger.

⟳ Target Reading Skill

Preview and Ask Questions
Ask two questions based on the underlined heading.

_____

_____

_____

✓ Reading Check

Underline the text that tells what made the 2000 presidential election unusual.

Who Wins an Election?

30 What does a candidate need to win? First, he or she must be a good leader. He or she must make good decisions. And he or she must raise a lot of money. Finally, being an **incumbent** helps a candidate's chance to win. An incumbent has a name that voters know. He 35 or she also has experience. A challenger often has little chance to win unless an incumbent has made mistakes.

<u>The Electoral College</u>

Voters do not choose the President directly. They elect people called **electors.** The electors vote for the President in the Electoral College.

40 The Electoral College has 538 electors. Each state has the same number of electors as it has members of Congress. Voters cast their ballots for a certain candidate on election day. But they are really voting for that candidate's team of electors. A candidate needs a 45 majority of electoral votes—270 or more—to win.

Candidates win or "carry" states as the votes are counted. That means that a candidate's whole team of electors has won in that state.

Many people question the Electoral College system. 50 They do not think the "winner-take-all" method of giving electoral votes from each state is fair. The 2000 election is an example. Al Gore received about 500,000 more votes than George W. Bush. Bush still became President. He had 271 electoral votes. Gore had only 267.

Review Questions

1. What are three sources of money for candidates for national office?

_____

2. How many electoral votes does a candidate for President need to win?

_____

Key Terms

incumbent (in KUM bunt) *n.* someone who already has the position for which he or she is running

electors (ih LEK terz) *n.* people who promise to cast votes for the candidate picked by voters

1. To vote, you must be
   A. at least 18 years old.
   B. a citizen of the United States.
   C. a resident of the state in which you are voting.
   D. all of the above

2. By voting, you
   A. run for public office.
   B. lead our government.
   C. say where you stand on issues.
   D. all of the above

3. From which of the following do many voters today receive most of their information about candidates?
   A. public places
   B. television
   C. ballot measures
   D. editorials

4. The campaign press secretary
   A. is in charge of the campaign.
   B. manages the media for the candidate.
   C. guides the campaign staff.
   D. raises money for the candidate.

5. Which determines the winner in a presidential election?
   A. Electoral College
   B. opinion polls
   C. party leaders
   D. members of Congress

Short Answer Question

Explain how the Electoral College works.

_____

_____

_____

_____

_____

_____

Reading Preview

Section 1
What Is Foreign Policy?

Objectives

1. Summarize the goals of foreign policy.

2. Identify and describe the tools of foreign policy.

Target Reading Skill

Identify Stated Main Ideas The main idea of a paragraph or section is its most important point. It includes all the other points in the paragraph or section. Writers often state the main idea directly. Look at this paragraph, for example.

> The United States forms military, political, and economic alliances with other countries. The North Atlantic Treaty Organization (NATO) is a military alliance. The Organization of American States (OAS) is a political alliance. The Organization for Economic Cooperation and Development (OECD) is an economic alliance.

The main idea is stated directly in the first sentence:

> The United States forms military, political, and economic alliances with other countries.

The other sentences in the paragraph provide examples, or details, that support this big idea. Underline the main idea of each paragraph as you read this section.

Vocabulary Strategy

Recognizing Word Origins Word origins can help you to understand the meaning of words. A word's origin is where it comes from. You will find the words *security* and *intelligence* in this section. Both words come from Latin words. *Security* comes from a word meaning "without care." *Intelligence* comes from a word meaning "understand." Knowing something about the origins of these words can help you understand their meaning. Use this knowledge and the context to understand the meanings of *security* and *intelligence* as you read.

Section 1 Summary

1 Each nation needs a plan for getting along with other nations. This plan is called a foreign policy. A nation's foreign policy describes its goals. And it explains how these goals will be met.

Goals of Foreign Policy

5 The United States has many foreign-policy goals.

- National <u>security</u> is most important. That means keeping our nation and its people safe.

- A second goal is to get nations to work for peace. A war anywhere can be a threat to all people.

10 • Increasing trade is a third goal. Trade helps the economy. It creates markets for our goods and services. This means profits for American business. Trade also brings us goods from other nations.

- Another goal is for other nations to respect human
15 rights. Freedom, justice, and equality are human rights. Many Americans think democracy is the best way to protect these rights. So we help other nations that try to create or keep a democratic government.

Tools of Foreign Policy

The military helps to defend us against **aggression**.
20 **Deterrence** is a key part of our foreign policy. It helps to protect our national security.

   The United States also uses these tools to meet its foreign policy goals.

- We form alliances with other nations. The North
25 Atlantic Treaty Organization (NATO) is a military alliance. The Organization of American States (OAS) is a political alliance. It helps its members work together peacefully.

Target Reading Skill

Identify Stated Main Ideas
Underline the sentence that states the main idea of the section *Goals of Foreign Policy.*

Vocabulary Strategy

Recognizing Word Origins If *se-* means "without" and *cur-* means "care," what you do think *security* means?

_____

_____

✓ Reading Check

List the foreign policy goals of the United States.

_____

_____

_____

_____

_____

Key Terms

aggression (uh greh shun) *n.* an attack or threat of attack by another country

deterrence (dih TER uns) *n.* keeping a strong defense so that other nations do not attack

Identify Stated Main Ideas
Underline two sentences that state the main idea of the bracketed paragraph.

✓ **Reading Check**

Circle one important tool of American foreign policy. Then bracket details that describe it.

- We use **diplomacy**. Nations send each other officials called diplomats. Diplomats talk about disputes and issues. Members of the Department of State usually carry out diplomacy. The President uses diplomacy with other heads of government at a **summit meeting**.

- We use **foreign aid**. We give or loan money to other nations. Foreign aid supports nations that are our friends. This may reduce the chance of revolution and war.

- Trade measures help us trade with other nations. They also help convince our trading partners to support our foreign policy. **Sanctions** stop or limit trade. Sanctions are used to change another nation's behavior.

- **Intelligence** protects national security. The Central Intelligence Agency (CIA) gathers data about other nations. Other groups also collect information. These include the Federal Bureau of Investigation (FBI) and the National Security Agency.

Review Questions

1. Explain the main goal of American foreign policy.

_____

_____

2. What tools help support American foreign policy?

_____

_____

Key Terms

diplomacy (duh PLŌ muh see) *n.* the relations and communications between countries

summit meeting (SUH mut MEE ting) *n.* a gathering at which the President meets with leaders of other nations

foreign aid (FOR un AYD) *n.* a program of giving military and economic help to other countries

sanctions (SAYNG shunz) *n.* actions that stop or limit trade with another nation in order to change that nation's behavior

intelligence (in TEL ih juns) *n.* information about another country and what it plans to do

Reading Preview

Section 2
Making Foreign Policy

Objectives

1. Describe the role of the executive branch in making foreign policy.
2. Examine the role of Congress in making foreign policy.
3. Explain how private groups and citizens can affect foreign policy.

Target Reading Skill

Identify Supporting Details Details support the main idea of a paragraph or section. These details give further information about the main idea. They may give examples or reasons. Read this paragraph.

> Several congressional committees are important in making foreign policy. The Senate Foreign Relations Committee, the House International Relations Committee, and the Armed Services committees in both houses are most involved. These committees hold hearings. They also write and study bills that affect our relations with other countries.

The main idea of the paragraph is underlined. All other details in the paragraph support this idea. The second sentence gives examples of important committees in Congress. The other sentences tell how the congressional committees help to make foreign policy.

As you read, look for details that support the main idea of each paragraph or section.

Vocabulary Strategy

Recognizing Word Origins Many words have come into the English language from other languages. You will read the words *diplomat* and *corps* in this section. Both came into English from the French. *Diplomat* can be traced to a word that has to do with documents about relations among nations. In French the word *corps* means "body." Think about these word origins when you come across the two words.

Section 2 Summary

© Pearson Education, Inc., Publishing as Pearson Prentice Hall. All rights reserved.

Target Reading Skill

Identify Supporting Details
Write MI next to the main idea of the bracketed paragraph. Write SD next to a detail that supports this idea.

Vocabulary Strategy

Recognizing Word Origins Think about the origins of *diplomat*. Use what you know to explain what a diplomat is.

_____

_____

_____

Vocabulary Strategy

Bracket the text that describes the President's role in setting foreign policy.

¹ Many people help to make our foreign policy. Some of these people are inside the government. Others are outside of it.

The Executive Branch

The Constitution gives the President the main job of ⁵ making foreign policy. The President:

- Sets foreign policy as commander in chief of the armed forces.
- Sets policy as the nation's chief <u>diplomat</u>.
- Shapes defense policies and meets with other leaders.
¹⁰ • Makes treaties and executive agreements.
- Chooses officials to represent us in other nations.
- Sends budget ideas to Congress for defense spending and foreign aid.

The President does not make decisions alone. ¹⁵ Departments and agencies of the executive branch help. The White House staff helps, too.

The Department of State gives advice on foreign policy. It also carries out foreign policy. The Secretary of State works closely with the President. He or she ²⁰ represents our nation in meetings with other nations. Experts on different parts of the world help the Secretary of State. The Department of State has about 16,000 workers in other nations.

The Department of Defense also helps. It gives ²⁵ advice about which weapons to make. It gives advice about where to place our troops. The **National Security Council** (NSC) advises the President on the nation's safety. It includes the Vice President. It also includes the Secretaries of State and Defense. The ³⁰ **National Security Advisor** is the head of the NSC.

Key Terms

National Security Council (NSC) (NASH uh nul sih KYOOR ih tee KOWN sul) *n.* group that helps the President make decisions about the country's safety

National Security Advisor (NASH uh nul sih KYOOR ih tee ad vī zer) *n.* the leader of the National Security Council

Role of Congress

Congress also helps to set foreign policy. Only Congress can declare war. The Senate has the power to approve or reject a treaty. The Senate must approve the President's choices for the underline diplomatic corps.

35 Committees in Congress also help to make foreign policy. These committees include the Senate Foreign Relations, the House International Relations, and the Armed Services committees. They write and study bills about foreign affairs. They hold hearings to learn more 40 about these issues.

Role of Private Groups

Private groups can shape foreign policy, too. Many have special interests that are affected by foreign policy. They want to have a say in what that policy will be.

Businesses that trade with other nations are interest-45 ed in foreign policy. Labor groups want foreign policy to protect jobs. Anti-nuclear groups, church groups, and human rights groups also try to affect foreign policy. People try to shape policy toward areas of the world they care about. For example, many Cuban 50 Americans have influenced our policy toward Cuba. These private groups can convince others to take action to support their goals. They can pressure members of Congress to vote in their favor on issues.

Being informed helps citizens to make better deci-55 sions. Citizens can learn about foreign countries and our policies toward them. They can follow world news. They can study, travel, or work abroad. They can run for office. They can vote for people with their views. They may also share views on issues with a member of 60 Congress.

Review Questions

1. Who in the executive branch helps make foreign policy?

_____

_____

2. Describe three ways that individual citizens can affect foreign policy.

_____

_____

Vocabulary Strategy

Recognizing Word Origins If *corps* means "body" in French, what do you think a diplomatic corps is?

_____

_____

✓ Reading Check

Underline three details that describe the role of Congress in setting foreign policy.

⊙ Target Reading Skill

Identify Supporting Details Put a check mark next to three details in the bracketed paragraph that tell about the role of private groups in setting foreign policy.

✓ Reading Check

List two ways an interest group can affect foreign policy.

_____

_____

_____

_____

Reading Preview

Section 3
Foreign Policy in Action

Objectives

1. Discuss the history of American foreign policy through World War II.

2. Learn about the Cold War.

3. Study regional challenges to American foreign policy.

4. Describe how American policy is leading the war on terrorism.

Target Reading Skill

Identify Implied Main Ideas Writers do not always state the main idea of a paragraph or section directly. Instead, the main idea is implied, or suggested, by the details. You must use the details to identify the main idea. Then you must state it yourself.

Use this diagram to identify implied main ideas as you read. Write down the details in a paragraph or section. Add them up to identify the main idea. Then state the main idea in one sentence.

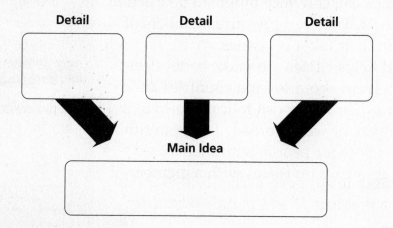

Detail   Detail   Detail

Main Idea

Vocabulary Strategy

Recognizing Word Origins What you know about a word's origins can help you to understand its meaning. You will find the words *league* and *establish* in this section. Both come from Latin, like many other English words. The word *league* can be traced to a word meaning "tie or bind together." The word *establish* is connected to a word meaning "stable or firm." Look for these words as you read. Use what you know about their origins to help you understand them.

Section 3 Summary

¹ Our foreign policy has changed over time. The United States has followed **isolationism** at times. At other times, it has taken an active part in world events.

Foreign Policy Through World War II

President Washington chose a position of **neutrality**.
⁵ Staying isolated was not easy. Leaders in Europe were taking over foreign lands. President Monroe responded with the Monroe Doctrine in 1823.

World War I forced our nation to get involved outside our borders. After the war, President Wilson
¹⁰ helped to found the <u>League</u> of Nations. The League was supposed to help keep peace. But Congress wanted to return to isolationism. It would not let us join the League.

World War II began in Europe. The United States
¹⁵ tried to stay out of it. Then the Japanese bombed Pearl Harbor, Hawaii, in 1941. We declared war. When the war ended in 1945, the United States was the richest and most powerful country in the world.

The Cold War

After World War II, the Soviet Union and the spread of
²⁰ communism were the main threats to peace. The Soviets took control of several Eastern European nations. It threatened others.

United States policy at this time was called **containment**. Giving money to other countries was the
²⁵ main tool for this policy at first. Then the United States used military strength to support it. The Cold War had begun. It was not a real war. It was mainly a battle of words and warnings.

Key Terms

isolationism (ī suh LAY shuh nih zum) *n.* a foreign policy that tries to limit relations with other countries

neutrality (noo TRA luh tee) *n.* a policy of not taking sides in wars between other countries

containment (kun TAYN munt) *n.* a policy of using armies and money to stop the spread of communism

---

Target Reading Skill

Identify Implied Main Ideas In one sentence, state the main idea of the section *Foreign Policy Through World War II.*

_____

_____

_____

Vocabulary Strategy

Recognizing Word Origins Think about what you know about the origins of the word *league.* What does the word mean here?

_____

_____

_____

✓ Reading Check

Underline the sentence that tells what caused the United States to abandon its policy of isolationism.

✓ Reading Check

Underline the sentence that explains why the Soviet Union seemed like a threat to the United States.

The 1970s was a time of **détente.** The United States and the Soviet Union began to get along. But both also continued to build their militaries.

There was great change in the 1980s and 1990s. Communist governments fell. Russia and other Soviet republics became independent. Russia and the United States became better friends.

Today's Challenges

Trade has increased between China and the United States. But China's treatment of its citizens has hurt relations between the two nations. People debate about how to react to China's poor human rights record.

Challenges to our foreign policy include economic and regional issues. Balancing trade with Japan is an important goal. Competing with China and the European Union is also vital. Regional challenges exist in Latin America, Eastern Europe, the Middle East, and Africa.

Leading the War on Terrorism

The United States now leads a war on terror. It works with other nations to stop attacks. It also works to stop the flow of money to terrorists.

It is not easy to <u>establish</u> a foreign policy goal today. Choices about foreign policy are harder now that the enemy is not easy to identify. Each problem has to be handled on its own.

Review Questions

1. What was the foreign policy of the early United States?

_____

_____

2. How is the United States leading the war on terrorism?

_____

_____

Key Term

détente (day TAHNT) *n.* improved relations between the United States and the Soviet Union

1. The main foreign-policy goal of the United States is
   A. world peace.
   B. national security.
   C. increasing trade.
   D. human rights.

2. The United States uses foreign aid to
   A. support nations that are our friends.
   B. increase American imports to other countries.
   C. gather information about other countries.
   D. all of the above

3. Which department of the executive branch carries out foreign policy?
   A. Department of Defense
   B. Department of Justice
   C. Department of State
   D. Department of the Treasury

4. Labor groups want foreign policy to protect
   A. certain areas of the world.
   B. jobs for Americans.
   C. people of diverse backgrounds.
   D. foreign service officers.

5. The goal of containment was to stop
   A. German aggression.
   B. European colonization.
   C. expansion to the west.
   D. the spread of communism.

Short Answer Question

How has the foreign policy of the United States changed since George Washington was President?

_____

_____

_____

_____

_____

_____

Reading Preview

Section 1
The Nations of the World

Objectives

1. Define what a nation is.
2. Explore the different histories of nations.
3. Discuss the process of economic development.

Target Reading Skill

Identify Contrasts Contrasts are differences. You look at how two things differ when you contrast them. You will read about developed nations and developing nations in this section. Both groups are nations. They differ in how they have developed. Their histories differ. Their economies differ. As you read, pay attention to details that describe these differences. List the differences in a chart like this.

Developed Nations	Developing Nations

Vocabulary Strategy

Using Word Parts You can often use word parts to figure out the meanings of words you do not recognize while reading. Word parts include roots, prefixes, and suffixes. A root is the base of a word. It has meaning by itself.

You will come across the words *unity, unit, nation,* and *native* in this section. The chart shows the Latin roots of these words.

Word	Root	Meaning of Root
unity	un-	one
unit		
nation	nat-	to be born
native		

Section 1 Summary

¹ The world is divided into nations. Each nation has borders. These borders are very important to the people who live within them.

What Is a Nation?

A nation is a group of people. These people share a
⁵ language, a history, and an identity. The group needs more than a sense of <u>unity</u> to be a nation. It must form a political <u>unit</u>.

Every nation has three basic features. First, it has a territory with borders. The borders define the nation's
¹⁰ land area. Second, a nation has a government. Third, a nation has **sovereignty**. Sovereignty means that the government has power within the nation's borders. It also has the power to deal with other nations.

All nations have a duty to protect their own inter-
¹⁵ ests. A nation must have power to look after its interests. National power takes many forms. Some nations gain power because they have valuable natural resources. Some gain power through their armies. Some become powerful by building a strong economy.
²⁰ People within a nation often feel a sense of **nationalism**. Culture, language, religion, and political tradition can add to this feeling.

The Different Histories of Nations

Some nations are rich. Others are poor. Nations have different climates, landscapes, languages, and religions.
²⁵ The histories of nations also differ.

Many American, African, and Asian nations were colonies at one time. A **colony** is a territory ruled by a more powerful nation. That nation is called a colonial power. Colonial powers wanted colonies to supply
³⁰ crops. They wanted colonies for natural resources such as oil. Colonies were also a source of cheap labor.

Vocabulary Strategy

Using Word Parts If the root *un-* means "one," what does *unity* mean? What is a *unit*?

_____

_____

✓ Reading Check

Number the three characteristics that all nations share.

↻ Target Reading Skill

Identify Contrasts Circle the text that contrasts nations.

✓ Reading Check

Bracket the sentences that explain why some nations became colonial powers.

Key Terms

sovereignty (SAHV run tee) *n.* the power to make and carry out laws within a country's borders
nationalism (NASH uh nuh liz um) *n.* pride in shared history
colony (KOL uh nee) *n.* a land ruled by a more powerful nation

Using Word Parts Think about the meaning of the root *nat-*. Explain the term *native peoples*.

_____

_____

_____

Identify Contrasts Write a C next to each of the two paragraphs that contrast the standard of living in developed nations with that of developing nations.

List the most important difference between developing and developed nations.

_____

_____

_____

People from the colonial power settled some colonies. The newcomers killed or pushed aside the people who already lived here. Soon there were more ³⁵ settlers than <u>native peoples</u>. A colonial power often forced its language and laws on a colony. It also forced native peoples to do hard work.

Economic Development

Nations today can be divided into "developed nations" and "developing nations." The main difference is their ⁴⁰ standard of living.

Developed nations have industry and modern technology. They make goods and services. Most people live in towns and cities. Many work in service jobs. Most people have enough money for their basic needs.

⁴⁵ Most people in developing nations are poor. Some developing nations do not have enough jobs for people. It is hard for many people to get an education. Many people are hungry.

Most developing nations were once colonies. They ⁵⁰ had weak economies when they became free. Their economies were set up to export resources. The resources were not used to improve the standard of living. Many also had political problems. Some colonies had people with different languages and religions all living together. ⁵⁵ These groups sometimes fought for power.

The poorer nations are trying to develop their economies. Richer nations and international groups are helping. This has improved life for many people in developing nations.

Review Questions

1. What is a nation?

_____

_____

2. Why did many developing nations have weak economies when they became independent?

_____

_____

Key Term

standard of living (STAN derd UV LIV ing) *n.* the amount and kinds of goods and services people can have

Reading Preview

Section 2 Relations Among and Within Nations

Objectives

1. Identify the types of conflict that arise among nations.
2. Explore competition among nations.
3. Discuss the Cold War and its aftermath.
4. Examine cooperation among nations.

Target Reading Skill

Make Comparisons Comparing two or more things helps you see how they are alike. Things that are alike have features in common. You will read about conflicts among nations in this section. Think about how the conflicts are alike. Then list what the conflicts have in common.

Vocabulary Strategy

Using Word Parts Many words can be broken into parts. The parts of a word can tell you something about its meaning. Prefixes, roots, and suffixes are word parts. Some words in this section have the same prefix but different roots. The prefix goes in front of the root and changes its meaning.

Word	Prefix	Root	Meaning of Word
conflict	con- com- "together" co-	-flict- "strike"	?
competition		-pet- "strive"	?
cooperation		-oper- "work"	?

Think about what you know about the parts of these words to understand their meanings as you read.

Vocabulary Strategy

Using Word Parts Explain the meaning of *conflict* using its prefix and root.

_____

_____

Target Reading Skill

Making Comparisons The section *Types of Conflict* compares types of conflicts. Bracket the sentence that tells how most conflicts are alike.

✓ Reading Check

Circle two types of conflict among or within nations.

Vocabulary Strategy

Using Word Parts Draw a line between the prefix and root of *competition*. Then explain its meaning.

_____

_____

_____

✓ Reading Check

Underline two possible consequences of international competition.

---

¹ Nations come into <u>conflict</u> in wars. They compete for power. They also cooperate in many ways.

Types of Conflict

Most conflicts are caused by one group's belief that another group is against it. This chart shows four types ⁵ of conflict among or within nations.

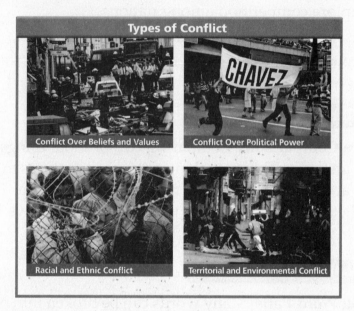

Types of Conflict

Conflict Over Beliefs and Values

Conflict Over Political Power

Racial and Ethnic Conflict

Territorial and Environmental Conflict

<u>Competition</u> Among Nations

Nations compete through trade. This can help by causing companies to improve the way they do business. It can harm if one nation believes the other is being unfair.

Nations also compete for military power. This can ¹⁰ increase tension between countries. It can lead to conflict. Today the buildup of weapons in North Korea and China is a concern.

The Cold War and Its Aftermath

The United States and the Soviet Union had been friends during World War II. After the war, the Soviet ¹⁵ Union supported **communism**. The United States supported democracy. Both nations also had strong armies. They saw each other as dangerous.

Key Term

communism (KAHM yuh niz um) *n.* a system in which the government owns and controls the resources

---

The Soviet Union set up a Communist government in East Germany and Eastern Europe. The Soviet Union and these nations formed the Warsaw Pact. The United States and the nations of Western Europe formed the North Atlantic Treaty Organization (NATO). Each alliance built up its army.

This superpower conflict was called the **Cold War**. It was fought with words, warnings, and a buildup of weapons. The Cold War broke into several "hot" wars. They included the Korean and Vietnam wars.

Political changes in the 1980s and 1990s ended the Cold War. The nations of Eastern Europe got rid of their Communist governments. They began to have free market economies. The Soviet Union fell apart. Its republics became independent.

Cooperation Among Nations

Many nations have formed trade groups. The European Union (EU) is an example. A trade group works for economic and political <u>cooperation</u> in a region. Another example is the North American Free Trade Agreement (NAFTA). It promotes trade among Canada, Mexico, and the United States.

Nations also work together to provide aid. Many nations helped the people of the former Soviet Union after the Cold War. Nations also joined to help refugees from the 1994 civil war in Rwanda.

Nations work together to promote peace. A **balance of power** may have helped to keep peace during the Cold War. Nations still work for peace today.

Review Questions

1. Describe two possible effects of competition for military power.

2. What developments ended the Cold War?

Key Terms

Cold War (KŌLD WOR) *n.* a struggle—like a real war but with no armed battles—between the U.S. and the Soviet Union

balance of power (BAL uns UV POW er) *n.* a case in which one powerful country's military offsets and balances another's

✓ **Reading Check**

Put a check mark next to the names of the nations on opposite sides in the Cold War.

Target Reading Skill

Make Comparisons Explain how the EU and NAFTA are alike.

_____

_____

Vocabulary Strategy

Using Word Parts Explain the meaning of *cooperation* based on its prefix and root.

_____

_____

_____

✓ **Reading Check**

List the three ways that nations work together.

1. _____

2. _____

3. _____

Reading Preview

Section 3 The Challenge of Interdependence

Objectives

1. Learn about the United Nations.
2. Explore the work of nongovernmental organizations.
3. Discuss the impact of these organizations.

Target Reading Skill

Identify Contrasts When you identify contrasts between things, you note their differences. You will read about different divisions, or parts, of the United Nations in this section. Each division has different powers or jobs.

You can use the diagram below to show contrasts, or differences, between two divisions of the United Nations. The shared, center part of the diagram shows a way the two divisions are alike. Both are part of the United Nations. The separate, outer parts of the diagram show differences.

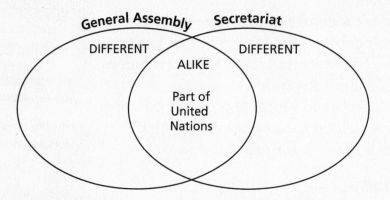

Vocabulary Strategy

Using Word Parts Breaking a word you do not know into parts may help you understand its meaning. You may know something about the meaning of the word's prefix, root, or suffix. You can use what you know to figure out the word's meaning.

You will come across the words *interdependent* and *international* in this section. Each contains the prefix *inter-*, which means "between or among." Put this information together with what you know about the other parts of each word.

Section 3 Summary

¹ Today's world is <u>interdependent</u>. The largest organization of nations working together is the United Nations.

The United Nations

The United Nations (UN) was created in 1945. The UN
has 189 member nations. That is almost every nation in
⁵ the world. One of its goals is to keep world peace. The
UN also works to promote justice and cooperation.

The UN has six major divisions. These are the
Security Council, the General Assembly, the Secretariat,
the Economic and Social Council, the International
¹⁰ Court of Justice, and the Trusteeship Council.

The Security Council is the most powerful. It can help
to settle conflicts. It may send a force of **peacekeepers**
to a country if war breaks out.

The Security Council has 15 members. Five are
¹⁵ always on the council. These are the United States,
Russia, Great Britain, China, and France. They are
called the "Big Five." Ten other members are elected to
two-year terms by the General Assembly. Nine votes
out of 15 are needed for the Security Council to
²⁰ approve an action. Each of the "Big Five" has veto
power. That means an action is defeated if one of the
"Big Five" votes against it.

Every member nation belongs to the General
Assembly. Each has one vote. This group discusses
²⁵ world problems. They also decide how the UN will
spend its money.

The Secretariat carries out daily tasks. People from
more than 150 countries work in the Secretariat. They
translate documents. They provide services to UN
³⁰ councils and agencies. They prepare reports.

The Economic and Social Council works to improve
standards of living. The Council has representatives
from 54 countries.

Vocabulary Strategy

Using Word Parts How do you
think an *interdependent* group of
nations works?

_____

_____

Target Reading Skill

Identify Contrasts Bracket the
sentences that tell how the
members of the Security
Council and the mem-
bers of the General
Assembly differ.

✓ Reading Check

Circle the names of the six
major divisions of the
United Nations.

Key Term

peacekeepers (PEES kee purz) *n.* members of the military whose
job is usually to help settle conflicts and maintain order in a region

Vocabulary Strategy

Using Word Parts Use the word parts of *international* to explain what international law is.

_____

_____

Target Reading Skill

Identify Contrasts Put a check mark next to the sentence that tells how the Trusteeship Council differs from other UN divisions.

✓ Reading Check

Bracket text that gives an example of a non-governmental organization and tells what it does.

✓ Reading Check

Number two obstacles in the way of international cooperation.

The International Court of Justice is the UN's judicial branch. It is often called the World Court. It is made up of 15 judges. They are from 15 different countries. The "Big Five" countries also have seats on this court.

The Trusteeship Council was set up to help govern territories formed after World War II. The Trusteeship Council is no longer a working part of the UN.

Non-Governmental Organizations

Private nongovernmental organizations (NGOs) also work on global problems. NGOs protect political and economic rights. They work to protect human rights. They fight hunger and disease. They deal with many other global problems. The Red Cross is one example of an NGO. It helps victims of war and natural disaster.

The Impact of Organizations

Countries must work together for organizations to solve world problems. Cooperation is not always easy. Nations usually do not want to lose any political power. They often want to make their own decisions when their security is involved. The UN has had trouble stopping conflicts for this reason.

The UN and other groups have had more success with economic problems than political problems. They have helped to teach farmers better ways to grow crops. They help countries build dams. And they help countries enter world trade.

Countries cooperate best in smaller groups limited to one region. Examples are NATO and the Organization of African Unity. Their members usually have more in common than larger organizations like the UN.

Review Questions

1. When dealing with what issue does the UN have the most success?

_____

_____

2. What is the "Big Five"?

_____

_____

Chapter 25 Assessment

1. Which of the following gives people a sense of nationalism?
   A. language
   B. political tradition
   C. culture
   D. all of the above

2. Most developing countries were once
   A. colonial powers.
   B. colonies.
   C. independent nations.
   D. none of the above

3. Which of the following is an example of an alliance?
   A. World War II
   B. the Warsaw Pact
   C. the International Court of Justice
   D. Latin America

4. Which of the following is an example of a trade group?
   A. NATO
   B. the UN
   C. the EU
   D. NGOs

5. The United Nations (UN) is
   A. the largest organization of nations working together.
   B. a summit meeting of leaders from many nations.
   C. a nongovernmental organization that helps nations.
   D. the first economic conference of developing nations.

Short Answer Question

Summarize the different ways that nations can work together.

_____

_____

_____

_____

_____